CW00704475

The Cracks Between What V
What We Are Supposed to E

The Cracks Between What We Are and What We Are Supposed to Be

Essays and Interviews

Harryette Mullen

Introduction by Hank Lazer

THE UNIVERSITY OF ALABAMA PRESS
Tuscaloosa

Typeface: Minion and Goudy

Cover: "The Flag is Bleeding," 1967. Faith Ringgold (c) 1967. Courtesy of the artist.
Cover design by: Michele Myatt Quinn
∞
The paper on which this book is printed meets the minimum requirements of
American National Standard for Information Sciences—Permanence of Paper for
Printed Library Materials, ANSI Z39.48-1984.

Library of Congress Cataloging-in-Publication Data

Mullen, Harryette Romell.
    The cracks between what we are and what we are supposed to be : essays and
interviews / Harryette Mullen ; introduction by Hank Lazer.
        p. cm. — (Modern and contemporary poetics)
    Includes bibliographical references.
    ISBN 978-0-8173-5713-9 (pbk.) — ISBN 978-0-8173-8617-7 (ebook) 1. Mullen,
Harryette Romell—Interviews. 2. Mullen, Harryette Romell—Criticism and interpretation. 3. Poets, American—20th century—Interviews. 4. African American women
poets—Interviews. 5. Literature and society—United States—History—20th century.
6. African American women—Intellectual life—20th century. I. Title.
    PS3563.U3954Z459 2012
    811'.54—dc23

                                                                    2012005533

This book is dedicated to family and friends. Without them I could never have written anything at all.

Contents

II. Longer Essays

III. Interviews

Acknowledgments

This book would not exist without the critical vision and active support of Charles Bernstein, Hank Lazer, and Dan Waterman. I am thankful to all of them for their dedicated effort on behalf of this work. Thanks as well to Kevin Fitzgerald for careful editing. I also thank my outstanding colleagues at UCLA and the members of my superlative writing group—Wendy Belcher, Mary Bucci Bush, Ellen Krout-Hasegawa, Geraldine Kudaka, Kathleen McHugh, and Alice Wexler—for their care and commitment over the years these essays were written. I appreciate as well the always supportive UCLA Friends of English. I gratefully acknowledge the innovative editors of the journals in which several of these essays first appeared.

1. "Imagining the Unimagined Reader: Writing to the Unborn and Including the Excluded." *boundary 2*, Spring 1999, 198–203.
2. "Poetry and Identity." *West Coast Line* 19, 1996, 85–89.
3. "Kinky Quatrains: The Making of *Muse & Drudge*." In *Ecstatic Occasions, Expedient Forms*. Ed. David Lehman. Ann Arbor: U Michigan P, 1996.
4. "Telegraphs from a Distracted Sibyl." *American Book Review*, vol. 17, no. 3, February/March 1996.
5. "If Lilies are Lily White: From the Stain of Miscegenation in 'Melanctha' to Stein's 'Clean Mixture' of White and Color in *Tender Buttons*." Presentation for *Gertrude Stein at the Millennium*, Washington University, Saint Louis, 1999. Also appeared online in *Mark(s)* <www.markszine.net>.
6. "Nine Syllables Label Sylvia: Reading Plath's 'Metaphors.'" *Chain*, 1997.
7. "Evaluation of an Unwritten Poem: Wislawa Szymborska in the Dialogue of Critical and Creative Thinkers." *The Explicator*. vol. 64, no. 2, Winter 2006, 112–15.

8. "Theme for the Oulipians." Presentation for CalArts Noulipo Conference, 2006. Also published in *The Noulipian Analects,* Los Angeles: Les Figues Press, 2007.

9. "When He Is Least Himself: Paul Laurence Dunbar and Double Consciousness in African-American Poetry." Presentation for Paul Laurence Dunbar Centennial Conference, Stanford University, 2006. Also published in *African American Review,* June 22, 2007.

10. "Truly Unruly Julie: The Innovative Rule-Breaking Poetry of Julie Patton." *American Poet,* Journal of Academy of American Poets, Fall 2001, 26–27.

11. "All Silence Says Music Will Follow: Listening to Lorenzo Thomas." Presentation at American Studies Association, Houston, Texas 2002.

12. "The Cracks Between What We Are and What We Are Supposed to Be: Stretching the Dialogue of African-American Poetry." Presentation at American Literature Association, Long Beach, California 2000; and Naropa University, Boulder, Colorado, 2000. Published in *How2* <www.asu.edu/pipercwcenter/how2journal>.

13. "African Signs and Spirit Writing." *Callaloo* 19.3, 1996, 670–689. Also reprinted in *African American Literary Theory: A Reader,* 2000, and *The Black Studies Reader,* 2004.

14. "Runaway Tongue: Resistant Orality in *Uncle Tom's Cabin, Our Nig, Incidents in the Life of a Slave Girl,* and *Beloved.*" Presentation at American Studies Association, New Orleans, 1990. Also reprinted in *The Culture of Sentiment: Race, Gender, and Sentimentality in Nineteenth-Century America,* ed. Shirley Samuels, New York: Oxford UP 1992, 244–64, 332–35. Copyright © 1992 by Oxford University Press, Inc. Used by permission of Oxford University Press, Inc.

15. "Optic White: Blackness and the Production of Whiteness." *diacritics,* 24.2–3, Summer-Fall 1994, 71–89. Also reprinted in *Cultural and Literary Critiques of the Concept of "Race,"* ed. Nathaniel E. Gates, New York: Garland Publishers, 1997.

16. "Phantom Pain: Nathaniel Mackey's *Bedouin Hornbook.*" *Talisman* 9, Fall 1992, 37–43.

17. "A Collective Force of Burning Ink: Will Alexander's *Asia & Haiti.*" *Callaloo* 22.2, 1999, 417–426.

18. "Incessant Elusives: The Oppositional Poetics of Erica Hunt and Will Alexander." Presentation at MELUS Europe Conference, Heidelberg, Germany, 1998. Also reprinted in *Holding Their Own,* eds. Dorothea Fischer-Hornung and Heike Raphael-Hernandez.

19. "'The Solo Mysterioso Blues': An Interview with Harryette Mullen" by Calvin Bedient. *Callaloo* 19.3, 1996, 651–669.

20. "An Interview with Harryette Mullen" by Daniel Kane. *What is Poetry?: Conversations with the American Avant-Garde,* New York: Teachers & Writers Collaborative, 2003, 126–137.

21. "An Interview with Harryette Mullen" by Elisabeth Frost. *Contemporary Literature* vol. 41, 2000, 397–421.

22. "An Interview with Harryette Mullen" by Cynthia Hogue. *Postmodern Culture,* 9.2, 1999.

23. "I Dream a World": A Conversation with Harryette Mullen by Nibir K. Ghosh. *Multicultural America,* Chandigarh: Unistar, 2005.

INTRODUCTION

Hank Lazer

Harryette Mullen's collection of essays and interviews is an important literary event. Like her poetry, Mullen's essays and interviews are written at several key intersections: speech and writing, innovation and race. Mullen notes that her work "continues to explore linguistic quirks and cultural references peculiar to American English as spoken by the multiethnic peoples of the United States" (6). As you will see, this collection provides abundant evidence of Mullen's vision of a multiethnic America. Mullen's politics is for linguistic inclusion: "I desire that my work appeal to an audience that is diverse and inclusive while at the same time wondering if human beings will ever learn how to be inclusive without repressing human diversity through cultural and linguistic imperialism" (6). While Mullen claims that her own "inclination is to pursue what is minor, marginal, idiosyncratic, trivial, debased, or aberrant in the language that I speak and write" (6), the results are hardly minor. Mullen is helping us all to imagine and to inhabit a multiethnic culture that has rid itself of xenophobia, and Mullen's exact provocation is to create a linguistic environment that promotes that acceptance and openness through its intellectual challenges and exemplary linguistic play.

Mullen's writing arrives in an era of charged identity politics, and she is determined to challenge overly simplified versions of identity. She interrogates and complicates identity: "The idea of identity informs my poetry, insofar as identity acts upon language, and language acts upon identity. It would be accurate to say that my poetry explores the reciprocity of language and culture" (6). Mullen, by her own description, is involved in a "construction and ultimate deconstruction of a representative black poetic voice" (51). Particularly in the essay "The Cracks Between What We Are and What We Are Supposed to Be," she takes up Aldon Nielsen's term "interrogate," which Mullen applies in its original sense of "standing between and asking ques-

tions." Her poetry and essays thereby participate in an interrogative practice where the writing is located "in a space between declarative representations of blackness and a critical engagement with the cultural and discursive
practices by which evolving identities are recognized, articulated, and defined." This writing of "'other blackness' (rather than 'black otherness')" constitutes a powerful, intelligent disturbance of any homogeneous sense of African American culture and identity. The result, as Mullen describes it, is to
allow "the meanings of blackness to proliferate and expand, thus stretching
black identity and making it more inclusive, but also allowing instability in
the definition of blackness" (68–69).

Mullen's essays interrogate governing assumptions about blackness: "Presumably for the African American writer there is no alternative to the production of this 'authentic black voice' but silence, invisibility, or self-effacement"
(79). In "African Signs and Spirit Writing," an important critique of Henry
Louis Gates' work, Mullen argues that "any theory of African American literature that privileges a speech-based poetics or the trope of orality to the exclusion of more writerly texts results in the impoverishment of the tradition"
(79-80). Mullen's own poetry is a crucial instance of writing and thinking
that interrogates the profoundly important intersection of speech and writing: "I am writing for the eye and the ear at once, at that intersection of orality and literacy, wanting to make sure that there is a troubled, disturbing aspect to the work so that it is never just a 'speakerly' or a 'writerly' text" (216).
Part of the pathway for Mullen to this intersection goes by way of Gertrude
Stein's writing, particularly *Tender Buttons,* although Mullen's consideration
of Stein remains a skeptical one—"although I claim her [Stein] as an ancestor, I cannot say that I am a devout ancestor worshipper" (26).

Along with exploring the relationship between speech-based and literary-
based text, Mullen also questions received notions and categories for poets
of color. She writes that "'formally innovative minority poets,' when visible
at all, are not likely to be perceived either as typical of a racial/ethnic group
or as representative of an aesthetic movement" (10). Or, put more directly,
"[t]he assumption remains, however unexamined, that 'avant-garde' poetry
is not 'black' and that 'black' poetry, however singular its 'voice,' is not 'formally innovative'" (11). It is hard to imagine this assumption remaining unexamined in light of the evidence presented by Mullen's poetry, essays, and
interviews. Her work, along with that of Aldon Nielsen and Lorenzo Thomas
(Mullen calls Thomas "my most immediate and influential model of a black
poet engaged in formal innovation" [12]), clearly demonstrates that "black"
and "innovative" are not mutually exclusive categories. I think that Mullen
is correct when she understands her own *Muse & Drudge* (1995) as a work

that "might alter or challenge that assumption [that "black" and "innovative" are separate categories], bridging what apparently has been imagined as a gap (or chasm?) between my work as a 'black' poet and my work as a 'formally innovative' poet" (12). This collection of essays and interviews further extends the supports and byways of that bridge into a well-linked thoroughfare with considerable interchange between both sides of that now much narrowed divide.

As you will see as you make your way through this collection, Mullen's essays and reviews establish important kinships, with earlier poets such as Lorenzo Thomas, Tom Dent, and Ishmael Reed, and with a range of contemporaries that include Nathaniel Mackey, Will Alexander, Jay Wright, Ed Roberson, Clarence Major, Julie Patton, C. S. Giscombe, Claudia Rankine, Mark McMorris, and Akilah Oliver. Mullen has written superb essays especially on the work of Mackey and Alexander, thereby making important, articulate interventions into contemporary taste and attention, extending the range of audibility and visibility for this particularly rich era of "formally innovative minority poets." Thus, Mullen's critical writing functions as activist research: partisan, partial, and ethical. In one sense, then, her work (essays and poetry) is an effort to "create an audience" for herself and others (228). In another sense, though, her writing—which is deeply informed by her probing scholarship, her knowledge of a broad range of music, her training in folklore, and her genealogical research—amounts to an idealistic or optimistic engagement designed to make her and us more whole: When asked, "'How do you know all this stuff?'" she replies, "it's because I've been searching. We feel incomplete, and we search to make ourselves, our knowledge, more complete" (203). I find that Mullen's writing inspires us, her readers, to take part in that ongoing search to make ourselves and our knowledge more complete; in this respect, her writing energizes our own reading and writing.

Ultimately, Mullen's work embodies a strikingly contemporary sense of a miscegenated culture. She acknowledges this as a crucial perspective in her own work: "A lot has been said of how American culture is a miscegenated culture, how it is a product of a mixing and mingling of diverse races and cultures and languages, and I would agree with that. I would say that, yes, my text is deliberately a multi-voiced text, a text that tries to express the actual diversity of my own experience living here, exposed to different cultures. *Mongrel* comes from 'among.' Among others. We are among; we are not along. We are all mongrels" (186). For Mullen, as a poet and essayist, that exploration of the possibilities for a hybrid, miscegenated textuality takes place at the linguistic intersection where different varieties of English interact; in her own words, her "poetic idiom is a product of American English and its vernaculars, including those associated with black speakers of American English" (5).

In "Imagining the Unimagined Reader: Writing to the Unborn and Including the Excluded," Mullen suggests that "about one-third of my pleasure as a writer comes from the work itself, the process of writing, a third from the response of my contemporaries, and another third in contemplating unknown readers who inhabit a future I will not live to see" (3). It is my hope that this new collection of essays and interviews creates an opportunity for additional responses from contemporaries as well as a means for future readers to join the conversations and considerations that Mullen's writing makes possible.

The Cracks Between What We Are and
What We Are Supposed to Be

I
Shorter Essays

I
Imagining the Unimagined Reader
Writing to the Unborn and Including the Excluded

The context for my work is not so much geographic as it is linguistic and cultural. I write beyond the range of my voice and the social boundaries of identity, yet within the limits imposed on my work and my imagination by language and its cultural significance. The idea of identity informs my poetry, insofar as identity acts upon language, and language acts upon identity. It would be accurate to say that my poetry explores the reciprocity of language and culture. My work is informed by my interactions with readers, writers, scholars, and critics, as well as my interest in the various possibilities for poetry in written and spoken American English.

I write for myself and others. An other is anyone who is not me. Anyone who is not me is like me in some ways and unlike me in other ways. I write, optimistically, for an imagined audience of known and unknown readers. Many of my imagined readers have yet to encounter my work. Most of them are not even born yet. About one-third of my pleasure as a writer comes from the work itself, the process of writing, a third from the response of my contemporaries, and another third in contemplating unknown readers who inhabit a future I will not live to see. When I read the words of African Americans who were slaves, I feel at once my similarity and difference. I experience simultaneously continuity and discontinuity with the past, which I imagine is similar to that of the unborn reader who might encounter my work in some possible future. There is another kind of experience I sometimes have when reading the words of authors who never imagined that someone like me might be included in the potential audience for their work, as when I read in Cirlot's *Dictionary of Symbols* that a "Negro" symbolizes the beast in the human. When I read words never meant for me, or anyone like me—words that exclude me, or anyone like me, as a possible reader—then I feel simul-

taneously my exclusion and my inclusion as a literate black woman, the unimagined reader of the text.

A future reader I imagine for my work is the offspring of an illiterate
woman. A significant percentage of the world's population remains illiterate,
the majority of them girls and women. An even greater number of people
have minimal access to books or the leisure to read them. In addition to
people who simply have no opportunity to be empowered by education, the
problem of illiteracy has expanded, as the late Paulo Freire pointed out, to
include nominally educated people who are unable to function as critical
readers. The disputes among what Hank Lazer calls "opposing poetries" provide examples of the proliferation of competing poetics representing competing and alternative literacies, of which the proliferation of illiteracies is a
side effect. E. D. Hirsch's "cultural literacy" franchise offered a panacea for
the anxieties of the educated and elite classes contemplating an increasingly
diverse and multicultural population, as well as for the anxieties of minorities resisting total assimilation of the dominant culture.

What constitutes literacy has always been determined by the powerful,
while illiteracy persists as an attribute of the disempowered. Economic and
social policies in the United States that widen the gap between the haves and
have-nots inevitably deepen the divide between the literate and the illiterate,
with the illiterate increasingly consigned to the criminal justice system. The
July 27, 1997, issue of the *Women's Review of Books* gathered a collection of
articles on U.S. prisons and activists working with incarcerated women and
their children, observing that, "As we approach the millennium, prisons are
among the country's biggest post-cold war growth industries. Within the
prison boom, women are the fastest-growing population, a trend due primarily to the so-called war on drugs." One article, "Literacy for Life," reports
on the work of Motheread, a North Carolina organization that helps women
in prison improve their own and their children's literacy skills. In addition
to the division of the literate and the illiterate, there is further division between the literate and the hyperliterate. The illiteracy that Motheread targets is of a more abject variety than that claimed by poet Sharon Doubiago,
a college-educated white woman with working-class roots, in an interview
in *Contemporary Literature*: "I read Helen in Egypt at eighteen. I've always
said, self-deprecatingly, that I didn't understand a word of it. I didn't know
any mythology. I was illiterate, although I was a Bible scholar."

I think I have a fairly accurate sense of the people who are reading my poetry now, because I am already acquainted with many of them. They are poets, critics, teachers, and students of literature. Some are readers interested
in the poetry of writers of color, or black writers more specifically, or women

writers. Some are readers who simply enjoy poetry. These known readers are the people I see at poetry readings and literature conferences, at art centers, colleges, and (more rarely) at bookstores. A few others only began to read my work because they are friends or members of my family. If they did not know me already, they probably would never have encountered my books in their normal everyday lives.

Aside from illiteracy, and the poverty that perpetuates it, which get my vote as urgent yet insufficiently recognized issues for writers and teachers of poetry, the major barriers to potential readers of my poetry are availability and language. All four of my poetry books, so far, have been published in relatively small editions by small presses and have been distributed mainly by mail order through the individual publishers and by Small Press Distribution in Berkeley. My books are very rarely found on bookstore shelves. When they are, it is usually a campus bookstore that orders books because I am scheduled to read at a particular college. These readings often occur in the context of a brief "residency" of up to a week, which might also include a public lecture on poetics; visits to writing, literature, and other classes; individual critiques of student writing; interviews for print or broadcast media; book signings; and various receptions and meals with interested faculty and students. Sometimes off-campus readings at community venues are also included in the residency. The variety of events, sponsored by different entities, allows more potential readers to be introduced to the work, and pragmatically combines funds from various departments and organizations to pay the expenses of travel, accommodations, and honorarium. Additionally, a few of my poems have appeared, with or without my permission, on the World Wide Web, thereby expanding my potential audience beyond those who see my work in books or periodicals.

For some potential readers, language is an even greater barrier than availability. It is possible that my poetry might become more available, but it is unlikely that my poems will become any more translatable. As long as my poems remain untranslated, they are accessible only to those who can read English. It is not that I am a linguistic chauvinist, by any means, but simply that, as a more or less monolingual speaker of American English, I am working within the language that is mine. With the exception of a handful of prose poems recently translated by Mexican poet Pedro Serrano and a few poems from my first book that were translated into Spanish for a bilingual anthology, my work exists only in English. I have sprinkled Spanish words into my poems but never enough to make the work bilingual. My poetic idiom is a product of American English and its vernaculars, including those associated with black speakers of American English.

As I continue to work conceptually with specific cultural and linguistic materials, rather than logical statement, linear narrative, or transparent lyrical expression, my work gets closer to what makes poetry so resistant to paraphrase, and thus, untranslatable. While I can appreciate the narrative drive of Homer and Virgil, the lyrical transparency of Sappho, Pablo Neruda, and Wislawa Szymborska and the democratic appeal of Walt Whitman and Langston Hughes, and while I certainly admire the qualities that allow these poets to connect with a foreign audience despite what is lost in translation, the qualities that I aspire to in my work seem to be precisely those that resist translation, that have to do with living, thinking, reading, and writing inside a particular language.

My desires as a poet are contradictory. I aspire to write poetry that would leave no insurmountable obstacle to comprehension and pleasure other than the ultimate limits of the reader's interest and linguistic competence. However, I do not necessarily approach this goal by employing a beautiful, pure, simple, or accessible literary language or by maintaining a clear, consistent, recognizable, or authentic voice in my work. At this point in my life, I am more interested in working with language per se than in developing or maintaining my own particular voice or style of writing, although I am aware that my poems may constitute a peculiar idiolect that can be identified as mine. I think of writing as a process that is synthetic rather than organic, artificial rather than natural, human rather than divine. My inclination is to pursue what is minor, marginal, idiosyncratic, trivial, debased, or aberrant in the language that I speak and write. I desire that my work appeal to an audience that is diverse and inclusive while at the same time wondering if human beings will ever learn how to be inclusive without repressing human diversity through cultural and linguistic imperialism.

Of course my fond desire that my work reach every interested reader on the planet from the present to the imagined future itself represents the imperialism of the poet's ego; and surely any poet who fantasizes a globally diverse audience should write poems that can be translated more easily. Although the phenomena that interest me are common to most languages, my work nevertheless continues to explore linguistic quirks and cultural references peculiar to American English as spoken by the multiethnic peoples of the United States. My poems often recycle familiar and humble materials in search of the poetry found in everyday language: puns, double entendres, taboo words, Freudian slips, jokes, riddles, proverbs, folk poetry, found poetry, idiomatic expressions, slang and jargon, coinages, neologisms, nonce words, portmanteaus, pidgins and creoles, nicknames, diminutives, baby talk, tongue twisters, children's rhyming games, imitative and onomatopoeic formations, syntactical and grammatical peculiarities, true and false etymologies, clichés, jingles, and slogans.

Whether in verse or prose poetry, I enjoy playing with the sounds and rhythms of words, creating aural patterns of repeating phonemes, and using the devices of assonance, consonance, alliteration, rhyme, and various echo effects. As a writer I sometimes practice a kind of linguistic archaeology of the metaphorical origins of words, a resurrection of dead metaphors that are buried in any language. I am curious about the "unconscious" of language, suggested by the various indirections of metaphor, metonymy, euphemism, periphrasis, and taboo word deformation. I am equally interested in the materiality of language itself, the physical presence of words and letters on the page, so I am fond of word games, such as acrostics, anagrams, paragrams, lipograms, univocalics, tautograms, charades, homophones, spoonerisms, and palindromes that draw attention to the manipulable properties of letters and words. I like the possibility of scrambled words and syntax, of secret or alternative meanings, of words hidden within other words, as in equivoque, cryptograms, and cryptomorphic riddles. Solving such word puzzles models the activity of different readers decoding and comprehending alternative messages from the same text.

Recently I have written a poem composed of what I call "aphasic similes," another poem that gets its syntactical structure from a line of African American folklore that I found in Vertamae Grosvenor's diaspora soul food cookbook, and also a prose poem inspired by certain stylistic tics of formula fiction writing, known as "Tom Swifties," after the hero of a series of books written for juvenile readers in the early twentieth century. An ongoing project is a poem titled "Jinglejangle" that catalogs over three hundred items created by what the dictionary calls "rhyming and jingling formation," which are examples of the poetic process in everyday language.

Although I happen to be working in what is currently the global language of international capitalism, or what some call "Imperial English," the quirks, contradictions, even the inanities, in the language of the declining Anglo-American empire are what interest me most. Writing in English does not assure me that my work will reach the unborn readers of the future (assuming optimistically that human beings and poetry have a future) for whom English may well be as dead as Latin, Ancient Greek, and Sumerian are for me. My poetry will not reach people who do not read English, or people who do not read poetry, whether they are literate or illiterate. Although some of my poems would not suffer if they were heard but not read, others ought to be seen as well as heard. Video and audiotapes of me reading my work are stored in various poetry archives, which would make the work available to anyone who can understand my spoken English, but these media documents happen to be as perishable as books and periodicals.

Not when I am writing, but after I have written, I consider who would be left out and excluded from the poem. Although it is not necessary or possible to include everyone, I find that it is useful to me as a writer to think about the fact that language, culture, and poetry always exclude as well as they include potential audiences. One reason I have avoided a singular style or voice for my poetry is the possibility of including a diverse audience of readers attracted to different poems and different aspects of the work. I try to leave room for unknown readers I can only imagine.

2
Poetry and Identity

Some poems I wrote over a decade ago are only now earning a few bucks (and I do mean a few) through their inclusion in anthologies of African American poets. Because of these recent nibbles (for which I am grateful), I have made an act of faith in the posterity of my work, legally naming my sister as my heir and executor of my literary estate. Anyone reading this knows that the living poet feels lucky to be paid in copies of the published work; but perhaps when I am dead, payments for future poetry permissions might help to sustain my sister, my nephews, or their children. My recent inclusion in these anthologies gives rise to this meditation on the various experiences of inclusion, exclusion, and marginality of a "formally innovative" black poet.

It has been argued that if publication in anthologies from commercial presses, reviews and other coverage in mass media, space on bookstore shelves, adoption into course curricula, and library acquisitions are the measures of success, it would seem that representative "black" poets are currently more assimilable into the "mainstream" than "formally innovative" poets of any hue. Although both the "avant-garde poet" and the "minority poet" may be perceived as "others" in relation to the "mainstream" (regardless of the distance and the different concerns that might separate avant-garde and minority poets), it would seem that the mainstream has far more to gain by appropriating minority poets who work in recognizable and accessible forms and who can thus be marketed to the broadest possible audience of readers.

MTV notwithstanding, textbooks and anthologies—the most commercial and lucrative venues for poetry publication (profitable for the publishers if not for the poets)—continue to be the primary means of reaching the broadest audience of people who read poetry. Poets are anthologized as representatives of their era, nationality, region, race, ethnicity, gender, class, and/or aesthetic affiliation; and anthologies are driven by realities of marketing, as well as by critical activity and curricular needs. In the anthology and text-book markets poets "of color," given their automatic representational status, have a distinct advantage over "formally innovative" poets, who appeal to no large or easily identifiable demographic segment of the literary market.

"Avant-garde" poets—to the extent that they can be gathered together and made comprehensible (given sufficient critical energy and academic accep-tance) as members of some distinctive and coherently articulated generation, school, or movement—can be packaged for mainly academic consumption in much the same manner that "poets of color" or "spoken word" practition-ers have been labeled and gathered into anthologies aimed at both main-stream and academic audiences. It would seem, however, that the "avant-garde poet of color" threatens the cohesiveness of the narratives that allow the mainstream audience to recognize, comprehend, or imagine a collective identity, purpose, and aesthetics for a literary group or movement, whether it is a group "of color" or a movement defined by its commitment to "formal innovation."

"Formally innovative minority poets," when visible at all, are not likely to be perceived either as typical of a racial/ethnic group or as representative of an aesthetic movement. Their unaccountable existence therefore strains the seams of the critical narratives necessary to make them (individually and collectively) comprehensible and thus teachable and marketable. In each generation the erasure of the anomalous black writer abets the construction of a continuous, internally consistent tradition, and it deprives the idiosyn-cratic minority artist of a history, compelling her to struggle even harder to construct a cultural context out of her own radical individuality. She is un-anticipated and often unacknowledged because of the imposed obscurity of her aesthetic antecedents.

Because my first book allowed me to be placed rather neatly within the category of "representative blackness" (as well as in the categories of "femi-nist" and "regional" poet), whereas my second and third books are more frequently described as "formally innovative" poetry rather than as "black poetry," I have had the sometimes unsettling experience of seeing my work divided into distinct taxonomies. Because I no longer write poems like the ones in *Tree Tall Woman* (Energy Earth, 1981), some readers perhaps per-ceive my world as "less black.

Evidently, publishers of African American anthologies are entirely un-interested in my more recent work, from *Trimmings* on. Only in the ear-lier poetry, represented by the work in *Tree Tall Woman* or similarly "speak-erly" poems, am I digestible as a black poet. Those seeking to incorporate me into an African American poetic tradition apparently overlook my two prose poem books, *Trimmings* (Tender Buttons, 1991) and *S*PeRM**K*T*

(Singing Horse, 1992), just as those who praise these books generally do not connect them to the emphatically ethnic poetic "voice" of *Tree Tall Woman*, which likely seems markedly inflected by race, class, gender, culture, and region compared to the more ambiguously located subjectivity of *Trimmings* and *S*PeRM**K*T*. The perceived gap that allows different parts of my work to be claimed or assimilated, ignored or rejected, by various readers is widened by the fact that not enough readers challenge or move beyond boundaries that continue to separate writing that appears in "black" or "minority," "mainstream," and "avant-garde" books and journals.

Poet and critic Rachel Blau DuPlessis generously includes me in her essay on contemporary women's poetry in the recent *Oxford Companion to Women's Writing in the United States*. A peculiar effect of the daunting constraints and demands of the encyclopedic essay, perhaps, is that I am not grouped with black women poets (of whom only Ntozake Shange is singled out as an exemplar of "experimental" writing). Instead, I am placed in a subcategory of formally innovative poets who are also women of color. Or rather (because "women of color" seems to occupy a separate category apart from innovative or experimental poets), I become an example of "innovative women poets of minority background," along with Mei-mei Berssenbrugge and Myung Mi Kim, as well as Erica Hunt (in fact, at different times I have read on the same program with the latter two).

Because I also work as a literary critic, I understand the desire to place each writer and her work in the proper critical cubbyhole: one constructs meaningful distinctions in order to articulate significant critical statements based on comparisons of different textual practices and traditions. As an African Americanist, I am aware that my scholarly discipline depends, in part, on defining what is distinct, particular, and continuous about our literary and cultural heritage; yet it concerns me to see how frequently even editors and critics with the best intentions participate in draining the category "black" or "African American" of its complex internal diversity by removing from the category anything so eccentric or innovative that it subverts a "traditional" or "canonical" notion of black or African American heritage. Excluding or ignoring the unconventional tends to homogenize the canon, marooning those divergent works that might be equally (or more) alien to the mainstream. Nor are such unanticipated works always likely to be embraced immediately by an "avant-garde" that might also view blackness as "otherness," even as, in making its own claim to diversity, it adopts the innovative artist of minority background as an exceptional comrade.

The assumption remains, however unexamined, that "avant-garde" poetry is not "black" and that "black" poetry, however singular its "voice," is not "formally innovative." It is my hope that *Muse & Drudge* (Singing Horse,

1995) might alter or challenge that assumption, bridging what apparently has been imagined as a gap (or chasm?) between my work as a "black" poet and my work as a "formally innovative" poet. I see this as a "Baraka vs. Jones" problem—although he has moved in the other direction. For me, the dilemma is similar to the conflict Ron Silliman discusses in *The New Sentence* between "codes of oppressed peoples" (a poetry with its own urgent aesthetics: hence the entire construction of the Harlem Renaissance, Negritude, and the Black Arts/Black Aesthetics movements) and so-called purely aesthetic schools (whose aesthetic mode itself can be read as a social code and an ideological weapon).

I felt that my latest poetic experiment must be successful when selections from *Muse & Drudge* were chosen to appear in "black" leaning journals *Callaloo* and *Mule teeth* as well as in mainstream publications seeking diversity and journals devoted to a racially unspecified "avant-garde." It's also encouraging when my work is solicited for new literary magazines and student-edited publications by young African Americans, Asian Americans, Latinos, and other members of racially diverse editorial collectives. I would single out Nathaniel Mackey's *Hambone* as exemplary in the welcome it has offered to challenging and idiosyncratic work from a diverse spectrum of writers. Mackey and Ishmael Reed, editor of *Quilt,* are two African American poet-editors (each with his own eccentric relation to black traditions) who published transitional poems that I wrote in the period between *Tree Tall Woman* and *Trimmings.* Is it a coincidence that both reside in California, where I myself was living when I began to write "differently" as I interrogated my previously unexamined black identity? Yet during this time it was Lorenzo Thomas—a poet born in Panama, reared in New York and transplanted to Houston, Texas—who became my most immediate and influential model of a black poet engaged in formal innovation.

My marginality as a black artist teaches me important lessons for my survival and integrity as an aesthetic innovator; and certainly my experience crossing boundaries as a participant-observer in the "mysterious" avant-garde has provided me with additional models, resources, alliances, and readers in my development as an African American artist whose work struggles to overcome aesthetic apartheid.

Feeling no nostalgia for segregation nor any need or desire to divest myself of my black identity and connections to black communities nor any particular stake in defending traditional "humanism," I hope that my work continues to challenge that deadly distinction between "blackness" and "humanity"—or "universality"—that is still imposed on black human beings.

3
Kinky Quatrains

The Making of *Muse & Drudge*

From *Muse & Drudge*

1.
O rose so drowsy in
my flower bed your pink
pajamas zig-zag
into fluent dreams of living ink

carve out your niche
reconfigure the hybrid
back in the kitchen
live alone, buy bread

your backbone slip
sliding silk hipped
to the discography
of archival sarcophagi

pregnant pause
conceived by doorknob insinuation
and no set animal
laminates on DNA

2.
marry at a hotel, annul 'em
nary hep male rose sullen
let alley roam, yell melon
dull normal fellow hammers omelette

divine sunrises
Osiris's irises
his splendid mistress
is his sis Isis.

creole cocoa loca
crayon gumbo boca
crayfish crayola
jumbo mocha-cola

warp maid fresh
fetish coquettish
a voyeur leers
at x-rated reels

3.
married the bear's daughter
and ain't got a quarter
now you're playing the dozens
with your uncle's cousins

sitting here marooned
in limbo quiombo
ace coon ballooned up
without a parachute

use your noodle for
more than a hatrack
act like you got the sense
God gave a gopher

couldn't fold the tablecloth
can't count my biscuits
think you're able to solve
a figure, go ahead and risk it

4.
when memory is unforgiving
mute eloquence
of taciturn ghosts
wreaks havoc on the living

intimidates intimates
polishing naked cactus
down below a bitter buffer
inferno never froze over

to deaden the shock
of enthusiastic knowledge
a soft body when struck
pale light or moderate

smooth as if by rubbing
thick downward curving
bare skin imitative
military coat made of this

5.
Jesus is my airplane
I shall feel no turbulence
though I fly in a squall
through the spleen of Satan

in a dream the book beckoned
opened for me to the page
where I read the words
that were to me a sign

houses of Heidelberg
outhouse cracked house
destroyed funhouse lost
and found house of dead dolls

two-headed dreamer
of second-sighted vision
through the veil
she heard her call

6.
just as I am I come
knee bent and body bowed
this here's sorrow's home
my body's southern song

cram all you can
into jelly jam
preserve a feeling
keep it sweet

so beautiful it was
presumptuous to alter
the shape of my pleasure
in doing or making

proceed with abandon
finding yourself where you are
and who you're playing for
what stray companion

Writing poetry for me is more a matter of texture than form. *Muse & Drudge* employs a ubiquitously traditional form, the quatrain or tetrastich, common to ballads and other folk poetry, and well represented within the history of English verse. I was attracted to the form primarily because I saw that, given the surface uniformity and constraint of the four-by-four format as a unit of composition (four quatrains per page), I could make these four-line stanzas quirky, irregular, and sensuously kinky in terms of polyrhythm (as opposed to regular meter) and polyvocality (as opposed to the persistence of a single lyric voice or narrative viewpoint). This form also allowed for a wide range of lexical choice and levels of diction (from the sacred to the profane), variation in line length, the various possibilities of rhyming or not rhyming, using end rhyme or internal rhyme, or odd lines of prose arranged as lines and stanzas to make "found poetry," as well as semantic and syntactic tensions within and between lines.

As in my prose poems *Trimmings* and *S*PeRM**K*T,* I continue to use what Stephen Yenser identified as "multivalent fragments," which produce a layered effect of multiple and sometimes contradictory semantic meanings and cultural allusions. I am also interested in the textural effects enabled by what Roman Jakobson called "subliminal verbal patterning" in literary and folk poetry. Folklorist John Holmes McDowell, referring to children's riddles, calls this aspect of the folk composition "riddling texture" or "aural composition . . . the palpable, sensuous organization . . . metrical and phonological patterning" of the verbal utterance.

My writing process is improvisatory, and certainly I have been influenced by instrumental and vocal improvisations of blues and jazz musicians. Some of the lines I write aspire to certain moments in jazz when scat becomes a kind of inspired speaking in tongues, or glossolalia, moments when utterance is pure music. Improvisatory methods I have used in poetry also follow from my interest in the literary techniques and experiments of Oulipo, as well as Saussure's investigation of anagrammatic, tabular readings of poetic texts, which has also influenced Steve McCaffery and Bernadette Mayer, poets whose work I have found useful for its playful preoccupation with the materiality and texture of writing.

Of course I follow in the tradition of poets, including Paul Lawrence Dunbar, James Weldon Johnson, Langston Hughes, Sterling Brown, Margaret Walker, Etheridge Knight, and Gwendolyn Brooks, who often worked with humble, common, and "folksy" materials, such as proverbs, prayers, folk sermons, lullabies, nursery rhymes and children's lore, blues, ballads, jokes, raps, riddles, and toasts. Although simple, such forms are striking in their mnemonic force, aural texture, and pervasive persistence. In a poetic text, simple things can be used for complex effects. I use all of these and other folk-based forms, allusively, along with their mutant offspring: clichés, political slogans, advertising jingles, tabloid headlines, and other linguistic readymades from the mass-culture dumpster. These I recycle in the spirit of Duchamp and Tyree Guyton's "Heidelberg Houses" in Detroit. Inverted, the urinal becomes a fountain; recontextualized in a gallery or museum, it can be a work of art. Guyton transformed a social landscape and dynamically exposed conflicting views about community when he took an abandoned shack used as a crack house and turned it into a life-sized dollhouse; he accomplished similar aims when he turned a vacant trash-strewn lot into a community art park and only then did politicians revile the lot as an eyesore. However, most influential to me personally is Lorenzo Thomas, whose attention to the communal drum and commitment to his own offbeat solo music demonstrates the flexibility of traditions, forms, and genres in the hands of an adept aesthetic innovator.

Muse & Drudge, like the jazz soloist who plays "mysterious" music, locates itself in a space where it is possible to pay dues, respects, and "props" to tradition while still claiming the freedom to wander to the other side of far.

4

Telegraphs from a Distracted Sibyl

I went to graduate school in Santa Cruz. Dipping into the Bay Area bouilla-baisse of aesthetically and politically engaged poets, artists, filmmakers, mu-sicians, and new age root workers, and getting all sorts of ideas and notions in my encounters with postmodern theory as a grad student, I rediscovered my favorite modernists, Jean Toomer, Melvin Tolson, and Gertrude Stein, and started on my second book, *Trimmings*, which is, in part, my way of giv-ing propers to our Ms. Gwendolyn Brooks, and talking back to Gertrude's *Tender Buttons* and *Melanctha*. My "girt/girdle" paragraph is also a tribute to Gertrude "Ma" Rainey, as well as Genie Stein. *Trimmings* was followed by *S*PeRM**K*T*, which is similar to its predecessor, but with a nastier at-titude, since it spews out the mass culture that has used my brain pan as its petri dish. (I could remember 20-year-old jingles but couldn't recite a line of Jay Wright or Ed Roberson to save my soul.)

Trimmings and *S*PeRM**K*T* are both prose poems and list poems. I par-ticularly enjoyed the challenge of transforming and recycling the list poem, a workshop cliché, from the compost heap of listless language and depicted devices. However, I freely admit that a persistent fear, as I composed these poems in prose, was that they might not be recognizable (despite my dotty improvs on Black English and my deliberate choice of a "trivial," "feminine" subject matter and a "minor" literary form). Like legal scholar Patricia Wil-liams, I occasionally dread that the greatest accolade, or even acceptance, the so-called mainstream culture can offer me is that, after I've been dead long enough, I might be remembered as white and/or male (or praised for hav-ing written "like" a white male). I suppose that's why I allowed the publica-tion of those frightful pictures of myself on the books.

In both texts, I adapted the prose poem, composed of my own kind of "new sentences," instead of using open or free verse forms. I also took the risk of abandoning the precisely located black female subjectivity of my first, folksy book—*Tree Tall Woman*—for something that looks more like the text of a telegraph from a distracted sibyl whose songs, if not her feet, are always shuffling. (In this respect I compare myself to Erica Hunt, whose *Local History* struck me as urgently urban, postmodern, and sibylline. Incidentally the sibyl was perhaps the first deconstructionist in the sense that she constantly deconstructed her own written texts, and her oracles, something like Ifa divination, or like what Ishmael Reed in *Mumbo Jumbo* calls "Jes Grew's text," were randomized fragments from her voluminous manuscripts, which some zealous literary censor later burned. A less complete annihilation, or what translator Diane Rayor calls "a collaboration of the poet and time," produced the tantalizingly spare lines of Sappho.)

I think of my first book as more a derivation and celebration of my mother's (spoken) voice than as the discovery of "my own voice" as a writer. In poetry I have no voice, only text. I like it that way, since I've always been a shy and disorganized speaker but a much bolder and more focused writer.

My next work, *Muse & Drudge* (also known as "Mules & Drugs") is a verse poem in quatrains that uses rhyme and rhythm inconsistently and, I hope, unpredictably; it *is* an attempt on my part to return to a more-or-less recognizably "colored," "negro," "black," or "African American" base of folk-street-blues-based riffs, rap, and rhetoric without returning to the specifically located subjectivity of my earlier work. I wanted to use all that I've learned since I strayed from the beaten to the off-beat path but still keep my promise to meet the devil at the crossroads and walk a mile in some other body's down-or-upbeat sneakers, as the case may be, with plenty of wordplay along the way. *Muse & Drudge* is, on the one hand, a pretty straightforward praise song to women of the African diaspora, although a good deal of it is less than flattering; on the other hand, it is a blues riff on Sappho as Sapphire. As an old bluesman said, with double-edged ambiguity, "If it wasn't for women, we wouldn't have the blues."

So I guess I'd say my literary background and practice as a writer, in short, has been something of a traditional, eclectic, folksy, trashy, classical, avant-garde, worldly, naive, unorthodox, spiritual, polymorphously perverse, mammy-made, jig-rig, and Rube Goldberg operation.

And I suppose I wouldn't have it any other way!

5

If Lilies are Lily White

From the Stain of Miscegenation in Stein's "Melanctha" to the "Clean Mixture" of White and Colored in Her *Tender Buttons*

I begin with the idea of color and race as different yet overlapping preoccupations in the two texts by Gertrude Stein with which I, as a black woman and as a poet, have the most intense relationship: "Melanctha" or *Tender Buttons*. Whether or not Stein shows her "true colors," so to speak, in either "Melanctha" or *Tender Buttons* is open to argument: "Melanctha," with its brash forays into African American vernacular and black female sexuality, has been read by Aldon Nielsen and others as an overtly racist text, while *Tender Buttons* is more widely celebrated by contemporary poets as a dazzling, cryptic, and insistently colorful work of verbal innovation.[1]

My reading of *Tender Buttons* is inextricably bound to my reading of "Melanctha," its precursor. Even though, in many respects, *Tender Buttons* appears to make a radical stylistic break from the narrative and syntactical structures of "Melanctha," I am interested in what I perceive to be an underlying thematic continuity that can be traced from one to the other. Stein's explicit interest in sexual and racial stereotypes in "Melanctha" unquestionably influences my response to *Tender Buttons*. If, as Nielsen argues—an argument with which I agree—"Melanctha" rests on a creaky foundation of racial and sexual fantasy, *Tender Buttons,* for all its poetic innovation and for all its departure from the overt social concerns of its predecessor, nevertheless continues Stein's concern with the impact of color on perception.

It has been said of modern art that "[c]olor was no longer used only to describe or define particular objects, but it could also function as an autonomous element that created a rhythm for the entire composition"; this description applies as well to *Tender Buttons*.[2] Color—as an attribute of physical objects, as a phenomenon of perception, as an aesthetic stimulus, as an artist's medium, as a set of descriptive adjectives within a literary text, and also as an indicator of racial and sexual identity—is a preoccupation of Stein's *Tender Buttons*. If "difference is spreading," as the text announces right at the beginning, with "A CARAFE, THAT IS A BLIND GLASS," then color as an indicator of difference is also spreading and pervasive in *Tender Buttons*.[3] While race is overt, visible, and superficial in "Melanctha," I would argue that it is also present, though more covert, invisible, and subliminal, in *Tender Buttons*.

Reading *Tender Buttons* through the lens provided by its race-conscious palimpsest "Melanctha," I am struck by a number of Stein's grammatically and syntactically subversive fragments, sentences, and paragraphs that beg to be read as possible meditations on race as well as sexuality. The first few pages offer such suggestive possibilities as "a single hurt color and an arrangement in a system of pointing" (461); "Dirty is yellow. A sign of more is not mentioned. A piece of coffee is not a detainer. The resemblance to yellow is dirtier and distincter. The clean mixture is whiter and not coal color, never more coal color than altogether" (463); and "If lilies are lily white if they exhaust noise and distance and even dust, if they dusty will dirt a surface that has no extreme grace, if they do this and it is not necessary it is not at all necessary if they do this they need a catalogue" (465).

Of course, my favorite fragment, and the key to understanding the relationship of *Tender Buttons* to "Melanctha" and my own relationship to Stein, is the small fragment titled "A PETTICOAT," which reads, in its entirety: "A light white, a disgrace, an ink spot, a rosy charm" (471). Here Stein combines a feminine metaphor of writing with images associated with female sexuality and reproduction: ink leaving its stain on white sheets of paper is equated with blood, as the writer is conflated with the menstruating woman, deflowered virgin, or mother giving birth. This brief utterance is remarkable for its compression and for its Rorschach-like power to evoke a narrative from the reader.

I see in this intriguing description (or series, or sequence, or set of appositives) a possible allusion to Manet's painting *Olympia*, which Picasso parodied in a drawing that places a nude black woman under the leering gaze of a white male. Picasso's sketch, almost a cartoon, uncovers and places in the foreground what Manet had left in the shadowy background of Olympia's reclining white nude. Stein's text suggests an image of vulnerable female sexuality as well as an equally vulnerable racial purity, which can be violated through the violation of the white woman's body. Of course, as a writer, Stein can be said to be on the side of the stain, the ink that deflowers the virgin page. For writers to write, ink and blood must be spilled. Innocence must give way to experience, and purity must be violated. The violence that Stein does to grammar, syntax, and meaning is part of *Tender Buttons's* comment on the entropy of domestic life, which is the housekeeper's futile task to manage.

What the brief passages I've quoted have in common is their association of color with dirt and purity or whiteness with vulnerability, given the constant threat of dirt and stains. These have been the traditional concerns of bourgeois American white women, who, as daughters, wives, mothers, and homemakers, are charged with the eternal maintenance of sexual and racial purity, which they pursue by patrolling their homes for telltale signs of dust or dirt. Stein caricatures this bourgeois obsession with domestic purity, but she does so at the expense of her black characters, as when the narrator of "Melanctha" repeatedly describes Rose as "decent" (although "unmoral"). Presumably Rose is "decent" because she is married and because of her habitual cleanliness—never mind that she is just too lazy, shiftless, and stupid to care for her newborn baby.[4]

In "Melanctha," color as a distinguishing physical characteristic establishes a hierarchy of intelligence and complexity among characters described as ranging from "real black" to "pale yellow." The dark-skinned Rose Johnson, described as "a real black, tall, well built, sullen, stupid, childlike and good looking negress" is contrasted with the "subtle, intelligent, attractive, half white girl Melanctha Herbert" (339–340). As others have pointed out, the "yellow girl" Melanctha and the "black Rosie," as well as other characters, correspond to the most deeply entrenched stereotypes about African Americans: those with darker complexions are imagined as alternately childish and brutish, and those with lighter skin are depicted as complex mixtures of sensitivity and tragedy, their visible fractions of whiteness somehow refining their sensibilities so that they suffer emotional pain unimaginable in their darker kin.[5]

Even the names of the two women refer to color: Rose Johnson suggests the erotic darkness of the female sex, on the one hand, while on the other hand Melanctha suggests the black and blue of melanin and melancholy. Stein's mode of textual composition freely exploits color as one in a list of possible descriptors, as a kind of shorthand that substitutes for the delineation of character. Rose is nothing more than an accumulation of epithets, as in: "coarse, decent, sullen, ordinary black Rose" and "unmoral, promiscuous, shiftless Rose" (340). She, in her simplicity, is contrasted with "pale yellow and mysterious" and "complex and desiring" Melanctha (343). The astonishing, almost giddy glibness of the strings of adjectives attached to each character might allow one to suppose that Stein had begun to interrogate the color coding of racial and sexual identity by calling attention to such formulaic characterizations.

If, as Stein said, *Tender Buttons* was in part a project intended to rid her of nouns, "Melanctha" is a text that splurges on adjectives.[6] One result of such excess is a striking demonstration that words used habitually to describe people may obscure far more than they reveal about their subjects. Each time a formulaic string is reiterated, the description carries less meaning, each inane repetition symptomatic of a lack of interest in these characters. Indeed, a lack of interest in the whole idea of character is apparent. In "Melanctha" the adjectives are not only more active than the verbs, they are even more active than the characters themselves, most of whom do little beyond fornicating, procreating, and indulging in the occasional razor fight.

Yet it is significant that Rose, an orphan reared in an affluent white household, and Melanctha, with her mixed racial heritage, depart in one notable respect from the stereotype of what Rose calls "common niggers." Both women are exiled from the realm of what Stein's narrator repeatedly calls "the wide abandoned laughter that makes the warm glow of negro sunshine." Stein depicts both Rose and Melanctha as exceptions to this particular rule of race: "Rose was never joyous with the earth-born boundless joy of Negroes. Hers was just the ordinary, any sort of woman laughter." The melancholy Melanctha is even more exceptional. She tells her friend Rose that she often thinks of killing herself because she is "so blue." These characters hover between extreme poles of emotional absurdities: the oxymoronic "negro sunshine" of happy darkies and the puzzling paradox of a black woman with white blood who looks yellow and who considers suicide because she is blue. Melanctha's mystery is tied to her fate as a stereotype. Stein has created her by repackaging the so-called tragic mulatto, a figure dating back to the literature of slavery, with jazzy ragtime rhythms of improvisational prose. Melanctha at first appears to be an avatar of female desire seeking its fulfillment outside the sanctuary of heterosexual marriage; she thereby anticipates white women's pursuit of sexual freedom in the jazz age. However, she eventually succumbs to her fate as a tragic mulatto, as the embodiment of racial and sexual taboo, as a social problem that can be corrected only with her death.

The best thing I can say about "Melanctha" is that its creation of awkward characters from the clichés and stereotypes of popular culture draws attention to their constructed subjectivity and also implicates any reader who fails to reach beyond the limits of the ordinary conventions by which meaning is constructed, including the set of conventions that attach social and cultural significance to color. Whether deliberately or not, Stein has put narrative expectations for human complexity in conflict with the racist stereotypes that bracket her characters.[7] What I find interesting about "Melanctha" is that even as the narrator invokes the sentimental stereotype of "negro sunshine," Stein immediately negates it in constructing the subjectivity of her characters. Whether color reveals or conceals identity is a question with which both "Melanctha" and *Tender Buttons* are engaged.

Three Lives, the text in which "Melanctha" is the middle story, was first published in 1909, the same year that Scott Joplin's "Maple Leaf Rag" sold half a million copies.[8] *Tender Buttons* followed in 1914. Carl Van Vechten, the controversial white advocate of black writers and artists of the Harlem Renaissance who also edited *Selected Writings of Gertrude Stein,* claimed credit for helping Stein find a publisher for *Tender Buttons* after he and Stein met in 1913. While textual evidence and anecdotal accounts suggest that Stein was far less interested in black people than Van Vechten, a dedicated negrophile if there ever was one, Stein experimented in "Melanctha" and *Tender Buttons* with themes of race and sexuality that would also preoccupy black writers of the Harlem Renaissance.

It was Van Vechten, the scandalous author of the novel *Nigger Heaven,* who symbolized more than any other single figure the Harlem Renaissance's association with downtown white thrill seekers who went slumming uptown to taste the forbidden joys of mongrel Manhattan.[9] It was Van Vechten whose influence on the artistic production of the Harlem Renaissance was seen as detrimental to the efforts of such black writers and intellectuals as Jessie Fauset and W. E. B. Du Bois, who felt that black art and literature should be positive and uplifting so as to normalize rather than exoticize black experience.[10] Although respectably bourgeois African Americans viewed Van Vechten's work as literary slumming, his protean role as godfather to the Harlem Renaissance, admirer of "Melanctha," and midwife to Stein's *Tender Buttons* suggests the degree to which race—particularly the social, cultural, and genetic mixing of the races—was a significant, if sometimes unarticulated, concern of modernism and modernist art.

In some respects, modernism can be seen as an aesthetic movement created out of a crisis of recognition and misrecognition as artists of various races increasingly found occasions to encounter one another as colleagues, collaborators, and competitors. In some cases, black and white artists whose education, experience, and interests were more similar than different almost seemed to conspire in creating colorfully exotic representations of blackness that exaggerated racial difference. Stein's and Van Vechten's works shared elements of exoticism and primitivism with certain works by Jean Toomer,

Claude McKay, and Langston Hughes. Richard Wright's professed admiration for "Melanctha" has often been cited by critics to defend Stein against charges of racism. Certainly the meaning of color varies according to its context, and racial epithets signify differently depending on who uses them and how they are handled; thus the color coding in Stein's "Melanctha" is more discomfiting even if it is less objectifying than Sterling Brown's adaptation of African American folk poetry in "Odyssey of Big Boy":

> Had stovepipe blond in Macon,
> Yaller gal in Marylan',
> In Richmond had a choklit brown,
> Called me huh monkey man—
> Huh big fool monkey man.
> Had two fair browns in Arkansaw
> And three in Tennessee,
> Had Creole gal in New Orleans,
> Sho Gawd did two time me—
> Lawd two time, fo' time me—[11]

If anything, Stein participates in a time-honored American tradition where white artists selectively appropriate elements of black vernacular expression, a move that has repeatedly stimulated black artists to reappropriate the expressive forms, syncopated rhythms, and improvisational eloquence associated with black folk and popular culture. This double movement of appropriation and reappropriation is suggested in Wright's account of his response to "Melanctha":

> The style was so insistent and original and sang so quaintly that I took the book home.
>
> As I read it my ears were opened for the first time to the magic of the spoken word. I began to hear the speech of my grandmother, who spoke a deep, pure Negro dialect. . . .
>
> All of my life I had been only half hearing, but Miss Stein's struggling words made the speech of the people around me vivid. From that moment on, in my attempts at writing, I was able to tap at will the vast pool of living words that swirled around me. (338)

While cultural assimilation has been the compulsory norm for European immigrants to the United States, miscegenation, the genetic mixing of the races, has always seemed dangerous in a white America that fears the visible trace of color that threatens to stain or taint the presumed purity of whiteness. Ingrained stereotypes about black identity reflect the desires and fears that white observers have projected onto black bodies, and certainly the tragic mulatto stereotype is less a comment on biracial identity than a conventional representation of a white person trapped in a racially tainted body. The curse of the tragic mulatto is his or her inability to enjoy the supposed hedonism of the black race due to the unfortunate interference of sensibilities inherited from the white progenitor. In a sense, American culture has been an ongoing production of "lily-white" mulattos untainted by physical traces of blackness who might combine the intelligence and refinement attributed to the white race with the capacity for pleasure attributed to the black.

In her transition from the explicit racial and sexual themes of "Melanctha" to the subtle pervasive themes of color and domestic eroticism in *Tender Buttons,* Stein, the daughter of European immigrants, recreates herself through an aesthetic mode of production as an American cultural mulatto, a modernist mongrel who, like Picasso, synthesizes a "clean mixture" of Africa and Europe through artistic rather than reproductive means. As someone who managed to be both bourgeois and bohemian, both a respected avant-garde artist and a popular author in demand on the lecture circuit, as well as a lesbian who settled happily into a domestic arrangement with a devoted spouse-equivalent, the public Gertrude Stein is quite the opposite of her creation, Melanctha, the recycled tragic mulatto. Melanctha never establishes a stable life nor experiences the pleasures of marriage, career, or family; instead she eventually dies of tuberculosis in "a home for poor consumptives" (457). Is Melanctha a representation of the sexual freedom that Stein desired for herself as well as an embodiment of Stein's worst fears as a woman living outside the legal institutions of marriage and patriarchy? Is Melanctha's ambiguous racial identity an analog of Stein's ambivalence about her own Jewish identity? If we take certain words from *Tender Buttons* and apply them to Melanctha, does this help determine whether her "resemblance to yellow is dirtier and distincter" than Stein's "clean mixture" of domestic order and syntactical disorder?

Tender Buttons remains an extraordinary source of creative energy for my poetry and me. Two of my books, *Trimmings* and *S*PeRM**K*T,* began as responses to *Tender Buttons.* I feel free to claim Gertrude as a literary foreparent, even though I am not so sure she would want to claim me as an heir. And although I claim her as an ancestor, I cannot say that I am a devout ancestor worshipper. Once I, as a reader, have confronted the sentimentally racist "negro sunshine" and "wide abandoned laughter" of "Melanctha," I am prepared to apply my own race-conscious reading to the cozily domestic image in *Tender Buttons* of "a white egg and a colored pan" (487). When I encounter in this charmingly disarming text a perplexing catalogue of unlikely items, akin to an eccentric shopping list, that includes "a white bird, a colored mine, a mixed orange, a dog," I examine it with the critical consciousness of America's "others" confronted with signs that once decreed, "No Jews, dogs, or niggers allowed" (486). My ancestors on the black side were corralled together with Gertrude Stein and Rin Tin Tin by the peculiar heterogeneity of this public prohibition. I can certainly imagine Gertrude laughing at its absurdity as she purchased her one-way ticket to Paris; and if I can imagine that, I suppose I can imagine myself laughing at every absurdity I find in "Melanctha." So I imagine myself laughing—in sunshine or in rain.

Notes

1. Among critical discussions of Stein, Aldon Nielsen's *Reading Race,* Sonia Saldivar-Hull's "Wrestling Your Ally: Gertrude Stein, Racism, and Feminist Critical Practice," and Milton Cohen's "Black Brutes and Mulatto Saints: The Racial Hierarchy of Stein's 'Melanctha'" critique the racial stereotyping in "Melanctha."

2. Curator's notes for an exhibit of paintings by Max Beckmann, shown with works of his more famous contemporaries, Leger, Delaunay, Rouault, Matisse, Braque, and Picasso. The Saint Louis Art Museum, February 1999.

3. *Selected Writings of Gertrude Stein*, p. 461. For subsequent quotations from this text, page numbers are in parentheses.

4. We are told that Rose owes her clean habits as well as her survival not to her parents but to the largesse of the white family that had employed her mother as a servant. When her mother dies, they decide to rear the "cute, attractive, good looking" orphan as their own. Contrasted with their benevolence, Rose's fatal neglect of her own infant is even more disturbing, despite the narrator's bland explanation that such deaths are common in black (and poor?) communities.

5. Although she is described as "half white" Melanctha's parents are both African Americans.

6. From Stein's *Lectures in America,* quoted in *Selected Writings of Gertrude Stein,* p. 460.

7. This conflict is worked out at the linguistic level, as Michael North argues in his discussion of Stein's synthesis of dialect and modernism in "Melanctha": "Stein raises a general suspicion about the way that language attaches attributes to things. . . . Though Stein includes in 'Melanctha' very little that could be recognized as black dialect, her whole linguistic strategy is to produce . . . tension between two quite different kinds of language. Thus the paradox on which Stein

constructs the peculiar dialect of 'Melanctha.' A patois with a very restricted vocabulary and a repetitious looping sentence structure it seems a kind of speech
that sticks almost superstitiously to the known and the familiar. And yet, the
more Stein's speakers reiterate the few simple words allotted to them, the more
unstable those words become." *The Dialect of Modernism,* pp. 74, 76. What is not
quite explicit here is that the language of the narrator is as impoverished by racial and sexual taboos and stereotypes as the speech of Stein's characters. A style
that seems playfully poetic in *Tender Buttons* seems willfully restrictive and un-
generous in "Melanctha."

8. See Carla Peterson, "The Remaking of Americans: Gertrude Stein's
'Melanctha' and African-American Musical Traditions."

9. With the possible exception of shipping magnate heir Nancy Cunard, who
financed and edited the 1934 anthology *Negro* and also published Ezra Pound
and Samuel Beckett. See Ann Douglas, *Terrible Honesty.*

10. Melanctha's suitor Jeff Campbell holds similar views of racial uplift. Their
doomed affair anticipates the argument between supporters of artistic freedom
and advocates of counter-racist art in the Harlem Renaissance.

11. *Collected Poems of Sterling Brown,* p. 21.

6
Nine Syllables Label Sylvia

Reading Plath's "Metaphors"

METAPHORS
I'm a riddle in nine syllables,
An elephant, a ponderous house,
A melon strolling on two tendrils.
O red fruit, ivory, fine timbers!
This loaf's big with its yeasty rising.
Money's new-minted in this fat purse.
I'm a means, a stage, a cow in calf.
I've eaten a bag of green apples,
Boarded a train there's no getting off.
                    Sylvia Plath, *Crossing the Water*

Plath's poem "Metaphors" is packed with metaphors: a different one for each line, sometimes two or three. Yet all are poetically equivalent, referring to the same unstated condition of pregnancy. The poet has compressed similes into metaphors so that conventional comparisons—"I'm as heavy as an elephant. I'm as big as a house. My belly looks like I've swallowed a watermelon"—are converted into metaphors representing an enormity that is both weighty and ridiculous—"I'm . . . an elephant . . . a ponderous house . . . a melon." These metaphors then generate the synecdoches of ivory, timbers, red fruit, which indicate the dismantling, destruction, or commodification of the metaphorical elephant, house, and melon. Subsequent metaphors communicate contradictory feelings of pride, self-worth, domesticity, radical transformation, illness, anticipation, anxiety, commitment, and resignation. The poem's title might also connect to pregnancy by functioning as a subliminal pun based on the etymological origins of the word *metaphor* (carry across; transfer): *meta*, meaning "involved with change," and *pherein*, meaning "to bear." This pun on metaphor/pregnancy, as well as on traditional tropes of the artist as creator and the poet as maker, might suggest that the first line derives from the word-guessing game charades, which relies on its players' alphabetical and cultural literacy.

    "Metaphors" technically is not a charade, although it incorporates the kind of opening challenge that signals a language game: "I'm a riddle in nine syllables." Charades requires players to solve a kind of riddle in which each syllable of the word to be guessed, and sometimes the word itself, is enigmatically described or dramatically represented. Usually one player offers hints based on breaking down words or phrases into smaller units of words, syllables, or letters: "My first [syllable] wears my second"; or "I am a word of twelve letters." The charade, in its association of words, syllables, and letters with numbers, has a cryptographic aspect, linking it to codes, ciphers, and puzzles that substitute numerals for alphabets as well as to the ancient riddling tradition.

Plath's poem shares certain features common to other types of cryptographic puzzles. It evokes language games from the ancient ritual incantations, charms, and spells of all cultures. In many traditional narratives, solving a riddle is a crucial test of the hero's ingenuity, often with life or death consequences. Such traditional heroes have been mostly male. A good example is Oedipus, whose solution to the Sphinx's riddle was "man," meaning humanity. In Plath's poem, however, it is the female poet who, by posing and embodying her own riddle, is both protagonist and sphinx. Her subliminal pun on bearing or carrying suggests magical correspondences between poetry and pregnancy. Plath's title, "Metaphors," and "pregnancy," the unstated word that names the poet's condition and is the answer to the poem's riddle, both contain nine letters. The poem is shaped formally and conceptually around the "magic" number nine (months, letters, syllables, lines), just as the poem's metaphors are figurative references to pregnancy. The poet's riddling metaphors follow the polite convention of discussing pregnancy indirectly through periphrasis and euphemism.

Plath's metaphors might apply to her poem as well as to herself as a pregnant poet, a poet with a head full of creative ideas. However playful in form, the content of the poem expresses conflicted emotions concerning the literal, figurative, or anticipated state of pregnancy. The anxiety extends to the conflicting roles of both vessel and creator, both riddle and riddler, inhabited by a pregnant woman or by an inspired artist. Here the conventional beginning statement of the charade provides a key that suggests an analogical relationship in which the poet is the tenor and her poem (with its riddling metaphors) the vehicle. The number nine—referring to letters in the title, lines in the poem, syllables per line, and months required for a full-term pregnancy—establishes a link between formal and linguistic elements of the poem and the poet's biography.

Although Plath did not become pregnant until some time after "Metaphors" was written, this poem marks a moment when she had tried and failed to conceive a child and thus underscores the association of the riddle-

poem with "magical" properties. "Metaphors" might have served as the poetic equivalent of the anticipated pregnancy or as a magic spell to bring about
the desired outcome. The poem could thus be read not only as a dreamlike
wish-fulfillment fantasy but also as a brainchild that affirms the poet's fer-
tile imagination. Although she is not literally "with child" when the poem is
written, Plath seems to insist that she is nevertheless pregnant with poetry.
The riddle format is appropriate for expressing the strangeness of pregnancy
as well as the poet's fear of the unknown territory she is about to enter. The
elusiveness of the riddle's answer might also correspond to a woman's frus-
tration when, after attempting to conceive, the pregnancy (both desired and
feared) fails to materialize.

What A. J. Greimas would call the poem's "negative complex isotopy,"
when the vehicle seems more real or more fully present in the poem than the
tenor, might correspond to the experience of a pregnant woman, estranged
from herself as her body undergoes its physiological transformation. The occult enigma of the riddle corresponds to a self disguised or hidden within an
altered body that appears ever stranger. That both "figures" keep changing
might be seen as another subliminal pun in the poem that again relates metaphor, the literary figure, to the pregnant poet's changing body. The puzzle of
the riddle, its manipulation of linguistic code, might also be associated with
the secret of life conceived within the body, the ability of living creatures to
reproduce through replication of their genetic code.

Although Plath's poem employs no perplexing obstruction, it resembles
traditional riddles, as it isolates and decontextualizes the metaphor and its
vehicle to the point that the tenor or literal referent remains latent, a puzzle
to be solved. The tenor is represented only by the pronoun shifter "I," which
refers explicitly to the metaphorical vehicles (elephant, house, melon, etc.)
or to the poem itself, a riddle composed of nine lines of nine syllables each.
Yet the reader is aware that logically and implicitly "I" refers also to the poet
as the tenor of all this poem's metaphors.

The number nine as well as the first person pronoun "I" are the slender
means by which the poem equates one isotopy with another. In this way
Plath's poem, like the charade word game, allows the meaning of the poem,
or the solution of the puzzle it poses for the reader, to turn on the minimal
units of meaning within a linguistic or numerical code: a single letter and a
single digit. (Coincidentally "I" is also the Roman numeral one, so that the
relationship of one and nine suggests movement from singularity to multiplicity as the poet and her metaphors go forth and multiply.) "I'm a riddle
in nine syllables" incorporates the language of the charade, equating "I" and
"riddle" while associating each with the number "nine."

Plath's poem makes a challenging and rewarding assignment for a literature or creative writing class. Sometimes I ask my students to write a brief
analysis of the poem in which they observe its formal properties and their relation to the poem's meaning. In addition to more obvious matters, I suggest
that they consider the relation of metaphors to riddles, charades, and word
games. I also ask students to write poems of their own using Plath's "Metaphors" as a model. Interestingly, some students who write brilliant formal
analyses of Plath's poem are unable to crack the riddle. Others can guess instantly the riddle's answer but may find it difficult to write critically about the
poem. Typically, the women in the class are more likely to solve the riddle
than the men. When the assignments come in, we discuss the results, and I
share my own response to the exercise, including poems imitating or mod-
eled on Plath's that, for pedagogical purposes, also explicate its significance
while solving Plath's riddle.

NINE SYLLABLES LABEL SYLVIA
Poet Sylvia Plath is pregnant.
Sylvia's pregnant with her poem.
Pregnancy is only nine letters.
Syllable, a metaphor for month?
Sylvia's nine pregnant syllables!
Pregnant: creative and inventive.
Poet and her poem, both pregnant.
Pregnant means filled and charged with meaning.
Sylvia is a pregnant poem.

SYLVIA'S STILL ON THE SYLLABUS
Of riddles, metaphors, conundrums.
Metaphor makes things equivalent:
Units of language, units of time.
She goes unnamed through periphrasis,
Metaphor and circumlocution;
Fashions cute euphemistic riddles,
Then leaves us to guess her syllables.
Sylvia's still a big enigma.

My imitations, by stating explicitly what remains implicit in "Metaphors,"
restore the reality of the tenor, Sylvia Plath, pregnant poet. Of course, one
obvious way I depart from the grammar of her poem is in my use of third

person rather than first, which thus changes the rhetorical situation, so there is no ambiguous "I" that might be the poet and/or her poem. My imitations respond to the poet's portrayal of herself and her poem as enigmas. While they follow Plath in other formal features, my poems do not leap from metaphor to metaphor from line to line; instead I acknowledge her implicit equation of metaphors and pregnancy, of poem and poet, of creation and procreation. My poems based on her model comment on her use of logogriph, but my imitations are not linguistically structured as riddles.

A convention of riddles is that objects may "speak" in the first person using metaphors that at once describe the object and obscure its identity. The inhibiting effect of such metaphors—or the riddle's clues—has been called obstruction or a "block element." A traditional riddle blocks or delays its solution by confusing us with mixed metaphors and incompatible isotopies. Obstruction does not absolutely prevent, but it does delay, the eventual solution. In traditional riddles, obscurity may result from an anthropomorphic description of an inanimate object or the reverse, as when Plath's pregnant speaker compares herself to a purse, watermelon, or house. Obscurity also occurs when the riddling description is a series of comparisons that conflict or appear incoherent on a literal level, although they accumulate coherence on a figurative level, as in Plath's "Metaphors." The mixture of descriptive metaphors at first generates confusion, but once the solution is reached, in retrospect the clues are all comprehensible as figurative comparisons.

A riddle's difficulty depends on the bizarre and obscure clues it provides. In the charade the word itself "speaks," providing clues for guessing its constituent parts. What puzzles us is that the charade scrambles relations between signifier and signified. In riddles and charades, the substitution of pronoun for noun allows the unnamed name to speak of itself. The pregnant poet appears only in the guise of metaphor: obscured yet latently present, as she is in the first-person pronoun. If the poem is a riddle or charade, it might be the poem or its objects speaking rather than (or as well as) the poet herself. "I am a riddle in nine syllables" is a literal description of each metaphorical line of the poem, as well as a metaphorical description of a literally pregnant poet.

I want to conclude by addressing more directly the poem's explicit conflict, a conflict that is underlined by the linguistic conventions of riddles, games, and puzzles: naming versus not naming. Plath's text is a periphrastic series of metaphors for pregnancy that results in a riddle-like poem that does not block the reader's ability to solve the puzzle; instead, it suggests the poet's ambivalence about pregnancy at an era when women were expected to be mothers but were discouraged from careers as poets or anything else. Poems written by women about pregnancy may be plentiful now, but when Plath wrote "Metaphors" the idea of a pregnant poet must have seemed far stranger than it does today. Perhaps it was a potent metaphor for the creativity of male poets who would never be literally pregnant or bear actual children. For a female poet it was almost unspeakable.

7
Evaluation of an Unwritten Poem

Wislawa Szymborska in the Dialogue of Creative and Critical Thinkers

From the ancient world to the Renaissance, when the sciences, arts, and humanities all spoke the same language, it was not unusual to find scientists writing poetry or to find poets, philosophers, and artists probing the universe with the curiosity of scientists. With their increasing specialization, the disciplines have diverged, resulting often in mutual incomprehension. As a poet who studied sociology as well as literature, Wislawa Szymborska, the 1996 winner of the Nobel Prize in Literature, is particularly interesting to consider in terms of the divergence of the arts and sciences or the dialogue of creative and critical thinkers. A number of Symborska's poems reflect on the rift between poetic and prosaic discursive modes and the clashing styles of creative-intuitive and critical-analytical thinkers. Perhaps the most explicitly antagonistic in its view of their separation is the following poem.

EVALUATION OF AN UNWRITTEN POEM
In the poem's opening words
the authoress asserts that while the Earth is small,
the sky is excessively large and
in it there are, I quote, "too many stars for our own good."

In her depiction of the sky, one detects a certain helplessness,
the authoress is lost in a terrifying expanse,
she is startled by the planets' lifelessness,
and within her mind (which can only be called imprecise)
a question soon arises:
whether we are, in the end, alone
under the sun, all suns that ever shone.

In spite of all the laws of probability!
And today's universally accepted assumptions!
In the face of the irrefutable evidence that may fall
into human hands any day now! That's poetry for you.

Meanwhile, our Lady Bard returns to Earth,
a planet, so she claims, which "makes its rounds without eyewitnesses,"
the only "science fiction that our cosmos can afford."
The despair of a Pascal (1623–1662, *note mine*)
is, the authoress implies, unrivalled
on any, say, Andromeda or Cassiopeia.

Our solitary existence exacerbates our sense of obligation
and raises the inevitable question, How are we to live et cetera,
since, "we can't avoid the void."
"'My God,' man calls out to Himself,
'have mercy on me, I beseech thee, show me the way . . .'"

The authoress is distressed by the thought of life squandered so freely,
as if our supplies were boundless.
She is likewise worried by wars, which are, in her perverse opinion,
always lost on both sides,
and by the "authoritorture" (*sic!*) of some people by others.
Her moralistic intentions glimmer throughout the poem.
They might shine brighter beneath a less naïve pen.

Not under this one, alas. Her fundamentally unpersuasive thesis
(that we may well be alone
under the sun, all suns that ever shone)
combined with her lackadaisical style (a mixture
of lofty rhetoric and ordinary speech)
forces the question: Whom might this piece convince?
The answer can only be: No one. Q.E.D.[1]

Szymborska dramatizes a classic conflict of creative and critical thinking. In a witty dissection of a nonexistent poem, she considers the value of literature or art versus logical analysis or scientific reasoning. The poet takes on the voice of an analytical reader who could be a literary critic with a scientific bent or a scientist critiquing the language of poetry. The speaker in the poem is a reader who values facts, reason, and precision over emotion, rhetoric, and the imprecision of metaphor. Regarding the poem as a logical argument or mathematical proof, this critical reader complains that it fails to meet its burden and thus is unpersuasive. Not only does this stern critic give the poem a low mark but the poet herself is also downgraded. Metaphors and ambiguities are not just dismissed as examples of imprecision; they are also cited as evidence of the poet's fuzzy thinking, her innately flawed judgment. The poet's intuitive rather than analytical approach fails to convince this reader of the poem's merit. What otherwise might be regarded as a poet's strengths, this speaker perceives as shortcomings: "That's poetry for you."

Unlike the exacting critic, the poet tries to support "perverse opinions" with a "naïve pen." Unlike the rational scientist, the poet feels overwhelmed by a vast uncaring universe and depressed by an inhumane world. She is "helpless," "lost," "startled," "distressed," "worried," and "moralistic." Her style is "lackadaisical." Her mind is "imprecise." Neither the everyday vernacular nor the "lofty rhetoric" of the poet meets rigorous standards of scientific discourse. Szymborska's poem also comments on a stereotypical divide between masculine and feminine cognitive styles. In terms made popular by John Gray's book *Men Are from Mars, Women Are from Venus,* the intuitive poet ("authoress" or "Lady Bard") is a Venusian female, while the rational critic presumably is a Martian male. Possibly he has missed the point, but at least this skeptical reader is duly attentive to the poem. He evaluates its content and language, dwelling on the questions it raises, however ridiculous or naïve they seem to him. Unfortunately the critic in Szymborska's poem is unable to appreciate the poet's work when he disagrees with its premise.

Szymborska's title, "Evaluation of an Unwritten Poem," could refer to the distance separating the discursive practice of the critic from that of the poet. The poem is diminished in the critic's text. What the critic comprehends may differ from what the poet actually wrote or intended. The critic mutes or silences the poet's voice, especially when other readers consult the critic before (or instead of) reading the poet's original text. The "unwritten poem" in this sense could be a poem that neither the critic nor the poet wrote but instead a product of their interaction. This phantom text could be a poem the critic wishes he had written or what the critic imagines the poet has written. Indeed it is possible that I am discussing not Szymborska's poem but the poem I imagine when I read the translation of her original text. The work of Harold Bloom suggests that a compelling interpretation of poetry often involves creative misinterpretation.[2] The critic's most creative act may be misreading the poet's text.

By taking on the voice of the sophisticated analytical reader, Szymborska the poet creates an implicit dialogue between critic and poet that functions as a double-edged critique of both. In the most literal, denotative reading of the poem, the fact-driven critic reveals the poet's vulnerability. However, an alternate meaning diverges from this initial interpretation. On the one hand, there is a critical or scientific thinker who analyzes the poet's psyche as well as the poem itself and concludes that both are lacking. On the other hand, the critical voice in this dramatic monologue is the creation of a poet who is familiar with the critic's disparagement.

The paradoxical title, "Evaluation of an Unwritten Poem," could be read as a comment on the conventional antagonism that is presumed to exist between artist and critic. Szymborska gently mocks both parties: the poet who takes liberties with language, inventing ungainly words like "authoritorture," as well as the fastidious critic who objects to such idiosyncratic usage. She acknowledges the poet's heartfelt abuse of language as well as the critic's splenetic abuse of the poet. The polysyllabic portmanteau word she coins might refer to the work of all authoritarians, including writers whose books browbeat readers and critics whose reviews manhandle authors. The voice of the critic in this poem overtly ridicules fuzzy-brained poets; but taken as a whole the text of the poem also satirizes critical readers who relish a poem only when intent on taking it apart. The title suggests the potential destructiveness of the critical enterprise, since in this case the critic's evaluation seems to have precluded a possible poem that remains unwritten. This elusive work of art exists only as a few scattered quotes and paraphrases from the "unwritten" text—shreds or fragments of an imaginary poem that never coalesced into a coherent or persuasive argument.

We could say that the critical reader performs a dismal autopsy on the dead or aborted poem while blaming the poet who failed to create a convincing work. Alternatively, we could say that the phantom poem remains unwritten, perhaps due to the poet's fear of the reader's harsh evaluation or condescending critique. And yet the peculiar title also calls attention to the secondary role of the critic, since it is impossible to evaluate an unwritten poem or critique a work of art that might have been but never was created. Until the artist actually produces the work, the critic has nothing to say about it. Yet what makes this poem particularly interesting to me is the overt way the poet has incorporated a critical voice into the creation of the poem.

Note that "Evaluation of an Unwritten Poem" is *not* the poem that Szymborska's critic scorns: instead the critic goes after a poem that might have been but that doesn't actually exist. Szymborska has written something quite different: a poem that acknowledges the inner dialogue of a psyche that contains both creative and critical voices—just as it expresses bipolar emotions of hope and despair. Although it would appear that the critic has overwhelmed the poet and destroyed a prospective poem in the making, ultimately this voice of the rational reader is an aspect of the poet and her creation. The poem that made it to the page is a result of a dialogue of the poet's voice with a critical voice that could be internal or external, or both. Poets who also work as critics may feel that their critical writing comes at the expense of poems that remain unwritten. Yet Szymborska's poem appropriates for its own ends the voice of the exasperated critic.

It is a truism that critical thinking requires precise analysis rather than fuzzy metaphor, while the creative process requires a suppression of the inner critic. Yet if we were expecting that the analytical critic values cold, hard facts over emotion and intuition, Szymborska's poem is a bit of a surprise. In this case it is the poet or creative thinker who has accepted the void, while the critic or rational thinker, having faith in science, embraces the hope that human beings are not alone in the universe, an idea as yet unproven. As it turns out, this critical reader's belief doesn't actually rely on facts but rather on "laws of probability," "today's universally accepted assumptions," and "the irrefutable evidence that may fall into human hands any day now!" Here it is the critic, despite his harsh assessment of the poet's art, who expresses what the poet might prefer to believe.[3] Such unfounded belief is not unlike the credo expressed in another poem of Szymborska's, an intriguing companion to the previous poem, almost its mirror image.

DISCOVERY
I believe in the great discovery.
I believe in the man who will make the discovery.
I believe in the fear of the man who will make the discovery.

I believe in his face going white,
His queasiness, his upper lip drenched in cold sweat.

I believe in the burning of his notes,
burning them into ashes,
burning them to the last scrap.

I believe in the scattering of numbers,
scattering them without regret.

I believe in the man's haste,
in the precision of his movements,
in his free will.

I believe in the shattering of tablets,
the pouring out of liquids,
the extinguishing of rays.

I am convinced this will end well,
that it will not be too late,
that it will take place without witnesses.

I'm sure no one will find out what happened,
not the wife, not the wall,
not even the bird that might squeal in its song.

I believe in the refusal to take part.
I believe in the ruined career.
I believe in the wasted years of work.
I believe in the secret taken to the grave.

These words soar for me beyond all rules
without seeking support from actual examples.

My faith is strong, blind, and without foundation.

In the previous poem, the critic's faith would destroy the poet's art. Here it is the poet whose belief, a "faith . . . without foundation," would negate the scientist's deadly discovery. As the poet (or "authoress") is female in the other poem, the scientist here is envisioned as male—specifically, a white male. Again the potential antagonism of the poet and the scientist gives way to a productive alliance, an implied dialogue of creative-intuitive and critical-analytical thinkers. However, the implicit dialogue in both cases relies paradoxically on the actual or imagined nullification or setting aside of the other's text. In the critic's dramatic monologue, a poem remains in a sense "unread" if not "unwritten," as the poem to which the critic refers is unavailable to any subsequent reader. Alarmed by the poet's emotions, the critic reduces the poem to nothing more than an inchoate argument that fails to persuade. It only proves the critic's point that the poet's mind is "imprecise."
    While the critic, at odds with the poet, speaks of an unmade or obliterated work of art in "Evaluation of an Unwritten Poem," in "Discovery" a scientific breakthrough is undone through the humane action of a scientist who shares the poet's vision. In the poet's fervent credo this man of science, who is no less a man of conscience, foresees the inevitable consequence of his find-

ings and burns his own notes in order to suppress the terrible knowledge of his discovery. Perhaps with good reason, the poet's faith in the benevolence of the scientist may be greater than the rational critic's faith in the logic of the poet. In the previous poem, an absolute faith in science leads the skeptical critic to dismiss the poet's imprecise art. Here the poet's uncorroborated faith in the scientist's integrity envisions the destruction of scientific data in order to avert the destruction of life as we know it. At stake in both poems are the survival and spiritual well-being of humanity.

These two poems offer insight into the dialogue of critical and creative thinkers, a dialogue within and between disciplines as well as within and between individuals. Although Szymborska's poetic monologues allude to a stereotypical conflict between critical and creative thinkers, these monologues also can be read as two halves of an interactive dialogue. Szymborska has used creative and critical thinking to examine both parts of the dialogue and then has merged them in her poetry, producing a synthesis of their divergent expressions. Above all, she observes what great critical and creative thinkers share in common: a search for truth and a concern for humanity.

Many if not most of the poets I know are also scholars, teachers, book reviewers, and critics; and in reality, many if not all scientists and other critical thinkers also enjoy the works of creative artists and poets. Although poets may choose a road less traveled, they seek truth as diligently as scientists, critics, or scholars—just as critical-analytical thinkers appreciate the truth found in literature and art. Once during an airplane flight I sat next to a physicist who told me how intensely he and his colleagues enjoy and appreciate poetry. He said that in some respects, both the poet and the physicist are searching for language to grasp a complex reality that is difficult to imagine, comprehend, or describe.

As someone who works as both a poet and a critic, I have found that the dialogue between artist and critic can be positive or negative: negative when either the creator or the critic speaks out of turn; positive when each allows the other to articulate its position without immediately offering a rebuttal. I don't work well when I anticipate too soon how critical readers might respond or when my inner critic rejects all of my ideas before I have a chance to explore them fully. It is counterproductive if the critic is too vocal as I'm struggling to get a poem started—or for that matter when I'm beginning a critical essay. An undisciplined inner critic can sabotage the creative brainstorming required to explore ideas and make associations without knowing exactly where they will lead. I find it useful at this stage to jot ideas into a notebook without stopping to evaluate or judge their worth. At times, I might commit myself to short bursts of freewriting to start the flow of ideas.

I might try writing a first draft on a computer with a darkened screen so as to avoid the impulse to go back over each sentence as it is written.

Only at a later stage, when scattered notes begin to take form as an initial draft, can I allow my inner critic a voice in revising and editing the draft. I listen to the critical voice as I try to select my best ideas and give them an appropriate shape and structure. As I begin a writing project, the creator is dominant; but by the end, the critic has become a prevailing influence. It sometimes happens that I have to work at both creative and critical writing together. In such cases, it is often helpful to tackle first the critical writing—or the critical tasks such as revising and editing. For me a good time to work on a creative writing project is just before falling asleep at night, especially after I've spent time doing critical writing, revising, or editing. I find that when my inner critic is exhausted and therefore unable to interfere, I can often work more productively on a creative project.

I will conclude with a third poem by Szymborska. This final piece offers further reflection on the creative or poetic versus the critical or prosaic.

WRITING A RESUME
What needs to be done?
Fill out the application
and enclose the resume.

Regardless of the length of life,
a resume is best kept short.

Concise, well-chosen facts are de rigueur.
Landscapes are replaced by addresses,
shaky memories give way to unshakable dates.

Of all your loves, mention only the marriage;
of all your children, only those who were born.

Who knows you matters more than whom you know.
Trips only if taken abroad.
Memberships in what but without why.
Honors, but not how they were earned.

Write as if you'd never talked to yourself
and always kept yourself at arm's length.

Pass over in silence your dogs, cats, birds,
dusty keepsakes, friends, and dreams.

Price, not worth,
and title, not what's inside.
His shoe size, not where he's off to,
that one you pass off as yourself.
In addition, a photograph with one ear showing.
What matters is its shape, not what it hears.
What is there to hear, anyway?
The clatter of paper shredders.

In this wittily sarcastic compilation of conventionally pragmatic advice for job seekers, Szymborska suggests that even the most mundane and practical writing may carry on a secret dialogue with the poetry of life.

Notes

1. Q.E.D. is an acronym that refers to the Latin phrase *quod erat demonstrandum*, which is translated literally: "that which was to be demonstrated." Q.E.D. is written after mathematical proofs to show that the result required for the proof to be complete has been obtained. A more colloquial translation might be "See, I told you so." All poems are quoted in their entirety from *View with a Grain of Sand: Selected Poems,* by Wislawa Szymborska, trans. Stanislaw Baranczak and Clare Cavanagh (New York: Harcourt Brace, 1995).

2. Bloom 1973 and 1975.

3. It might amuse Szymborska to know that in 2004 a group of Swedish poets broadcast their work into outer space: "Apparently hoping to find and impress some Swedish-speaking aliens, a group of poets in Stockholm have beamed readings of their work into outer space. The poets gathered at an observatory on Nov. 16 and aimed their transmission at Vega, a star that is 25 light years from earth. 'I can't think of anything more adequate than poetry to communicate what it means to be human,' Daniel Sjolin, editor of the Swedish poetry magazine *Lyrikvannen,* told Reuters." *World Magazine,* November 2004.

8
Theme for the Oulipians

(Presented at the CalArts Noulipo Conference, 2006)

Langston Hughes has his "Theme for English B." This is my "Theme for the Oulipians." My connection to Oulipo is tenuous at best—more like nonexistent. I'm definitely not a member of Oulipo. I have the same initials as Harry Mathews; that's about as close as I get to an Oulipo connection. I did meet Harry Mathews at the Poetry Project in New York on April 18, 1996. I know the exact date because he was nice enough to sign and date a copy of one of his books for me. I'm more familiar with Umbra and the Black Arts Movement, the Beats, the Black Mountain poets, the New York School, and the Language poets, and even the connections I have to those groups were mediated by people like Nathaniel Mackey, one of my professors at UC Santa Cruz, and Lorenzo Thomas, a friend I met when we both worked in Texas in the Artists in Schools program. I'm not an Oulipian, but I'm proof that their ideas have far-reaching influence among poets and writers.

A long time ago, the first books by a member of Oulipo that I read were Italo Calvino's *Invisible Cities* and *If on a Winter's Night a Traveler.* But at that time I'd never heard of Oulipo and didn't know that Calvino was a member of the group. I think at the time I associated Calvino's work with another experimental novel that I found by accident in a used bookstore, Julio Cortazar's *Hopscotch.* I believe I liked these books because they were like games—hopscotch was a game I played as a child—and also because of their poeticity. Their structure and their rules and their playful strangeness made their prose more poetic. I think of poetry as the ultimate rule-governed writing because a poem is subject to all the rules of grammar, spelling, punctuation, rhetoric, and so forth that govern any text; on top of that the poem is also subject to additional rules specific to literature and to poetry. And what makes poetry even more complex is that the poet can choose to break any of those rules in the act of creating the poem.

I can remember that, years after finding Calvino's novels at Half-Price Books, when I first heard of Oulipo and Oulipians I thought of them in relation to the Eulipians in Rahsaan Roland Kirk's jazz classic, "Theme for the Eulipians," the ones he calls "the artists, the actors, and the journeymen" who come from a planet in another galaxy, Eulipia. I'm not an Oulipian, but I can call myself an Eulipian. I think I first heard of Oulipo when I was a graduate student at Santa Cruz from 1985 to 1988. But I didn't hear about Oulipo in the classroom; it was during a discussion with some Language poets I met in the Bay Area who were friends of Nate Mackey's, people whose work he was publishing in his journal *Hambone*. Because of them, I looked for books by and about Oulipo, whatever I could find: I read Roussel's *New Impressions of Africa,* because I'd heard it was racist. And I also got hold of Perec's lipogram novel, *A Void,* and *Life, A User's Manual,* and Queneau's *Exercises in Style.*

Oulipo was useful to me because its members not only had invented new kinds of literary structures and devices but also had investigated all kinds of artifice in literature dating back to ancient texts. The most liberating aspect of Oulipo for me was their demystification of "inspiration" in favor of "potential literature." This puts less stress on writing as a product and more emphasis on writing as a process that might result in a work of literature. The Oulipo dictionary game, S+7, inspired several poems in my book, *Sleeping with the Dictionary.* However, not one of those poems is written strictly according to the S+7 formula. For me, constraints, procedures, and language games are just ways to get past a block or impasse in the process of writing.

When I think of the degrees of separation between Oulipo and myself, I also think of my friendship with Barbara Henning who is, I believe, a friend of Harry Mathews. He was nice enough to write a blurb for her novel. Barbara Henning used to edit a poetry journal called *Long News in the Short Century* from about 1991–94. I first met her at the Nuyorican Poets Cafe where she was sitting at a table with my friend Lorenzo Thomas. Barbara invited me to submit some of my work to her journal, and she published me in one issue with Harry Mathews and in another issue with Bernadette Mayer.

I definitely knew about Oulipo by then, because I recognized that two poems in this journal, collaboratively written by Bernadette Mayer and Philip Good, were S+7 texts. That is, they were written according to the Oulipo dictionary game. In that game, an existing text is transformed into a poetic word salad by substituting for each substantive or noun in the original text the seventh noun down from it in a dictionary, preferably an unabridged dictionary.

Some of what I know about Oulipo I think I got by way of Bernadette Mayer's long list of writing experiments and exercises, which included ideas such as taking a walk for fourteen blocks and writing a line for each block. I don't know what Bernadette calls it, but I call it a pedestrian sonnet—perfect for New York poets. Here in Los Angeles, I suggest to my students that they write their lines while riding a bus, as I have done with my poem "#6 Sepulveda"; so I guess I've turned this exercise back toward its Oulipo origins on the Paris Metro.

At the 2006 Noulipo Conference, along with her translations of Catullus, Bernadette read the two poems that I first saw in Barbara Henning's journal, "Before Sextet" and "After Sextet." I've used those poems in my creative writing class at UCLA when we talk about Oulipo, S+7, and collaboration. I give students copies of both poems and ask them to explain how they think the poems were created. The students start out reading the poems silently, but I can tell that they get it when they start laughing out loud. They understand immediately that these poems are based on instructions for safe sex, that the original text consists of step-by-step instructions for the proper way to put on and then remove a condom.

After further discussion, students begin to understand that the dictionary is also a source text for S+7 poems. We discuss how a seemingly arbitrary game of word substitution turns a very prosaic text into poetry. Thus the substitution of "sextet" for "sex" and "conductor" for "condom" creates a musical metaphor in which "sexual performance" takes on other meanings. Practicing safe sex thus becomes a kind of poetic duet between two poets of opposite sexes, Bernadette Mayer and Philip Good, who enact a kind of lubricated intercourse between two prosaic texts, the condom instructions and the dictionary, within a social-historical context that includes a fear of contracting HIV. This is a useful example of the improvisational verve and serious play that can occur in a poem that mixes one lexicon with another in a way that seems arbitrary yet is nevertheless subject to interpretation.

The idea of a collaboration between poet and text—which can occur when a poet uses practically any kind of text as a starting point—allowed me to put together my book, *Sleeping with the Dictionary*. As I've said, this book includes several poems inspired by the Oulipo dictionary game S+7 though not a single one of them is written strictly according to the Oulipo rule. What I borrowed from Oulipo was the idea of textual transformation, an idea that returned me to two of my favorite books from childhood, *Alice in Wonder-*

land and *Through the Looking Glass,* when I realized that S+7 was a way to transform any text into something resembling Lewis Carroll's "Jabberwocky."

What's so striking about "Jabberwocky" and also about S+7 is the durability of grammatical and linguistic structures. Even when a good portion of a text is replaced with nonsense, a very strong residue remains of the sense of the original text. At the same time the words substituted, however arbitrary, nonsensical, and meaningless, add layers of poetic texture, potential metaphor, and meaning to the text. In this manner whatever was lost of the original is supplemented and enriched by what is substituted in its place. Following a rule or a set of rules, however arbitrary, can make poetry more poetic or can make a work of prose more intriguing.

While Oulipo members have invented a number of literary games, their activities also highlight the existence in world literature of such textual strategies as acrostics and anagrams. Sandra Cisneros told me once that I was the first reader to notice the acrostic in one of her short stories in *Woman Hollering Creek.* "Tin Tan Tan," the penultimate story in the collection, is presented by the author as an acrostic prose poem written to Lupita by Rogelio Velasquez. "Lupita" is the familiar diminutive of "Lupe," which is short for "Guadalupe"; she is an artist who works at a community cultural center in San Antonio, Texas. Rogelio Velasquez is the pen name of Flavio Munguia, a pest exterminator who dabbles in poetry. Flavio and Lupe are characters in the last story in *Woman Hollering Creek,* "Bien Pretty." Since I have assigned this book to students, I know that many readers not only miss the obvious acrostic, but they also miss the connection between the two stories, which the acrostic signals. Since I'm a Texan, I also know that Guadalupe is the name of the community arts center where Cisneros worked when she first moved to San Antonio. So the acrostic not only connects the two stories; it also signals the author's connection to the narrator of "Bien Pretty." A literary device that might seem arbitrary or contrived to some readers, if they notice it at all, actually marks a place in the text where fiction intersects with the author's autobiography.

I can't be sure of the exact genesis of the anagram poems that Terrance Hayes has written, but I believe they might be a result of his participation in a workshop I taught in three consecutive years, from 1999 to 2001, for Cave Canem, an organization of African American poets organized by Toi Derricotte and Cornelius Eady. Among other things, we discussed the Oulipian interest in the persistence of the ludic principle in literature, as well as their systematic investigation and documentation of games, procedures, and devices including acrostics, lipograms, and anagrams. Our discussion also included African American poets whose work includes similar playful devices, poets such as Russell Atkins, Julia Fields, and Julie Patton. One example I used was Bob Kaufman's poem "Oregon," which riffs on words—*Negro* and *green*—that are near anagrams of the word *Oregon*. I suggested that instead of using rhyme, a poem could be held together with anagrams. The traditional use of end rhyme is to draw attention to significant words in a poem. Anagrams could be a subtle and intriguing way of emphasizing significant words without making them visibly and audibly prominent as end rhymes.

Perhaps that discussion had something to do with the anagram poems in Terrance Hayes's book *Hip Logic,* published in 2002. In these poems, Hayes ends each line with a word that is a partial anagram of the word that serves as the poem's title. I'll conclude with an example from his book *Hip Logic.* The title of the poem is "Segregate," and the end words for each line are: *tree, gate, rest, gear, stare, eager, greets, tear (gas), geese, rage,* and *agree.*

SEGREGATE
On the first morning of school there is a young tree-
frog waiting patiently at the front gate.
Since this means there will be no classes for the rest
of the day, the children dump their school gear
in their lockers & hustle to the windows to stare.
The girls are eager to transform him with a kiss; the boys eager
to see him on the basketball court. But their principal greets
him with a "Get the Hell out of here!" A security guard fetches the tear-
gas. Some of the older teachers crowd the doorway like befuddled geese.
"You belong in the swamps not our schools!" they rage.
But clearly the cool-blooded Amphibian-American does not agree.

9

When He Is Least Himself

Paul Laurence Dunbar and Double Consciousness in African American Poetry

(Presented at the Paul Laurence Dunbar Centennial Conference, Stanford University, 2006)

Like Paul Laurence Dunbar and like many people who don't consider themselves to be poets, I began writing poetry as a child. Although Dunbar was not a poet I tried to emulate when I wrote my first poems, and although he is not among my consciously chosen ancestor poets, he certainly contributed to my poetic inheritance. I recognize now that his poetry was an influence so pervasive in my upbringing that I never felt the need to claim him as my own. I grew up in Fort Worth, Texas—one of the cities with a Dunbar High School, though no one in my family attended this school.[1] My grandparents and parents were schooled in Dunbar's poetry, a perennial favorite in the repertoire of black school and church programs. Dunbar's name and poetry would have been especially present in the lives of my Texas-born maternal grandfather, who was pastor of a Baptist church; my Pennsylvania-born maternal grandmother, who was the daughter of a minister, married another minister and actively participated in the black women's club movement; my Alabama-born paternal grandmother, who was an elementary school teacher; and my parents, who met as undergraduates at a historically black college in Alabama, where the artist David Driskell was one of their teachers and the poet Calvin Hernton was their classmate.[2] While reading a collection of my family's letters for a genealogy project, I noted my relatives' habit of using "Black Heritage" stamps, including the 1975 Paul Laurence Dunbar commemorative stamp. I may be in the last generation of African Americans who were routinely required to memorize and recite poetry as we were growing up. In my household, such recitations along with piano and ballet lessons, visits to museums and art galleries, and trips to the symphony and opera sought to broaden our horizons, to educate, uplift, and civilize us. Dunbar's "Little

Brown Baby" and "When Malindy Sings" were among the popular poems frequently recited in performances at school, at church, and at various community events, along with Langston Hughes's "Dream Deferred" and "Mother
to Son," Margaret Walker's "For My People," Gwendolyn Brooks' "We Real
Cool" and "Negro Hero" (about the Texan World War II hero Dorie Miller),
and James Weldon Johnson's "The Creation" and "The Prodigal Son" from
God's Trombones.

These poets—along with Lewis Carroll, Edward Lear, Mother Goose, and
jump rope rhymes learned on the playground—were in the background of
my childhood when I wrote my first rhyming verses in the form of home-
made and hand-drawn greeting cards. As a child dabbling in poetry, it never
occurred to me to write poems in black vernacular, despite the prevalence of
Dunbar's dialect poetry. If I had to label it, the linguistic norm in my household
might be described as "African American standard English," and it seemed
to me that Dunbar's work, whether in standard or vernacular dialects, represented an archaic form of American English. The Dunbar poems I knew
were a handful of favorites published in anthologies. As I became more interested in poetry, Dunbar receded into the background, along with other
staples of my childhood. I don't recall ever seeing a complete collection of his
work until much later, when I discovered that his poetry had a much greater
range than the poems I recalled from church and school recitals.[3]

Paul Laurence Dunbar's troubled life and poetry, which dealt with segregated linguistic domains, embodies and articulates a state that W. E. B. Du
Bois called "double consciousness." This psychic condition can be described
as African Americans' awareness of a social negation that contradicts our
view of ourselves. Double consciousness is the historical self-awareness of
African Americans who are struggling to overcome a legacy of slavery and
discrimination as they also claim the rights, responsibilities, and benefits
of freedom. Dunbar's knowledge of slavery was thankfully secondhand. He
wrote about slave life from the vantage point of freedom, as the offspring of
former slaves; for the most part, his focus was not on the oppression of the
slave system but rather on the humanity of the slave and the culture of the
African American folk community. Although Dunbar was sometimes con-
founded by the overwhelming popularity of his vernacular poems at the expense of his poems in standard English, his poetry indicates that an appreciation of black folk life was compatible with his identity as a cultured and
literate African American. In that way he is certainly a precursor to our present embrace of multicultural literacy.

While Phillis Wheatley's poetry demonstrated that an African-born slave
could master the tradition of English poetry, Dunbar's poetry, like Charles
Chesnutt's stories in *The Conjure Woman,* represents an innovative use of

literary code switching from standard English to nonstandard and regional dialects, including black vernacular. Such code switching indicates these writers' interest in a dialogical writing practice that foregrounds and encourages critical examination of African American double consciousness. Double consciousness implies not only self-awareness but also a keen awareness of the power of others to use legal and extralegal means, including intimidation and violence, to define and delimit the self. The writing of Dunbar and Chesnutt, along with that of Du Bois, brought to the tradition of African American literature a complex investigation of the linguistic, literary, social, and cultural construction of black and white identities. Dunbar and Chesnutt juxtapose standard and nonstandard dialects not only for comic effect or to demonstrate multicultural fluency but also to underscore social inequities that maintain hierarchies of power.

While I have a greater appreciation for Dunbar and Chesnutt today, when I began writing poetry my more immediate influences were writers of the Black Arts Movement, especially poets such as Lorenzo Thomas, Tom Dent, and Ishmael Reed. Their activity in the Umbra Writers Workshop helped to create a critical mass for that movement of black writers and artists. It was because of the Black Arts Movement that I began to think of writing poetry in what could be called a "black voice" or my own construction and ultimate deconstruction of a representative black poetic voice. Amiri Baraka, June Jordan, and Ntozake Shange were among the most instructive writers of the Black Arts Movement in terms of their search for, or construction of, a black voice in literature. It appeared to me that their personal struggle was to overcome and resolve the condition and internal conflict that Du Bois called double consciousness by creating a unitary black or colored self that was capable of rejecting or denouncing nearly everything of European origin while praising and enhancing blackness.

In this struggle for a coherent and positive black identity, standard English and traditional European verse forms became symbols of an oppressive dominant culture that socially conscious black poets must abandon in order to decolonize their minds. And yet Dunbar persistently wrote poems in standard literary English; he felt doing so was a way to expand his repertoire while resisting the white critic's dictum that the black poet's skill was best suited to express and preserve in literary form a familiar voice of the black folk community. In his often-quoted review of Dunbar's second poetry collection, *Majors and Minors,* William Dean Howells wrote:

> I shall not do this unknown but not ungifted poet the injury of comparing him with [Robert] Burns, yet I do not think that one can read his Negro pieces without feeling that they are of like impulse and in-

spiration with the work of Burns when he was most Burns, when he was most Scotch, when he was most peasant. When Burns was least himself, he wrote literary English, and Mr. Dunbar writes literary English when he is least himself.

I'd like to juxtapose this passage from Howells's review with a quotation from Oscar Wilde: "Man is least himself when he talks in his own person. Give him a mask, and he will tell you the truth."

Howells, a white critic, would define and limit black poetry according to what he regarded as the appropriate black voice, but Wilde's emphasis on artifice and performance acknowledges a complex relationship between truth and art. Whether or not Dunbar told "the truth" with or without his mask is less important to me than the fact that he allowed himself to explore a variety of literary forms and genres, just as he was willing and able to develop a variety of literary voices, whether or not they conformed to any particular concept of racial or ethnic authenticity. Readers and critics who would restrict Dunbar's expression devalue the complexity, the ambition, and the embrace of diversity that his writing represents.

As the Howells' quote above demonstrates, Dunbar was frequently compared to Robert Burns, a popular figure known for writing poetry in Scottish dialect, but Dunbar grew weary of the comparison. According to a newspaper editor who was one of Dunbar's admirers, Burns wrote great poems about humble subjects. This friend's advice to Dunbar was to consider that while many poets have written about great subjects such as love and death, Dunbar's particular gift was to tell a white audience "what that old Negro with a banjo is thinking."[4]

Dunbar had plenty of mentors and advisors telling him what to do; yet it is important to note how steadily he followed his own guidance, even when it meant producing unpopular work. I find inspiration in his literary range and ambition, in the reach of his writing beyond his own voice, in his ability to empathize with others, in his willingness as a writer to imagine and explore what was "least himself." So I'd like to conclude by looking briefly at a Dunbar poem, "Speakin' at de Cou't-house," in which he turns the tables on the common scenario of white observers ridiculing black speakers. Rather, a black narrator gives a humorous account of the speech of a white politician campaigning for office on his record as a Civil War hero.

SPEAKIN' AT DE COU'T-HOUSE
Dey been speakin' at de cou't-house,
An' laws-a-massy me,

'T'was de beatness kin' o' doin's
Dat evah I did see.
Of cose I had to be dah
In de middle o' de crowd,
An' I hallohed wid de othahs,
W'en de speakah riz and bowed.

I was kind o' disapp'inted
At de smallness of de man,
Case I'd allus pictered great folks
On a mo' expansive plan;
But I t'ought I could respect him
An' tek in de wo'ds he said,
Fu' dey sho was somp'n knowin'
In de bald spot on his haid.

But hit did seem so't o' funny
Aftah waitin' fu' a week
Dat de people kep' on shoutin'
So de man des could n't speak;
De ho'ns dey blared a little,
Den dey let loose on de drums,—
Some one tol' me dey was playin'
"See de conkerin' hero comes."
"Well," says I, "you all is white folks,
But you's sutny actin' queer,
What's de use of heroes comin'
Ef dey cain't talk w'en dey's here?"

Aftah while dey let him open,
An' dat man he waded in,
An he fit de wahs all ovah
Winnin' victeries lak sin.

W'en he come down to de present,
Den he made de feathahs fly.
He des waded in on money,
An' he played de ta'iff high.
An' he said de colah question,
Hit was ovah, solved, an' done,

Dat de dahky was his brothah,
Evah blessed mothah's son.

Well he settled all de trouble
Dat's been pesterin' de lan',
Den he set down mid de cheerin'
An' de playin' of de ban.'
I was feelin' moughty happy
'Twell I hyeahed somebody speak,
"Well, dat's his side of de bus'ness,
But you wait for Jones nex' week."
(Braxton 205)

With slight revision, "Speakin' at de Cou't-house" might stand as a commentary on current political discourse. The scene, if not timeless, has a generic familiarity. Addressing a boisterous crowd gathered in the town square, the candidate for office, presumably a Union veteran of the Civil War, recites his military exploits as credentials of patriotism and fitness for leadership. He mentions race only to declare it no longer a problem. He then focuses his energy and rhetorical skill on economic issues, such as tariffs, of primary concern to business interests.[5] Other than the suggestion that this scene occurs after the Civil War—probably after Reconstruction and most likely in a Northern state—the dramatic situation lacks a specific context that would help determine the politics of the black vernacular speaker listening to the white candidate's oration or, by extension, the political situation of African Americans at large. Dunbar's alert observer gives a lively account of the event. Yet given the apparent naiveté of the narrator's observations, it is unclear exactly what—besides the excitement of the occasion—draws such a black man, woman, or child to this pageant of traditional Americana.[6]

One can imagine Dunbar as a young boy attracted to the courthouse square by the music of the band, the thrill of the crowd, and the opportunity to see and hear "great folks," as the event is recalled with youthful enthusiasm. The narrator of the poem feels that the campaigning politician deserves respect not only for service to his country but also for physical signs of maturity such as a balding head. Like the white orator in the poem, the poet's father also was a veteran; but if Joshua Dunbar returned from the Civil War a conquering hero, his life as a black freedman in Ohio eventually settled into a vicious cycle of poverty, illness, and alcoholism. Dunbar's poetry was, among other things, a means of figurative and literal escape from the desperate circumstances of his early life; but the young Dunbar was also an enterprising journalist, and his collected prose offers a bracing tonic to balance the sweetness of much of his poetry. As editor of the short-lived *Dayton Tattler*, a weekly newspaper he founded with his high school classmate Orville Wright, Dunbar advocated black political activism and supported the Republican Party.[7]

African American voters' loyalty to the party of Lincoln, a legacy of the Civil War, ended decisively with the Depression-era politics of Franklin D. Roosevelt. In Dunbar's lifetime (1872–1906), with the exception of Democrat Grover Cleveland, every president of the United States, from Ulysses S. Grant to Theodore Roosevelt, was a Republican. While African Americans in the North and those newly enfranchised in the South helped to elect Republicans such as Grant, unrepentant Southern rebels threatened the lives of black men who dared exercise their right to vote and to run for public office. By the end of Reconstruction, Southern white men had regained political dominance through legal and extralegal means. It is left to the reader's imagination whether the dialect speaker in Dunbar's poem attends the courthouse rally as a potential voter or as a mere spectator of a political process that historically restricted the franchise to white male property owners.[8] As the poem's narrator observes, even in the North it was politically expedient before and after the Civil War to ignore "the color question." Is it any wonder that Dunbar and others felt ambivalent about their African American identity?

Notes

1. I was delighted to learn, in a recent conversation, that Ohio-born poet Marilyn Nelson has fond memories of attending Fort Worth's Dunbar High School when her father, a Tuskegee airman, was assigned to a nearby military base.

2. In his first teaching position Driskell was only a little older than his students at Talladega College. Hernton, nicknamed "Socrates" by Talladega classmates, later became an original member of the Society of Umbra, a catalyst for the Black Arts Movement.

3. I can identify with the experience of Arna Bontemps: "The name of Paul Laurence Dunbar was in every sense a household word in the black communities around Los Angeles when I was growing up here. It was not, however, a bookish word. It was a spoken word. And in those days it was associated with recitations which never failed to delight when we heard or said them at parties or on programs for the entertainment of the church-folk and their guests." Maya Angelou may hold a similar place in contemporary black communities. I seem to recall that in the school and church programs I attended where Dunbar poems were recited, the vernacular was toned down so that the dialect poems sounded

closer to contemporary African American English. It is likely that our black public school and Sunday school teachers adapted the Dunbar texts for student performances.

4. Cunningham writes: "One day Paul went down to see Mr. Charles Dennis, editor of the *Chicago News-Record*. As he had done in his letters, Mr. Dennis urged Paul to continue writing Negro dialect. Paul said he wanted to write of higher things than dialect permitted. Mr. Dennis tapped his fingers together and nodded. 'That's all right,' he said. 'Do that, too. But a lot of poets can write about life and love and death. You're the only one who can tell us what that old Negro is thinking about when he plays his banjo. Don't forget that Burns wrote about a field mouse. Couldn't be anything lower than that, eh? But Burns made it into poetry'" (98).

5. Dunbar's speaker may refer to the 1890 McKinley Tariff, introduced to Congress by William McKinley, Republican representative from Ohio, future U.S. president, and Civil War veteran of the Twenty-Third Ohio Volunteer Infantry. Intended to protect American industry from foreign competition, the tariff resulted in higher prices for many consumer goods and widespread discontent with the Republican Party, which in turn contributed to Democrat Grover Cleveland's victory over incumbent Republican President Benjamin Harrison in 1892.

6. In "The Poet and the Myths," Darwin T. Turner asserts that "The Lawyers' Ways," a poem with similar language and observations, is narrated by a white dialect speaker, while "Speakin' at de Cou't House" is in the voice of a black dialect speaker. According to Turner, these two narrators are equally targets of Dunbar's satire. I would note that trial lawyers and political orators also are targets of the satirical humor of the observant narrators of both poems. Although relations of power in such texts may be less complex than in one such as "Antebellum Sermon," nevertheless, in "The Lawyers' Ways" and "Speakin' at de Cou't House," Dunbar allows space for naïve speakers who may be young, black, poor, uneducated, and/or marginalized to lampoon or critique more powerful public speakers.

7. Dunbar also served for a short time as editor of the Indianapolis *World* in 1895. The second issue of the *Tattler* includes a brief item titled "Misplaced Zeal," a joke about a political orator who mistakes a supporter's cheering for heckling and has the "traitor" thrown out (*Dayton Tattler* 1890).

8. The right to vote was granted to all male citizens, regardless of race, color, or previous condition of servitude, in 1870 with ratification of the Fifteenth Amendment to the U.S. Constitution. The Nineteenth Amendment, guaranteeing women the right to vote, was not ratified until 1920.

10
Truly Unruly Julie

The Innovative Rule-Breaking Poetry of Julie Patton

Like certain jazz musicians who play "outside" the tradition, Julie Patton may be more familiar to Europeans than to readers in the United States. Her witty and musical poems, such as "Alphabet Soup," "Poor G," "Your Language Is Too Flowery," and "I Wrote that Shit," are joyful excursions to the land of Oo-Bla-Dee, which she often recites or sings in scripted and improvised performance. "Oxford Re-Verse" and "B" might be described as visually graphic sound poetry that plays with connections between writing and speech and similarities between the historical English dialects of British poets and the contemporary vernaculars of African Americans.

As her titles suggest, Patton applies whimsical intelligence to the raw material of her art. She is enchanted with words, enthralled by the alphabet, and attentive to the self-reflexive aspect of writing as aesthetic practice and process. Her poetry combines eclectic cultural influences, offbeat humor, adventurous experiment, and playful fascination with the magical properties of the spoken and written word. Like Thelonious Monk, Sun Ra, or Abbey Lincoln, Patton is an artistic free spirit, aware of, but unhampered by, tradition, and in touch with the "mysterious," which Clarence Major, in his dictionary of African American slang *Juba to Jive*, defines as "anything—especially music—that is 'weird' or innovative or avant garde."

In addition to her work as a poet, Julie Patton is also a multimedia visual and performance artist whose work includes poetic assemblages of artfully destroyed books. Through this variation on the artist's book, Patton comments on the writer's published and perishable life and work as well as the priorities of our electronic age. In these works, she assembles hardbound volumes with pages that are scorched and charred, or shredded and braided, or sealed shut with melted wax, or piled up and strewn with flowers as if they were burial mounds, memorials to the dead.

Patton is also a brilliant vocalist who has toured Europe with jazz musician Don Byron and performed in New York City with a Goth band. At Naropa Institute, the Buddhist college in Boulder, Colorado, where she is an occasional visiting writer at the Jack Kerouac School of Disembodied Poetics, Patton is famous for her orchestration of a site-specific opera collaboratively written and performed by her class of creative writing students. She is invited frequently as a visiting writer to the Schule für Dichtung (Vienna Poetry School), in Wien, Austria, and has also visited the Universidad de Antioquia's Escuela de Poesia (as part of the annual Festival Internacional de Poesia) and the Escuela Popular de Arte, both in Medellín, Colombia. At New York University, as an adjunct faculty member, Patton has taught a variety of innovative courses that address cultural production and technology.

Recent critical books by Nathaniel Mackey and Aldon Nielsen have addressed the often overlooked experimental poetry written by African Americans, and their observations apply even more emphatically to black women. Patton is one of a handful of African American women writers (including Adrienne Kennedy, Jayne Cortez, Charlotte Carter, Erica Hunt, Akilah Oliver, and a more recent generation including Suzan-Lori Parks, Renee Gladman, giovanni singleton, Tracie Morris, Miriam Jones, Janice Lowe, and Artress Bethany White) whose work is profoundly influenced by avant-garde movements. We may soon look forward to other accomplished and emerging poets from all over the map to discover one another at Cave Canem, a poetry workshop/retreat founded by Toi Derricotte and Cornelius Eady. After leading workshops at Cave Canem in June 1999, I spent two weeks at the Virginia Center for Creative Arts, where poet and critic Jonathan Monroe had gathered together a group of poets including Julie Patton. Julie was someone I had met on a few previous occasions during visits to New York City. Until those two weeks with the group in Virginia, our most extended contact had been a walk up the spiral ramp of the Guggenheim Museum to see a retrospective show of Robert Rauschenberg's work, and a late-night conversation in the apartment of Julie's Lower East Side neighbors, poet Erica Hunt and jazz musician Marty Ehrlich.

Our concurrent residencies at VCCA gave me the opportunity to appreciate the full spectrum of Julie's various modes of creation. I also learned that creativity runs in her family: one of her sisters sang with Mercer Ellington's band and her mother is a painter, whose work has appeared on the cover of the literary magazine *Callaloo*. Julie Patton grew up in Cleveland, Ohio, the home of innovative African American artists including playwright Adrienne Kennedy and poet Russell Atkins. Patton's mother, Virgie Patton-Ezelle, is a visual artist who had a long association with Karamu House, which was

founded as a multicultural arts institution and later became an important regional center for the Black Arts Movement that flourished in the late 1960s
and 1970s. It can be said that Julie Patton was nurtured in a rich artistic tradition and that her experimental creativity draws upon an inheritance of cultural sophistication as well as her own curiosity, intellect, and delightful invention.

The mysterious Julie Patton has a gift for life, having miraculously survived a frightening brush with death in the Paris Metro as well as several
months as a resident of an abandoned building in Manhattan. On another
occasion in Europe, she and her companions were rounded up at gunpoint
and held as suspected terrorists. I keep telling her that she must write her
memoirs, just as she has always urged Russell Atkins to find an archive for
his manuscripts and other papers safer than the unplugged refrigerator where
they were stored when she last visited him at home in Cleveland. Without
such efforts, the lives and works of innovative African American artists are
too often overlooked, and a valuable part of our literature and history may
be lost.

11
All Silence Says Music Will Follow

Listening to Lorenzo Thomas

Having myself been born in the univocalic state of Alabama, it is my pleasure to speak today of my own experience of listening to and reading the work of Lorenzo Thomas, a poet born in the univocalic nation of Panama. Lorenzo has written about Panama and its poets in "The Marvelous Land of Indefinitions," a poem collected in his 1979 book *Chances Are Few*. According to a website I consulted, *panama* is an indigenous word that means "abundance of fish and butterflies," which gives an indication of what the local attractions were in the days before Spanish architecture and the history summed up in the clever palindrome, "A man, a plan, a canal, Panama!" I imagine that some day in the future, the birthplace of Lorenzo Thomas will be one of the attractions on the visitor's guided tour. For me to come here to Houston from Los Angeles, where I live now, is to return to the state where I grew up and became a poet, as well as to return to the city where I became acquainted with the exemplary life and work of Lorenzo Thomas.[1] In one of the indigenous languages of this continent, *Texas* or *tejas* means "friends" or "allies," and in another indigenous language, *Alabama* means "tribal town," or more literally, "I make a clearing."

Like many Americans, neither Lorenzo nor I grew up in the places where we were born. His family moved from Panama to New York, mine from Alabama to Texas. So here I am, a poet and critic who was born in the "tribal town" of Florence, Alabama, and who grew up in the cow town of Fort Worth, returning to a city named for a Texas Anglo hero, trying to "make a clearing" to speak as both a poet and a critic about the work of a friend and ally I met in Texas, the poet and critic Lorenzo Thomas. Among the poets of Texas who I met when I was starting out, Lorenzo was one whose life and work demonstrated most emphatically how the poet can think, move, and write beyond the tribal town, beyond the boundaries of a regional or even a national identity. At the same time, in his observation of social and cultural phenomena and in his awareness of his surroundings, Lorenzo can be the most local of poets. He was thinking globally and acting locally long before it became a slogan on a bumper sticker. He was influential in encouraging my own sense of freedom from restrictions often imposed by a tribe or town, while also offering a model of the poet as community activist through his work with the Houston Blues Festival, Pacifica Radio, state and city arts councils, various associations of poets and writers, as well as numerous grassroots organizations.

Lorenzo Thomas was one of the messengers who brought the Black Arts movement below the Mason Dixon Line. He was one of the poets published in *Black Fire,* the signature anthology of the Black Arts movement edited by Larry Neal and Amiri Baraka. Because of Lorenzo, I knew that the innovative poets of Umbra had gathered together in New York even before the official beginning of the Black Arts movement; and because of Lorenzo, I knew that the Black Arts movement had connections to the other schools of "New American Poetry" collected in Donald Allen's 1960 anthology. Through LeRoi Jones/Amiri Baraka—the only black poet included in Allen's anthology—the Black Arts movement was connected through associations between Jones/Baraka and Charles Olson, Frank O'Hara, Allen Ginsberg, and Lorenzo Thomas to Black Mountain, the New York School, and Beat poetry, as well as to Umbra.

Lorenzo and I met in the state of Texas, my home from age three until I left for graduate school in California. Texas has been the home of Lorenzo Thomas more or less since he left New York in the 1970s. At this point he has lived in Texas about as long as I did. Although I'm no longer sure whether we first met in Houston or in Austin, where I first began attending poetry readings, I can say that I have known Lorenzo Thomas since at least 1980, and that I had the privilege to get closer to Lorenzo and his poetry in the year that I lived in Houston and began to work in the Texas Artists in Schools Program. I first encountered his work when he performed it at readings in places like Houston, Austin, Galveston, and Beaumont. A little later when I began to read his books, I appreciated even more the complexity and diversity of his work as well as his animated style of delivery that appeals to nonliterary as well as literary audiences. Lorenzo's eclectic practice of mixing classical, vernacular, and innovative styles has been a positive influence on my own work as a poet.

So I sing of Lorenzo Thomas, the definitive poet of the Marvelous Land of Indefinitions. I sing of the New World Orpheus composing lyrics for all sentient beings including spirits of the living and the dead, as well as mutely prophetic banana trees. I sing of the poet who writes with the voice of a prophet crying out in the wilderness, warning us of consequences, whether or not we choose to listen. I sing of the urban psalmist who goes on singing his song in what he calls "a heathen voice," singing his song in a strange land that grows ever stranger, as in the following poem from 1966 titled, "Song":

> You asked me to sing
> Then you seemed not
> To hear; to have gone out
> From the edge of my voice
>
> And I was singing
> There I was singing
> In a heathen voice
> You could not hear
> Though you requested
>
> The song—it was for them.
> Although they refuse you
> And the song I made for you
> Tangled in their tongue
>
> They wd mire themselves in the spring
> Rains, as I sit here folding and
> Unfolding my nose in your gardens
>
> I wouldn't mind it so bad
>
> Each word is cheapened
> In the air, sounding like
> Language that riots and
> Screams in the dark city
>
> Thoughts they requested
> Concepts that rule them
>
> Since I can't have you
> I will steal what you have

In 1967 in a poem titled "Onion Bucket," he wrote "All silence says music will follow," which suggests to me a dialectical relationship between life and death, between art and the void of meaninglessness, and suggests to any blocked writer that the blank page is ready to receive our creation. In the poetry of Lorenzo Thomas, there is often an implicit soundtrack behind the words, an allusive, unheard but remembered music that helps to establish the mood, location, or social context of a given moment in the poet's observant participation. The musical influences so pervasive in his poetry include jazz, blues, R&B, rock, reggae, calypso, zydeco, disco, country western, western classical music, and even muzak. Often some particular musical allusion allows the poet to define an intimate or social space, or the poem's speaker may borrow a theme or a rhetorical stance from a specific type of music, as in "Blues Cadet" and "MMDCCXIII ½." (The title of the latter appears to be a street address, 2713 ½, written in Roman numerals.) In these poems, whether the blues is directly or indirectly evoked, and whether or not the poem itself includes blues allusions, the space of home is defined as a blues space whenever the poet sings of the emotional discord and estrangement that occurs when individuals fail to connect. The poet sings the blues when love is off-key and a house is not a home. In "Blues Cadet," its title and its epigraph *after Sonny Boy Williamson* alert us to the poem's origins in the blues. The colloquial voice, intimate address to an absent love, and household metaphors used by the poem's troubled speaker would be appropriate for a traditional blues singer: "I've worn out the pictures on the carpet / Just pacing in my room // Ever since you went away." In "2713 ½" something close to a classical metrical pattern can be felt in the lines, yet under this speaker's more formal diction it is still possible to hear the blues:

The cruelty of ages past affects us now
Whoever it was who lived here lived a mean life,
Each door has locks designed for keys unknown

Our living room was once somebody's home
Our bedroom, someone's only room
Our kitchen had a hasp upon its door.

Door to a kitchen?

And our lives are hasped and boundaried
Because of ancient locks and madnesses
Of slumlord greed and desperate privacies

Which one is madness? Depends on who you are.
We find we cannot stay, the both of us, in the same room
Dance, like electrons, out of each other's way.

The cruelties of ages past affect us now.

Two poems in *Chances Are Few,* "Wheeling" and "The Rule of Thumb,"
are especially attentive to the social cues that music provides. In both poems,
music serves as a warning to the poet on the road that he is traveling through
possibly dangerous terrain. In "Wheeling" (which might refer to Wheeling,
West Virginia, as well as the act of steering a car), the impossibility of finding a jazz or R&B station on the radio alerts the weary traveler to the threat
of being stranded as a black stranger in white territory or the danger of falling asleep at the wheel while driving at night with the only available stations
carrying country western music or fundamentalist sermons, as the following excerpt suggests:

That's redneck music man just wait
You awake just in time
To see the next exit
And remark similar signs

You have seen somewhere
Before. This awakens
The driver and evoked

Gratitude from the death seat
Where I been riding
Alone with the bland view
Of the landscape of that
Highway so like any other
And so dull
. . . .
Welcome back to God's country
Wait. I'm trying to find the soul
Plus the tape died

About twenty miles down the road

The batteries couldn't stand
All that ignorance in the air
. . . .

In "The Rule of Thumb," the smooth, worn-out sound of hotel lobby muzak—depersonalized recordings of Tin Pan Alley torch songs—amplifies the loneliness and isolation of the speaker, who spends a blue Monday night drinking beer and watching television alone in his room at a mostly vacant motel on the outskirts of Tulsa. There's no way the smooth muzak, with its absence of true grit, can soothe this solitary traveler. If anything, the sound of it leaves him "on edge," in what for him is a different kind of blues space, a place so impersonal and so blandly white that it gives him the blues:

Tonight's only Monday
An off day in the motel game
Just like in life,
Blue Monday Blue Monday
But no heart-rending music
No "Rocks In My Bed"
. . . .

No

Torchy songs sputter down
Smooth as faded denim
Muzak
Annoying ooze into the lobby
As very few people check in
. . . .
On edge on the outskirts of town,
Those few behind doors,
Whose windows glow,
Are watching Melissa Manchester
Once again flunk the Memorex test
Wishing they had instead
Gone to Europe for the Silver Jubilee
To buy a cup with the Queen's mug
Upon it.

Was Lorenzo Thomas being ironic or prophetic when he wrote, "All silence says music will follow / No one acts under any compulsion"? In his case it is not necessary to choose between irony and prophecy or between silence and music. In our everyday communication, perhaps our highest aspiration is to be true to ourselves and to tell the truth to others. As speakers and writers, we hope to use language precisely, to say exactly what we mean. At our most rigorous, we want to communicate accurately and factually. At such critical moments, we strive to give an honest account of our perceptions. At best, we try not to betray our own best intentions. At best, we speak the truth as we know it. At our most sincere, we can only hope to say what we mean. And yet, I think that's why we require poetry, prophecy, and song, where it is possible to say more than we mean. The ability of such utterances to exceed meaning is what gives them significance beyond the range of our immediate time, place, and intentions. I'm going to end with a medley of lyrics, a cento composed of lines from four of Lorenzo's poems: "Onion Bucket" and "Cosmic Communion" from *The Bathers*, and "Class Action" and "Guilt" from *Chances Are Few*:

> All silence says music will follow.
> No one acts under any compulsion.[2]

> What shall I do but speak
> In Africa, the juju spirits shout through us
> Our screams speak rapture of their presence,
> Not our pain (which is unutterable).

> If no one speaks, the truth will still
> Be true.[3]

> But all I want to talk about
> Would be unspeakable things[4]

> "Just like a song
> You are capable
> Of deep incredible
> Vastly beautied
> Conceptions

> You will hear yourselves
> Speaking and it will be
> Like a song. You will be

You must remember this
As you awaken."[5]

Notes

1. This paper was originally prepared for the Lorenzo Thomas Panel at the American Studies Association Conference, which took place in Houston on November 15, 2002.

2. "Onion Bucket," *The Bathers, Book II, The Bathers*, p. 53

3. "Class Action," *Chances Are Few*, pp. 106, 108

4. "Guilt," *Chances Are Few*, p. 56

5. "Cosmic Communion," *The Bathers, Book III, Euphemysticism*, p. 138–39.

12

The Cracks Between What We Are and What We Are Supposed to Be

Stretching the Dialogue of African American Poetry

In *Black Chant: Languages of African-American Postmodernism* (1997), Aldon Nielsen makes a significant contribution to discussions of African American literary production by supplying a literary history for alternate traditions of African American poetry. If both the recently diversified contemporary mainstream canon and the recently established African American canon tend to include poets who are selected as representatives of blackness, Nielsen focuses his critical study on "poets whose works interrogate what literary society conceives to be blackness, what languages and what forms are critically associated with constructions of cultural blackness"(168). The aesthetic and intellectual practices of these writers and their readers enable them to explore the possibilities and limits of prevailing discourses and arm them with the flexibility to be interrogative as well as declarative.

In taking up the term that Nielsen uses, "interrogate," I want to apply it in its original sense of "standing between and asking questions." I would suggest that poets whose work is interrogative in this way have located their poetry in a space between declarative representations of blackness and a critical engagement with the cultural and discursive practices by which evolving identities are recognized, articulated, and defined. The works of these poets have contributed to a dialogue—a discourse on black alterity—that was initiated on the margins of both the mainstream culture and the traditional or popular culture of African Americans. This discourse of "other blackness" (rather than "black otherness") has recently begun to move into a larger discussion of the multiplicity and dissonance—the flipside of unity or homogeneity—of African American cultures and identities.

The exploratory interrogation of black identity as a social, cultural, and discursive formation raises critical questions about conventional representations of black identity. These questions not only allow the meanings of blackness to proliferate and expand, thus stretching black identity and making it more inclusive, but also allow instability in the definition of blackness. If the Black Arts Movement of the 1960s and '70s was primarily concerned with defining and empowering blackness while helping to reverse the cultural "whitewashing" of African Americans, several poets associated with this movement defined blackness specifically in ways that celebrated young militant black male heterosexuals and their supportive female comrades, partners, and admirers but at the same time frequently alienated other elements of the African American communities they ostensibly hoped to organize and empower. Perhaps this orientation of the movement sought to recruit an army of cultural warriors by framing black art as a safely masculine arena for young men who might otherwise have avoided what was regarded in some quarters as an effeminate activity.

In their attempt to purge African Americans of cultural whiteness, some proponents of black power vilified middle-class and homosexual lifestyles, seeing both as examples of blackness tainted and emasculated by decadent whiteness. Two primary sources for the most galvanizing rhetoric and influential styles of the Black Power and Black Arts movements, Malcolm X and Amiri Baraka, regarded themselves as having been corrupted by their earlier association with whiteness, queer sexualities, and a square middle-class background. Both men renamed themselves, creating new identities that inverted previously held values: Malcolm Little fled the middle-class pretensions of Boston's black strivers, first transforming himself into a conked, reefer-smoking, lindy-hopping zoot suiter, and later converting and becoming a minister of the Nation of Islam, accepting Elijah Muhammad's demonization of the white race; LeRoi Jones repudiated the black bourgeoisie and white bohemia, as allegorized in his 1964 play *Dutchman*. Although both eventually modified their radical positions, they contributed to the extreme rhetoric of radical black movements of the 1960s, as seen in the revolutionary style and swagger of militant leaders of the Black Panther political party. These charismatic leaders offered themselves as case studies for the project of purifying black identity and black culture of the contaminating effects of white domination, with which they often conflated bourgeois culture, homosexuality, and the Judeo-Christian religious tradition.

My remarks will focus not primarily on formally innovative work but on recent black poetry that has been enabled by theoretical discourse and avant-garde practices. Black poets who began to publish in the 1990s have started to incorporate into a more accessible poetic language the critical interrogation of cultural meanings of blackness. These poets are investigating the boundaries of racial and cultural identity and articulating precisely the positions of class and sexuality that were excluded from the center of blackness as defined in the Black Arts Movement. While additional names might be added to this discussion, I have selected as examples of this development in poetry the work of Elizabeth Alexander, G. E. Patterson, Akilah Oliver, and Suheir Hammad.

Of these, Alexander is the most widely known and published, with two well-received books, inclusion in several anthologies, and the academic credentials that led to a faculty position at the University of Chicago. Patterson is a well-regarded emerging poet who has been a fellow at the MacDowell Colony and whose first book has been noted in a publication cosponsored by the Academy of American Poets. Hammad, another emerging poet, has published a first book that contains several poems that employ the urban vernacular style of hip hop and spoken-word performance. Oliver, an adjunct faculty member at Naropa University, has the most edgily disjunctive poetics of this group. Her work also emerges from a performance background, in her case as a founding member of the multiracial avant-garde feminist group The Sacred Naked Nature Girls, whose collaborative work examines the social inscription of identity on the bodies of women.

With two published books of poetry, *The Venus Hottentot* (1990) and *Body of Life* (1996), Elizabeth Alexander has given us work of clarity and complexity that is at once pleasurably accessible and intellectually sophisticated. Her poetry offers a thoughtful meditation on the contradictions of postmodern identity, with the poet—herself the offspring of a materially comfortable and socially conscious black family—negotiating between popular culture's bipolar representations of blackness as a signifier of lack, deprivation, and negation versus blackness as a signifier of conspicuous consumption, unaccustomed privilege, and unrestrained excess. Between these opposing signs, she posits her intimate knowledge of black humanity and her observation and experience of creativity, energy, imagination, and pleasure as well as desire, unfulfilled yearning, and unmet need.

In poems such as "Nineteen"*(The Venus Hottentot)*, "Haircut," (*Body of Life*, 60–61), "Six Yellow Stanzas"(*Body of Life*, 51–54), and "Race" (*Giant Steps*, 19–20), Alexander finds in the location between cultural representations of whiteness and blackness the occasion to reaffirm her African American identity as she simultaneously articulates her class identification as a product of the black and "high yellow" bourgeoisie. Alexander claims all of her experience as a variety of black experience: memories of debutante balls and dreams of giving birth to a yellow baby in "Six Yellow Stanzas"; a youthful sexual encounter with an older black working-class man, a Vietnam veteran she meets on her first job away from home, in "Nineteen." In another poem, "Haircut," a haircut in Harlem allows the poet to imagine herself as a New York "fly-girl" as she travels on the IRT, self-consciously *buys black* in Harlem's black-owned businesses, and insistently connects her personal and family history to the aesthetic, cultural, and historical movements of Harlem's black community, where her unkinky hair and "riny" complexion blend into the continuum of textures and hues that constitute blackness. In "Race," Alexander's embrace of her own particular black experience extends to include even the once-taboo mention of a relative who passed as a white man.

Through her participation in Cave Canem, a workshop retreat for African American poets founded by Toi Derricotte and Cornelius Eady, Alexander has also served as a mentor for emerging black poets, including one I want to include in this discussion of interrogative poets, G. E. Patterson. In a cover blurb for his 1999 poetry collection, *Tug*, Alexander wrote, "These poems are wide-ranging in voice, style, and epistemology, surprising as so many turns." Derricotte also contributed an endorsement:

> Many of these poems seem autobiographical. Yet, on second reading, one is not sure. Are these the poems of an ordinary black man's life, or is there a tug between several possible, even alternative, lives? . . . I am so happy for this exploration which digs deep into the cracks between what we are and what we are supposed to be.

Among the poems in Patterson's book, the one titled "Autobiography of a Black Man" is a clearly fictional, hyperbolically generic "autobiography" that offers a sardonic critique of popular culture's conflicting representations of black men as admired and despised exemplars of reckless masculinity:

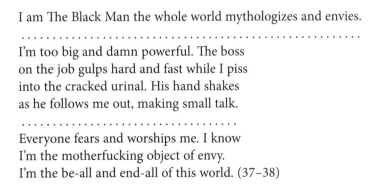

I am The Black Man the whole world mythologizes and envies.
. . . .
I'm too big and damn powerful. The boss
on the job gulps hard and fast while I piss
into the cracked urinal. His hand shakes
as he follows me out, making small talk.
. . . .
Everyone fears and worships me. I know
I'm the motherfucking object of envy.
I'm the be-all and end-all of this world. (37–38)

It is a position from which Patterson himself feels estranged, for as a young gay black man he is "desperate to be festive and loved" ("And," 64).

Also writing from a perspective of queer sexuality, Akilah Oliver opens her poetry collection *The She Said Dialogues: Flesh Memory* (1999) with a theoretical statement of the poet's intention to "investigate the non-linear synapses between desire, memory, blackness (as both a personal identity and a non-essentialist historical notion), sexuality, and language." She situates her text:

> in the on-going work I've been doing in performance . . . as it relates to a critical interrogation of the African-American literary/performative tradition. . . . The work I've been doing consciously seeks to disrupt this tradition, to play not only with language and form, but with the representational idioms of "blackness," "femaleness," "homogeneity" . . . as a kind of insurgent text within the African American literary tradition. I see the dialogues as part of the emerging outsider tradition in black literature which restates memory and identity in a post-Civil Rights framework. A framework which is multiplicitous . . . . Stretching the dialogue . . . . Making itself up as it goes. (4–5)

This statement indicates her familiarity with theoretical discourses of avant-garde performance and formally innovative writing practices, a critical awareness that enters into poems such as "she said loss, lost"(26–27) and "so where do you enter memory" (46–47). With the examples of Pat Parker and Audre Lorde behind her (two of the many brave poets who emerged at a time when the conflicting radical interests of the Black Power, feminist, and sexual identity movements left a minefield of contested space for lesbians of color), Oliver confronts the complications inherent in her own identity as a black woman born in St. Louis and raised in South Central Los Angeles who is trying to parent her son in the driven snow of Boulder, Colorado, while involved in an interracial lesbian relationship.

Oliver's work explores the possibilities for freedom, innovation, and critical thinking in the conscious choice of outsider status; in this manner she investigates escape from the sometimes oppressive spaces in which black people have learned to survive to the sanitized spaces of affluence that white privilege affords, a space in which it is possible for a struggling artist to live off the fat of the land. Oliver recalls a journal entry in which she recorded her son's first response to Boulder: "It looks so nice, it must be hiding something."[1] Like a tourist with an expired visa, Oliver turned a visit to Boulder into an extended stay instead of returning to a Los Angeles home rocked by earthquakes and riots. Although her sense of writing as insurrection was inspired by the insurgent poetry of the Black Arts Movement, Oliver's trans-

gressive text challenges the essentialist identity politics of black cultural na-
tionalism as much as it interrogates how white privilege operates in a place
"so nice, it must be hiding something."

Oliver sees her work as necessarily transgressive: it requires an intersection of the sacred and profane to create a discursive space for the inclusion
of all of her spiritual and physical, personal and political, and individual
and collective selves. The poet articulates her own sense of erotic desire and
transcendence, aware that her existence violates what others cherish as sacred truth. As in the work of Chicana author Cherrie Moraga, Oliver's poetry
profanes patriarchal religion as it sacralizes lesbian sexuality; in this manner
she seeks to escape the controlling discourse of church fathers regarding the
separation of body and soul, the divine right of masculine power and privilege, the holiness of celibacy, the sanctity of heterosexual marriage, and the
sin of homosexuality. Oliver also questions the secular significance of "black
soul" given the pervasive influence of African Americans on mainstream
popular culture and the global impact of black performers and musicians.

> tina turner on acid yodeling in arabic
> . . . my favorite line already happened.
> on the radio a voice sounds like a teasing three year old
> & the horn section goes nanananana. all cocky. closed fisted
> salutes. how come nobody mentioned clitorectomy with
> they dashikis on. like we were afraid a close look. a criticism. a rejection
>   of a fixed ritual would pop the bubble.
> dreams are fragile like that. concealing as much as they
> reveal. colors proscribed in song. imagining the world as
> placed. fixed.
>
> you a visitor in a landscape you don't control.
> i want to know what the eyes smelled at the bottom of the
> ships. i've seen that look of terror before. any asshole on
> the bus pants hanging off his butt. X terrorizing a fashion
> statement on hats & tee shirts. any black boy beautiful or
> ugly could be of my blood. one meaning of blackness. This
> arbitrariness of circumstance. know it's all possible &
> nothing's true.
> ("she said loss, lost," 26)
>
> . . . i need to flick myself in such a way that the moans
> eat me alive. no witnesses. church hats. round boxes stuffed

in closets. my mother told me i was a girl. i wanted to call
her god but the timing never seemed right . . . in the marketplace
    of dreams isis found oriris' penis. fragmented. i want a myth that
    would not
explain some thing. to enter the church doors on my knees.
i want jesus to fill me up. want the holy ghost to shout in
tongues. want to flick in the pulpit.
("so where do you enter memory," 46)

Finally, I want to turn to a poet whose inclusion in discussions of "black poetry" gives us an occasion to ask to what extent "blackness" functions as a political rather than a racial or cultural designation. Let us look at two of her poems:

YO BABY YO
poppin that yo baby yo
yo baby yo?
me to turn around you expect after
you show me no kind of respect?

the sneakers you wearin cost more than
the soul you sold to pay for them?

. . . yo baby yo
yo brotha yo
them gold chains
are tighter than you think.
(42)

BROWN BREAD HERO
may i have a vegetable hero?
no white
rye or wheat
brown
yeah a brown bread hero
brown
born and bred
no mayonnaise thank you
never liked it as much as
mustard i'll take spicy yellow on sweet brown mustard over

bland fatty mayo
anyday

no cheese please
cheese is to the west
the spice of the east
why smother in cheese
when i can enhance
spice dance
with turmeric sumac or curry
no mucous building cheese on my hero
I vegetables of the brown earth
between two layers of brown bread
no flesh of creatures
no white bread
no salt no sauce
thank you

a brown bread hero
brown born and bred
white has never been
my hero.
(59–60)

These two poems, from *Born Palestinian, Born Black* (1996), were written by Suheir Hammad, a daughter of Palestinian refugees who was born in Jordan and lived for a time in Beirut before moving with her family to Brooklyn.

On the one hand, her work suggests an expansive definition of blackness that encompasses more than race. Identification as black may also have to do with such issues as shared experience, cultural fluency, political solidarity, and styles of verbal performance. In "Brown Bread Hero," Hammad's aversion to the smothering blandness that she associates with the dominant culture's ideology of whiteness takes her into the political and cultural terrain of liberatory darkness. (Perhaps she also alludes to lactose intolerance, a genetic trait common to peoples of African, Middle Eastern, and Mediterranean descent that distinguishes their traditional dietary preferences from those of Northern Europeans.)

On the other hand, Hammad's verbal performance in "Yo Baby Yo" points to the constructedness of black language, black voice, and black experience (or any other language, voice, and experience), reminding us that indeed blackness is a social construction, that any language, culture, or dialect is acquired. Hammad's poem might be read as an illustration of the availability of contemporary black vernacular and its formulaic tropes to others besides African American speakers and writers or, less generously, as a caricature of urban black vernacular that is uncomfortably similar to that found throughout mainstream popular culture, including that used on the gold and platinum CDs of hip hop artists.

Suheir Hammad, Akilah Oliver, G. E. Patterson, and Elizabeth Alexander have all written poems that trouble the waters of blackness. These poets give us opportunities to reexamine the boundaries that were drawn in order to define the declarative blackness celebrated in the Black Arts Movement. Questioning such boundaries of class, sexuality, and even race itself, they all indicate in different ways and from different individual positions that blackness has become a space for critical and aesthetic interrogation, both from within and outside the canon of African American literature.

Notes

1. Conversation with author, July 3, 2000.

II
Longer Essays

13
African Signs and Spirit Writing

The recording of an authentic black voice, a voice of deliverance from
the deafening discursive silence which an "enlightened" Europe cited
as proof of the absence of the African's humanity, was the millennial
instrument of transformation through which the African would become
the European, the slave become the ex-slave, the brute animal become
the human being. So central was this idea to the birth of the black
literary tradition that four of the first five eighteenth-century slave
narratives drew upon the figure of the voice in the text as crucial "scenes
of instruction" in the development of the slave on his road to freedom.
James Gronniosaw in 1770, John Marrant in 1785, Ottobah Cuguano
in 1787, Olaudah Equiano in 1789, and John Jea in 1815, all draw upon
the figure of the voice in the text. . . . That the figure of the talking book
recurs in these . . . black eighteenth-century texts says much about the
degree of "intertextuality" in early black letters, more than we heretofore
thought. Equally important, however, this figure itself underscores the
established correlation between silence and blackness we have been
tracing, as well as the urgent need to make the text speak, the process by
which the slave marked his distance from the master.

> Henry Louis Gates, introduction to Charles Davis's
> *The Slave's Narrative*, 26–27

The influential scholar Henry Louis Gates argues that black literary traditions
privilege orality. This critical position has become something of a common-
place, in part because it is based on accurate observation. From the "talking
book" featured in early slave narratives to "dialect poetry" and the "speakerly text," the African American tradition that Gates constructs and can-
onizes is that which seeks to "speak" to readers with an "authentic black
voice." Presumably for the African American writer there is no alternative
to the production of this "authentic black voice" but silence, invisibility, or
self-effacement. This speech-based and racially inflected aesthetic that produces a "black poetic diction" requires that the writer acknowledge and reproduce in the text a significant difference between the spoken and written
language of African Americans and that of other Americans. Without dis-
puting, as George Schuyler did in his satiric novel *Black No More*, that such
a difference exists, I would like to argue that any theory of African American literature that privileges a speech-based poetics or the trope of orality

to the exclusion of more writerly texts results in the impoverishment of the tradition. While Gates includes in his canon a consummately writerly text such as Ralph Ellison's *Invisible Man* because it also functions brilliantly as a speakerly text, and while Gates appreciates Zora Neale Hurston and celebrates Sterling A. Brown, he cannot champion Jean Toomer's *Cane* with the same degree of enthusiasm.[1] I would not worry so much about the criteria Gates has set for inclusion in his canon if it did not seem to me that the requirement that a black text be "speakerly" will inevitably exclude certain African American texts that draw more on the culture of books, writing, and print than they do on the culture of orality.

Another concern I have about Gates's argument is its seeming acceptance of an erroneous Eurocentric assumption that African cultures developed no indigenous writing or script systems. Although he is well aware of Job Ben Solomon, a captive African sold into slavery in Maryland and later ransomed and returned to Africa after it was discovered that he was literate in Arabic, Gates seems to overlook the possibility that non-Islamic slaves might also have been familiar with writing or indigenous script systems used for various religious purposes in their own cultural contexts. While laws forbidding anyone to teach African American slaves born in the United States to read or write enforced their institutionalized illiteracy, such illiteracy cannot be accepted as given, although to speak of non-Islamic Africans as literate would require broader definitions of writing than Western scholars such as Walter J. Ong might find acceptable.

This essay explores connections between African signs and African American spirit writing, traditions that may be traced more readily within the contexts of the visual arts and art history. In those contexts perhaps more continuity exists between African and African American forms of visual expression than exists within a canon of African American literature or literary criticism, since the loss of African languages by African Americans constitutes a much more decisive rupture.

As a literary critic, another part of my project is to read the narratives of former slaves, including their spiritual narratives, as precursors of complementary traditions of African American literacy; at the same time, I must keep in mind that much of what is considered most authentically African in traditional African American culture has been preserved and maintained through extraliterary forms, and has in fact often been the creation of illiterate or marginally literate African Americans whose aesthetic impact is all the more astonishing given their exclusion from the educational, cultural, and political institutions of the dominant bourgeois white culture of the United States. Looking at parallel traditions of African American literacy, at those inaugurated by the narratives of former slaves and by visionary texts produced mainly in the nineteenth century, for possible answers, I am asking this larger question: how has the Western view of writing as a rational technology historically been received and transformed by African Americans whose primary means of cultural transmission have been oral and visual rather than written, and for whom graphic systems have been associated not with instrumental human communication but with techniques of spiritual power and spirit possession? In other words, how, historically, have African Americans' attitudes toward literacy as well as their own efforts to acquire, use, and interiorize the technologies of literacy been shaped by what art historian Robert Farris Thompson calls "the flash of the spirit of a certain people armed with improvisatory drive and brilliance"?[2]

The narratives of former slaves offer one possible answer to this question.[3] Another possibility and an alternative tradition are suggested by what Thompson notes, that in African American folk culture the printed text may provide ritual protection, as newspapers were used by "back-home architects" who "papered the walls of their cabins with newsprint to confuse jealous spirits with an excess of information," and writing may be employed to enclose and confine evil presences, as in the spirit-script of visionary artist J. B. Murray.[4] In Murray's noncommunicative spirit-writing or "textual glossolalia," which looks like illiterate scribbling or a handwriting exercise, Thompson finds an African American manifestation of what may be a surviving element of Kongo prophetic practices, in which an illegible script produced in a trancelike state functions as a graphic representation of spirit possession, what another critic calls "a visual equivalent to speaking in tongues" (Adele 14). In order to construct a cultural and material history of the embrace and transmutation of writing technologies by African Americans, one might ask how writing and text functioned in a folk milieu that valued a script for its cryptographic incomprehensibility and uniqueness rather than for its legibility or reproducibility. One might ask, in other words, how the uniformity of print was received by a folk culture in which perfect symmetry and straight, unbroken lines were avoided, that had an aesthetic preference for irregularity and variation that folklorist Gladys-Marie Fry attributes to "the folk belief of plantation slaves that evil spirits follow straight lines" (67).[5]

Thompson imaginatively suggests that, just as in African and diasporic forms of oral expression—from the pygmy yodel to the field holler of the slave; from the blues wail to the gospel hum; from the bebopping scat of the jazz singer to the nonsense riffs erupting in the performance of the rap, dub, or reggae artist—it is apparent that the voice may be "unshackled" from meaningful words or from the pragmatic function of language as a conveyor of cognitive information, and the written text, as spirit-script, may be un-shackled from any phonetic representation of human speech or graphic representation of language. "Music brings down the spirit upon a prepared point in traditional Kongo culture," Thompson states. I might add that a reading of nineteenth-century African American spiritual narratives suggests that, like music, the act of reading or writing as well as the process of acquiring literacy itself may be a means for the visionary writer to attract a powerful presence to inhabit a spiritually focused imagination or a blank sheet of paper. Jarena Lee recalls the moment of her conversion, a flash of the spirit that was inspired by hearing the Bible read aloud in church: "At the reading of the Psalms, a ray of renewed conviction darted into my soul" (Andrews 27). Zilpha Elaw, attending a camp meeting, experienced a "trance or ec-stasy" that resulted in an unprecedented feeling of empowerment:

> [My] heart and soul were rendered completely spotless—as clean as a sheet of white paper, and I felt as if I had never sinned in all my life.... When the prayer meeting afterwards commenced, the Lord opened my mouth in public prayer; and while I was thus engaged, it seemed as if I heard my God rustling in the tops of the mulberry-trees. Oh how precious was this day to my soul! (Andrews 67).

Through the appropriation of public symbols and participation in main-stream cultural discourses, an African American tradition of literacy as a secular technology and a tool for political empowerment coexists with a parallel tradition of visionary literacy as a spiritual practice in which divine inspiration, associated with Judeo-Christian biblical tradition, is syncretically merged with African traditions of spirit possession. Such is the case in the "spirit-writing" of Gertrude Morgan (1900–1980) and J. B. Murray (1910–1988), African American visionary folk artists who were, respectively, literate and illiterate practitioners of what Robert Farris Thompson calls "arts of defense and affirmation" and "arts of black yearning" for transcendence and freedom.

The tradition of African American secular literacy may be traced to the narratives of former slaves, with the 1845 narrative of Frederick Douglass serving as the paradigmatic text of the genre. The alternative tradition of visionary literacy may be traced to narratives and journals of spiritual awakening and religious conversion written by freeborn and emancipated Africans and African Americans in the eighteenth and nineteenth centuries. Each of these traditions of literacy, the sacred and the secular, has a specific relation to African and diasporic orality as well as to the institutionalized illiteracy that resulted from the systematic exclusion of African Americans from equal educational opportunities. Both traditions have a common origin in the early narratives of African captives for whom emancipation was associated with conversion to the equally potent religions of Christianity and literacy.[6] By the nineteenth century, the bonds linking religious conversion and legal emancipation had been broken as masters complained that it made no economic sense to free slaves simply because they had become fellow Christians. It remained for nineteenth-century former slaves, notably Douglass, to perceive that the legal codes forbidding literacy and social mobility to slaves were a secular analogue to the threat of spiritual alienation that had motivated Olaudah Equiano and others to learn to read in order to "talk to" the Bible.

The narratives of former slaves signal a decisive movement of literate African Americans toward self-empowerment through the tools and technologies of literacy that are productive of bourgeois subjectivity, and away from the degradation imposed by slavery and compulsory illiteracy. The zealous pursuit of literacy embodied by these former slaves, particularly Douglass, is an astute response to the disastrous assault on the collective cultural identities of African captives. That assault was conducted by the dominant bourgeois white culture, which characterized those coherent African traditional aesthetic and spiritual systems that remained within slave culture as the superstitious beliefs of primitive people. This assault in effect submerged, fragmented, or rendered irrelevant the orally transmitted forms of knowledge brought by Africans from their various ethnic groups.

Alongside the largely secular and overtly political narratives of former slaves, which of necessity are concerned with what happens to the slave's body, an alternate tradition of visionary literacy exists in the tradition of African American spiritual autobiography. That literary tradition concerned itself not with the legal status of the material body but with the shackles placed on the soul and on the spiritual expressiveness of the freeborn or emancipated African American, whose religious conversion, sanctification, and worship were expected to conform to the stringent standards of the white Christian establishment. Until the founding of black churches and the calling of black preachers and until the white clergy loosened its strictures against emotional displays of religious enthusiasm, African American worship had been constrained in its expressive forms and rituals, which included communal dancing, the call and response by which the community and its leaders mutually affirmed one another, and the spontaneous vocalizations of the spirit-possessed. For African American visionary writers and artists, the Bible, as sacred text and sublime speech, as the written record of a divine voice inspiring its authors to write and its readers to speak holy words, mediates the historical and mythic dislocation from primarily oral cultures to one in which literacy has the power of a fetish.

Although equally zealous in their pursuit of freedom through literacy, spiritual autobiographers, unlike most former-slave narrators, often forsake a "bourgeois perception" of reality (Lowe) for "things unseen" or "signs in the heavens." Because of the stress they place on visionary experience, these texts have as much in common with the practice of literate and illiterate African American visionary folk artists as with contemporaneous narratives written or dictated by emancipated or fugitive slaves in the eighteenth and nineteenth centuries. For visionary artists, as for these spiritual autobiographers, the artwork or text is an extension of their call to preach. Both function as a spiritual signature or divine imprimatur, superceding human authority. The writer as well as the artist can become "an inspired device for the subconscious spirit," the African ancestor-spirit whose black yearning, unleashed as glossolalia, would be regarded in the dominant culture as *mumbo jumbo.* Through the visionary artist or writer who serves as a medium, it is possible for the surviving spirit of African cultural traditions "to manifest itself on the physical plane" through the artist's materials or the materiality of the writing process. The work of such individuals, while resonating with ancient traditions, "is conceived out of [a] deeply intuitive calling and spiritual need" (Nasisse).

In addition to stressing spiritual and personal over material and political forms of power, visionary writers were also much more likely to attribute their literacy to supernatural agency rather than to the difficult and tedious work Douglass details in his attempt to "get hold of a book" and grasp the instrumentality of literacy (278). The secular tradition of the narratives of former slaves is exemplified by Douglass, who substituted abolitionist tracts for the Bible (Olaudah Equiano's "talking book") as the text of desire that motivated him to acquire literacy, and who learned to write by copying the penmanship of his young master, literally "writing in the spaces" of the master's copybook.[7]

> I got hold of a book entitled "The Columbian Orator." Every opportunity I got, I used to read this book. . . . During this time, my copybook was the board fence, brick wall, and pavement; my pen and ink was a lump of chalk. With these, I learned mainly how to write. . . . By this time, my little Master Thomas had gone to school, and learned how to write, and had written over a number of copybooks. . . . When left

thus [unsupervised in the master's house], I used to spend the time in writing in the spaces left in master Thomas's copybook, copying what he had written. I continued to do this until I could write a hand very similar to that of Master Thomas. Thus, after a long, tedious effort for years, I finally succeeded in learning how to write. (Douglass 278–281)[8]

Through his emphasis on the quotidian, his naming of the mundane material objects employed in his campaign of disciplinary self-instruction, and his substitution of abolitionist writings where previous narratives had placed the Bible as the text motivating the narrator to become literate, Douglass refigures and secularizes the trope of divine instruction employed in the spiritual autobiographies of some free-born or manumitted African Americans who claimed to have acquired literacy by supernatural means: through divine intervention after earnest prayer. The ethnographic and historical research that documents continuities between African and African American aesthetic and spiritual practices now makes it possible to explore how, in the eighteenth and nineteenth centuries, Africans and African Americans who converted to Anglo-American Protestantism as well as Latin Catholic Christianity and interiorized Western-style literacy may have transformed and refigured indigenous African concepts of protective religious writing. Maude Southwell Wahlman writes that:

In Africa, among the Mande, Fon, Ejagham, and Kongo peoples, indigenous and imported writing is associated with knowledge, power, and intelligence, and thus is considered sacred and protective. African signs were sewn, dyed, painted or woven into cloth; and Central African artifacts were often read as aspects of a Kongo religious cosmogram. . . . In Nigeria, the Ejagham people are known for their 400-year-old writing system, called *Nsibidi* (Talbot, 1912). It was most likely invented by women since one sees it on their secret society buildings, fans, calabashes, skin-covered masks, textiles, and costumes made for secret societies. . . . In the New World various mixtures of West African *(Vai)* and Nigerian *(Nsibidi)* scripts and the Kongo cosmogram fused to create numerous new scripts. (29–30)

This phenomenon has been most extensively documented in the Latin Catholic traditions in which religious syncretism thrives through the identification of Catholic saints with African deities, as well as through the church's hospitality to mysticism and the incorporation of indigenous paganisms into elaborately layered and localized rites and rituals. Yet it can also be demonstrated that even the more austere traditions of Anglo-American Protestant worship, particularly after the establishment of black churches, produced African American syncretisms of African, European, and indigenous Native American spiritual practices. African American preaching styles, call and response, spirituals, gospel singing, baptism and funeral rites, and ritual possession by "the Holy Ghost" are examples of such Protestant syncretisms. Particularly in its insistence on grassroots literacy training as an aspect of religious conversion and sanctification, with Bible reading the means through which the Holy Word would be transmitted directly to each individual, Protestantism fostered in African American religious tropologies the figuring of acquisition and interiorization of literacy as a Christian form of spirit-possession compatible with African mystical traditions.

The tradition of spiritual writers includes John Jea, Jarena Lee, Zilpha Elaw, Julia Foote, and Rebecca Cox Jackson, whose spirituality links them to illiterate visionaries Harriet Tubman, Sojourner Truth, and Harriet Powers, to literate insurrectionists such as Nat Turner and Denmark Vesey, and to twentieth-century visionary artists such as J. B. Murray and Gertrude Morgan. By comparing similarities in the imagery of visionary folk artists with the religious visions of nineteenth-century mystics, it is possible to see a continuum of syncretic survival whereby African spiritual traditions and aesthetic systems hid and thrived in the interstices of accepted Christian practices. According to Andy Nasisse:

> The overwhelming evidence that certain images and religious ideas encoded in the work of Black American visions has verifiable trans-Atlantic connections to specific cultures in Africa . . . gives additional support to the notion that these images surface from a collective source. . . . Although many of these Africanisms could have been taught and otherwise handed down through generations, there are numerous signs of the presence of tribal elements which seem to have spontaneously generated in an individual's art. (11)

Maude Southwell Wahlman locates visionary African American art in a "creolized" tradition that blends cultural and aesthetic traditions of Africans, Native Americans, and Europeans. Because the artists, some of them illiterate, "could not always articulate the African traditions that shaped their visions, dreams, and arts," they have seemed "idiosyncratic" to art critics and art historians schooled in European and Euro-American traditions (28–29).

The creolized tradition of visionary folk artists that has been "transmitted somewhat randomly through the generations . . . resulted in the retention of original African motifs although the symbolic meanings of the images were sometimes lost" (Adele 13).

This syncretic or creolized tradition is manifested in a most visually striking way in the work of African American quilters. The narrative quilts of Harriet Powers offer a fascinating example of artifacts that incorporate African techniques and design elements, while also expressing the spiritual preoccupations of an artistically gifted individual. Powers, who could neither read nor write, was born into slavery in 1837 and died in 1911. According to folklorist Gladys-Marie Fry, "Harriet Powers's quilt['s form] a direct link to the tapestries traditionally made by the Fon people of Abomey, the ancient capital of Dahomey, West Africa" (85). Sterling Stuckey asserts that both Dahomean and Bakongo traditions are evident in Powers's Bible story quilts. He writes:

> Dahomean influence . . . appeared in a form and a place in which whites would least expect African religious expression of any kind— in the quilts of slave women. Fashioned from throw-away cloth, slave quilts were used to clothe mysteries, to enfold those baptized with reinforcing symbols of their faith. Such quilts in Georgia bore a remarkable resemblance to Dahomean applique cloth. Harriet Powers's Bible quilt is a brilliant example both of that tradition and of Bakongo tradition, combining the two so naturally as to reflect the coming together of Dahomean and Bakongo people in American slavery. . . . Thus, her quilt is a symbol of the fusion of African ethnic traditions in slavery and later. . . . When asked about the meaning of her quilt, Harriet Powers responded at considerable length and in much detail, asserting that the quilt in every particular is Christian. (91–92)

The two extant Powers quilts memorialize historical, celestial, mythic, and biblical events, all drawn into the composition through the artist's imaginative system of visual representation. Powers's beautifully executed pictographic quilts also form an interesting link between folk material culture and the culture of literacy. Combining the distinctive applique techniques of Dahomean textile art with the distinctly American narrative quilt, Powers constructed visual narratives that could almost be described as storyboards. In the quilts themselves, textile approaches textuality; dictated notes record Powers's recital of the local, biblical, and apocryphal stories that inspired the series of narrative frames, which "read" from left to right and top to bottom in her two extant quilts, now held in the collections of the Smithsonian Institution and the Boston Museum of Fine Arts.

While I reject Nasisse's speculation that there may be some "genetic" reason for the recurrent images found in visionary folk art and their continuity with similar imagery found in African art and artifacts (other than the inherited tendency of human beings to make and preserve cultural symbols), certainly the persistence of such "Africanisms" in the work of Southern folk artists suggests that African cultural systems were not utterly destroyed by slavery; rather, they survived in fragmentary, dispersed, and marginalized forms that continue to exist alongside the dominant cultural traditions that also significantly influence African American cultural production.

Sterling Stuckey, following Thompson's insight, argues that African American culture was formed not only through the syncretism of African with European and indigenous native traditions but also through the fusion of traditional practices that were familiar and comprehensible to individuals from different African ethnolinguistic groups. The slave community actually served to consolidate, reinforce, and preserve certain African customs that diverse cultural systems had shared in common, such as burial rituals that included decorating graves with seashells, glass, or crockery. Stuckey writes:

> Slaves found objects in North America similar to the shells and close enough to the earthenware of West Africa to decorate the grave in an African manner. . . . Africans from different points of the continent shared this vision, which could have *strengthened* an African trait under the conditions of North American slavery. . . . Being on good terms with the ancestral spirits was an overarching conceptual concern for Africans everywhere in slavery. . . . No one has yet demonstrated that skilled slaves sought to cut themselves off from their spiritual base in the slave community. If skilled slaves did not remove themselves from that base they remained connected to the African heritage on the profoundest possible level. (Stuckey 42–43, emphasis in original)

What may seem to be the "spontaneous generation" of African symbols in the work of African American folk artists may in fact indicate that the folk tradition has served as a repository of African spiritual practices since the arrival of the first captive Africans to this country. Such seemingly idiosyncratic imagery, which nevertheless alludes to dispersed and hidden fragments of coherent cultural systems, generally does not appear in the secular tradition initiated in the materially based narratives of former slaves, which tend to distance the narrator from "slave superstition" or "heathen" African spirituality, while providing a rationale for displays of emotion by African Americans. While Christianity strongly influences African American spirituality, it is also evident that the visionary tradition allows within its spiritual matrix a space for a syncretic African-based spirituality or diasporic consciousness that a secular narrator such as Frederick Douglass specifically rejects as slave "superstition."

In his recollection of an incident in which an African-born slave offers and Douglass accepts a special root to serve as a protective charm against being whipped by the overseer, Douglass progressively dissociates himself from this superstitious belief in the power of the ritual object. At the same time he self-consciously uses his text to suggest that his increasing grasp of literacy allowed him eventually to transfer his youthful belief in the power associated in African cultures with ritual objects to the power associated in bourgeois Western culture with writing. First the written pass, which the slaves, significantly, swallow after a failed escape attempt, and finally the text of the narrative itself take on this aura of power that Douglass associates with his interiorization of literacy and its technologies.

Douglass's text registers cultural hybridity even as the narrator rejects the devalued alternative consciousness of the African captive in his determined pursuit of bourgeois subjectivity, the basic prerequisite of citizenship. His ambivalent portrayal of his own youthful belief in a spiritual technique, one that is later displaced by a belief in the greater efficacy of literacy, might be read as Douglass's gloss on the failure of slave insurrections led by Denmark Vesey and Nat Turner.[9] Vesey, a free black, and Turner, a slave, sought to forge leadership at the interface of African orality/spirituality and an African American visionary literacy founded on a prophetic reading of the Bible. Vesey's co-conspirator Gullah Jack, known among slaves as "the little man who can't be killed, shot, or taken," was, according to slave testimony, "born a conjuror and a physician, in his own country [Angola]," and possessed "a charm which rendered him invulnerable." Turner's insurrection relied on his reading of "signs in the heavens" and "hieroglyphic characters" he had "found on the leaves in the woods," which corresponded with "the figures [he] had seen in the heavens" as well as his application of biblical prophecy to the historical circumstance of slavery in the United States. Eric Foner speculates that Turner "may have inherited some of his rebelliousness from his parents, for according to local tradition, his African-born mother had to be restrained from killing her infant son rather than see him a slave and his father escaped when Nat was a boy." In his dictated 1831 "confession," Turner notes that his family and the slave community had implicitly equated his predilection for prophetic vision with his precocious aptitude for literacy (41–50). Although, like Douglass, he stressed his own extraordinary and individual brilliance, the leader of the most famous insurrection of slaves in the United States suggested that his uncanny knowledge of events that "had happened before I was born," quick intelligence, and easy acquisition of literacy were perceived by the African American community as miraculous spiritual gifts, which signaled that "I surely would be a prophet."

> To a mind like mine, restless, inquisitive and observant of every thing that was passing, it is easy to suppose that religion was the subject to which it would be directed, and although this subject principally occupied my thoughts—there was nothing that I saw or heard to which my attention was not directed—The manner in which I learned to read and write, not only had great influence on my own mind, as I acquired it with the most perfect ease, so much so, that I have no recollection whatever of learning the alphabet—but to the astonishment of the family, one day, when a book was shewn to me to keep me from crying, I began spelling the names of different objects—this was a source of wonder to all in the neighborhood, particularly the blacks—and this learning was constantly improved at all opportunities. (*Nat Turner* 41–42)

While the black community that nurtured Nat Turner viewed literacy as compatible and continuous with African spiritual practice, Douglass's text stresses the divergence of the letter from the spirit as African spiritual traditions are uprooted by bourgeois literacy. Douglass's loss of faith in African power and knowledge is also echoed in Henry Bibb's *Narrative*, when as a young man Bibb tries but is disappointed by the inefficacy of charms procured from a slave conjuror. Given the stereotypical association of rational thought and behavior with masculinity as well as with humanity, men more than women may have felt obliged to portray themselves in their narratives as rational rather than emotional or spiritual beings. Interestingly, at least two women who had been slaves, the illiterate Mary Prince and the literate Harriet Jacobs, included in their narratives tributes to the knowledge and skill of black women who practiced arts of traditional healing among the slaves.

Yet Robert Farris Thompson's insightful study of continuities between African and African American art, drawing on ethnographic research that regards cultural practices as coherent and comprehensible social "texts," suggests an alternate possibility for comprehensively "reading" African American traditions of literacy. Rather than presuming that Western knowledge and literacy simply displaced African ignorance and illiteracy, as Douglass seems to imply, the visionary tradition, which encompasses both literate and illiterate spiritual practitioners, suggests alternatively that African American literacy might be continuous rather than discontinuous with African ways of knowing and with traditional systems of oral and visual communication that represent natural and supernatural forces as participants in an extra-linguistic dialogue with human beings. Following the work of Melville Herskovits, as well as folklorist Zora Neale Hurston, Robert Farris Thompson has emphasized that ritual objects are invested with communicative power through the association of the names or qualities of objects with other objects, qualities, or actions.

> Kongo ritual experts have always worked with visionary objects. They call such objects *minkisi* (*nkisi* in the singular). . . . The powers of such experts also resided in the ability to read and write the *nkisi* language of visual astonishment. Such signs *(bidimbu)* include chalked ideographs, plus myriad symbolic objects linked to mystic actions, through puns, on the name of the object and the sound of a verb. For example, a priest might place a grain *(luzibu)* in an *nkisi* so that it might spiritually open *(zibula)* up an affair. But Kongo writing also sometimes included mysterious ciphers, received by a person in a state of spiritual possession. This was "writing in the spirit," sometimes referred to as "visual glossolalia," this was writing as if copied from "a billboard in the sky." (101)

Nat Turner's prophetic interpretation of "signs in the heavens" suggests that the members of slave communities found in the text of the Bible a resonance with aspects of African spiritual techniques (41–50). Douglass's secular interpretation of the visionary object may have overlooked the spiritual power of the *nkisi* "visual language," a power suggested in the multivalent significance of the *root,* which might have been used by the conjuror in ritual practice to indicate the strength that comes of being *rooted* in a coherent culture and kinship structure.[10] In the twisted appearance of the gnarled root may be found an analogue, within nature, to the mystic scribbling that represents for J. B. Murray the possibility of mediumistic communication with the supernatural.

> "High John the Conqueror" or "Johnny the Conqueroo" is a gnarled root sold for love and gambling. "When you see a twisted root within a charm," Nigerian elder Fu-Kiau Bunseki told Robert Farris Thompson,

"you know, like a tornado hidden in an egg, that this *nkisi* is very very strong." (*Flash of the Spirit*, p. 131). [Contemporary African American artist Alison] Saar has adapted this idea to a political image of Black power, a continuation of the concept of the extraordinary buried in the ordinary.[11]

The root's purported "magic" might lie simply in the power of language to aid in visualization as a healing technique or as a psychological tool for self-affirmation. Only recently has scientific experiment demonstrated the effectiveness of visualization and affirmation as techniques to achieve mental and physical health. Surely the African American root doctor's "arts of defense and affirmation" also served as arts of survival for slaves barred from access to political power, reliant on religion for institutional structure, and dependent on their own visionary powers of imagination to "make a way out of no way" and thus conjure a better future for their descendants. Contemporary African Americans, armed with technical skill and the tools of secular analysis, may equally rely on the inspiration they derive from these African arts for "creative strategies of cohesion and survival" (Piper 19).

The transmission of two important African religious concepts—religious writing and healing charms—provides an important example of the influence of African cultural traditions on African American visionary arts. Arts preserve cultural traditions even though the social context of traditions may change. In Africa the deeper significance of religious symbolism was revealed to those who had earned the title of elder. When religious ideas reappeared in the New World, they took different forms and meanings and were transmitted in different ways. They survived because they were essential tools of survival, and they were thus encoded in a multiplicity of forms: visual arts, songs, dance, and black speech. African American visionary arts can perhaps be classified into those more influenced by African script traditions or those more influenced by African charm traditions (Wahlman 29).

If it can be demonstrated that aspects of African religious practice, such as spirit possession, survive in contemporary worship in many black churches, then it may not be too great a stretch to suppose that similar spiritual values, including even a "miniaturization" of spirit possession, might also survive in a compatible tradition of visionary writing. The ability to produce knowledge through "readings" of signs offered by the natural world, as well as the freedom African American visionaries have found in submission to a spiritual force experienced as the interiorization of an external, self-validating power, certainly have resonance with attributes Timothy Simone identifies with African cultural systems.

Imprecision, fuzziness, and incomprehension were the very conditions that made it possible [for people in traditional African cultures] to develop a viable knowledge of social relations. Instead of these conditions being a problem to solve by resolute knowledge, they were viewed as the necessary limits to knowledge itself, determined by the value in which such knowledge was held, and the attitudes taken toward it.

There were choices among readings to be made. People looked for the best way to read things. Each reading was to add something else that could be said, neither to the detriment, exclusion, or undoing of any other reading.

Because he voices the thoughts of others, the speaker is not implicated, constrained, or held back in the speaking. He can make something happen—invent, undermine, posit, play—without it seeming that he is the one doing it. Therefore, no matter what happens as a result of the speaking, he is never fully captured, analyzed, apprehended, or pinned down by the listeners. Although this notion sounds like a Western deconstructive position toward identity in general, the difference in the Songhai context is that this notion is consciously recognized as the precondition for speaking in general and descriptive of the psychological orientation assumed toward speaking. (153–54)

Of course, the Greek and Semitic cultures on which classical Western civilization is founded and that carried on a dialogue with Africa through Egypt viewed the inspired writer as the instrument of a divine spirit; and outside of scientific or critical discourses, this view of the artist still pertains, at least residually, in discussions of creativity. Also sometimes overlooked in discussions of African American syncretism is the extent to which African cultures themselves typically have little interest in purity or orthodoxy but have frequently sought to mesh tradition with exogenous influences.[12]

In his work on the mystic writing of modern Kango prophets, Thompson describes the prophets' submission to a trancelike state and his production of texts, which is said to reflect "vibrations of the spirit. . . . These texts themselves embody *mayembo* (spiritual ecstasy) or *zakama* (spiritual happiness). . . . [The spirit] leaves a unique impress . . . this is what ecstasy might read like in transcription" (Thompson 101). The Kongo concepts, *mayembo* and *zakama,* spiritual ecstasy and spiritual happiness, are paramount in the mystical experiences of the African American preachers Jarena Lee, Zilpha Elaw, and Julia Foote, whose spiritual autobiographies are collected by William L. Andrews in *Sisters of the Spirit.* Each of these women had been disciplined and silenced during a childhood spent as an indentured servant in a white household, and each used literacy to prepare herself for the visitation of the spirit that would "unbridle" the tongue and allow the reader of the Word to speak in God's name. Jarena Lee, in a spiritual autobiography published in 1836, asserts that her ecstatic experiences (which include visual, aural, and tactile impressions she believes are personal communications with God) derive from her continual preoccupation with spiritual matters.

> As to the nature of uncommon impressions, which the reader cannot but have noticed, and possibly sneered at in the course of these pages, they may be accounted for in this way: It is known that the blind have the sense of hearing in a manner much more acute than those who can see: also their sense of feeling is exceedingly fine, and is found to detect any roughness on the smoothest surface, where those who can see can find none. So it may be with such as [I] am, who has never had more than three months schooling; and wishing to know much of the way and law of God, have therefore watched the more closely the operations of the spirit, and have in consequence been fed thereby. (Andrews 48)

For Julia Foote, the pursuit of literacy led to self-fulfillment through the fulfillment of her spiritual aspirations:

> I was a poor reader and a poor writer; but the dear Holy Spirit helped me by quickening my mental faculties. The more my besetting sin troubled me, the more anxious I became for an education. I believed that, if I were educated, God could make me understand what I needed; for, in spite of what others said, it would come to me, now and then, that I needed something more than what I had, but what that something was I could not tell. (Andrews 182)

Against the prevailing association of blackness with ignorance and sin, Zilpha Elaw, much like Nat Turner, boldly asserts her intellectual authority and her intimacy with spiritual power: "At the commencement of my religious course, I was deplorably ignorant and dark; but the Lord himself was graciously pleased to become my teacher, instructing me by his Holy Spirit, in the knowledge of the Holy Scriptures. It was not by the aid of human instruments that I was first drawn to Christ; and it was by the Lord alone that I was upheld, confirmed, instructed, sanctified, and directed" (Andrews 60). These writers are less interested than Douglass or other former-slave narrators in providing credible documentary evidence of their literacy; they are more interested in establishing a claim to direct spiritual communication with the divine. Such claims authorized their spiritual literacy and ranged from attributing rapid learning to an eagerness to read the Bible, to outright miracles of sudden comprehension, or to instruction in the form of spiritual guides sent in dreams or visions. Jarena Lee experienced her call to preach in a vision "which was presented to [her] so plainly as if it had been a literal fact." This vision had as its sequel a dream in which she responds to the call:

> In consequence of this, my mind became so exercised that during the night following, I took a text, and preached in my sleep. I thought there stood before me a great multitude, while I expounded to them the things of religion. So violent were my exertions, that I awoke from the sound of my own voice, which also awoke the family of the house where I resided. (Andrews 35)

Similar preoccupations with spiritual awakening pervade the journals of Rebecca Cox Jackson, the founder of an African American Shaker community. Jean Humez argues persuasively that the Shaker religion attracted Jackson in part because of its emphasis on sexual and racial equality. With the Shakers, who acknowledged her "gifts of power" as a "spirit-instrument," Jackson found support and encouragement for her desire to lead a self-sufficient black community. It is also worth noting that, although the requirement of celibacy would have discouraged most African Americans from joining the Shakers, theirs was virtually the only Christian religion that incorporated ecstatic dance into its worship. Most Protestant sects absolutely prohibited dancing; yet more than one African American convert found the forbidden pleasure of dance a strong temptation. In his introduction, William Andrews writes:

> Zilpha Elaw's parents made a vow to give up dancing and joined the Methodist church after a nearly fatal accident occurred on their way home from a frolic. Later, Elaw's older sister "would run away from home and go to dances—a place forbidden to us all," and Elaw herself, as a youthful Christian, "yielded to the persuasions of the old fiddler," but soon repented her supposed sin: "Had I persisted in dancing, I believe God would have smitten me dead on the spot. . . . What good is all this dissipation of the body and mind? Does dancing help to make you a better Christian?" (Andrews 178)

Among Rebecca Cox Jackson's gifts was that of literacy, which she explained as the result of divine instruction. Jackson wrote in her spiritual journal, kept from 1830 to 1864, that "the gift of literacy" came to her after praying to God when her literate brother, who was always too tired or too busy to teach her to read, failed to take accurate dictation of her spoken words when asked to write a letter. (The letter-writing sessions suggest to the reader of her journals the actual material site of her acquisition of literacy, as she alertly watches her brother write down her spoken words and then has him read them back to her.)

> After I received the blessing of God, I had a great desire to read the Bible. . . . And my brother so tired when he would come home that he had not power so to do, and it would grieve me. Then I would pray to God to give me power over my feelings that I might not think hard of my brother. Then I would be comforted. So I went to get my brother to write my letters and to read them. So he was awriting a letter in answer to one he had just read. I told him what to put in. Then I asked him to read. He did. I said, "Thee has put in more than I told thee." This he done several times. I then said, "I don't want thee to *word* my letter. I only want thee to *write* it." Then he said, "Sister, thee is the hardest one I ever wrote for!" These words, together with the manner that he had wrote my letter, pierced my soul like a sword. . . . And these words were spoken in my heart, "Be faithful, and the time shall come when you can write." . . . One day I was sitting finishing a dress in haste and in prayer. This word was spoken in my mind, "Who learned the first man on earth?" "Why God." "He is unchangeable, and if He learned the first man to read, He can learn you." I laid down my dress, picked up my Bible, ran upstairs, opened it, and kneeled down with it pressed to my breast, prayed earnestly to Almighty God if it was consisting to His holy will, to learn me to read His holy word. And when I looked on the word, I began to read. (107–8)

In her "dream of three books and a holy one," Jackson, who acquired literacy after age thirty-five, recalled:

> A white man took me by my right hand and led me on the north side of the room, where sat a square table. On it lay a book open. And he said to me, "Thou shall be instructed in the book, from Genesis to Revelations." And he took me on the west side, where stood a table. And it was like the first. And said, "Yea, thou shall be instructed from the beginning of creation to the end of time." And then he took me on the east side of the room also, where stood a table and book like the two

first, and said, "I will instruct thee—yea, thou shall be instructed from the beginning of all things to the end of all things. Yea, thou shall be well instructed, I will instruct." (146)

Jackson's image of the "holy one" who leads and instructs is sustained by the missionary efforts of white preachers as well as representations of the Christian deity and his angelic assistants. The association of literacy with white men (whose authority seems to be emphasized by the multiplication of books in Jackson's dream and by the symbolic significance of the square table and the right hand) is also common to early writings of African captives such as Equiano, who wrote in his 1792 narrative, "I had often seen my master and Dick employed in reading; and I had a great curiosity to talk to the books, as I thought they did; and so to learn how all things had a beginning" (43).

Yet Jackson differs from Equiano, and from Douglass, who, with the help of white boys and women, steals the thunder of white men. What distinguishes her representation of the acquisition of literacy is her belief that she learned to read not from any actual white person or persons in her community, nor even from her literate kindred, but from heavenly messengers (visualized as white and male) who appeared in dreams to instruct her. More often, Jackson's inspiration to acquire literacy is represented as "words spoken in [her] heart," and the extent to which both literacy and Christianity reinforced the authority of male speakers is suggested by the fact that even this inner voice of self-empowerment is described as words of "a tender father" (107–8). Thus the struggle for self-authorization is as dramatic for freeborn or emancipated visionary writers as it is for the former-slave narrators. Yet it is striking to note that their reliance on visions, dreams, inner voices, and possession by the Holy Spirit for the empowerment to speak and write may be seen also as attempts by African Americans, in the process of acquiring literacy, to fuse the inspiriting techniques of Christian prayer and biblical textuality with African traditions of oral and visual expressiveness. Protestantism in particular seems to have reinforced certain African cultural uses of "spirit-writing" while fostering an African American visionary literacy that values and legitimates the protective power of writing over the use of ritual objects. Such objects or charms are now more closely associated in African American culture with the persistence of African spiritual practices, while the links connecting African American visionary literacy to African script systems have, until recently, been obscured. The secular tradition of the blues paradoxically has circulated certain spiritual knowledge concerning the use of the *mojo,* while the Protestant religious tradition, with its emphasis on textuality, has been quite instrumental in promoting secular literacy among African Americans.

African American literature of the nineteenth century registers the emergence of a specifically African American culture marked by a productive tension between individuality and collectivity and between the sacred and secular aspects of everyday life. African cultures had worked to integrate these tensions seamlessly through communal rituals that forged collective identities and assured human beings of their significance in the universe. Certainly the former-slave narrators' entry into the public discourse on slavery and freedom was politically and historically crucial, and their writings continue to resonate in the "call and response" that Robert Stepto designated as the characteristic mode of African American literary influence. Yet it is also thanks to the complementary traditions of folk and visionary artists and writers who have preserved aspects of African and diasporic cultural consciousness in their syncretically visual and visionary works that the secular and spiritual traditions of African American literacy have begun once again to merge aesthetically, not in collective ritual, but in the work of contemporary visual and performance artists, including: Xenobia Bailey, Romare Bearden, John Biggers, Houston Conwill, Mel Edwards, David Hammons, Philip Jones, Ed Love, Robbie McCauley, Alison Saar, Betye Saar, Joyce Scott, Lorna Simpson, Renee Stout, Michael Cummings, Jawole Willa, Jo Zollar, and others (whose works have been studied by art critics, curators, and art historians, including Mary Schmidt Campbell, Kellie Jones, Kinshasha Conwill, Judith McWillie, Lowery Sims, Alvia Wardlaw, and Judith Wilson). This includes as well the work of contemporary African American writers such as Toni Cade Bambara, Octavia Butler, Randall Kenan, Ishmael Reed, Adrienne Kennedy, Nathaniel Mackey, Toni Morrison, Gloria Naylor, Ntozake Shange, and Alice Walker, in whose works and texts it is possible to read "the persistence of vision" (Kirsten Mullen 10–13).

Notes

1. See Henry Louis Gates's *Figures in Black.*

2. See Thompson's *Flash of the Spirit* and "The Song That Named the Land."

3. I have written more extensively about this tradition in *Gender and the Subjugated Body: Readings of Race, Subjectivity, and Difference in the Construction of Slave Narratives* (Ph.D. dissertation, University of California, Santa Cruz, 1990).

4. Similarly, the elaborately decorative, asymmetrically gridlike "devil houses" drawn in bichromatic red and blue pencil by illiterate prison artist Frank Jones were meant to confine and imprison the dangerous "spirits" that Jones had seen since childhood, as a result of having been "born with a veil over his left eye." Lynne Adele speculates, "[l]ike the individuals Jones encountered in his physical world, the inhabitants of his spiritual world were often dangerous. The haints tormented and haunted Jones, but by capturing them on paper and enclosing them in the cell-like rooms of the houses, he could render them harmless" (42). Jones and Murray may share the African American aesthetic of quiltmakers such as Pecolia Warner, whose work, according to Maude Southwell Wahlman, employs "multiple patterning, asymmetry, and unpredictable rhythms and tensions similar to those found in other Afro-American visual arts and in blues, jazz, Black English, and dance." Traditionally, African American tropes expressing tension between discontinuity and continuity, innovation and tradition, individuality and community, movement and stasis, passage and confinement, and inclusion and exclusion are addressed not only in the literary canon but also in the work of illiterate quilters and painters who improvise various idiosyncratic, irregular rhythms on the stable, containing structure of the grid. According to Wahlman, "Multiple patterning, and vestiges of script-like forms and designs, are especially evident in Afro-American [folk] paintings" (33).

5. See also Ruth Bass's "Mojo" and "The Little Man."

6. See Angelo Costanzo's *Surprizing Narrative: Olaudah Equiano and the Beginnings of Black Autobiography.*

7. See Gates's *The Signifying Monkey* (127–169).

8. Douglass's acquisition of literacy alienates him from the culture of plantation slaves, whose attempt to create culture and community is increasingly viewed by the narrator as mere accommodation to their enslavement. Recent scholarship has expanded to include a consideration of a broader spectrum of the slave community in addition to extraordinary individuals, such as Douglass, whose literacy and public stature allowed his immediate entry into the historical record. With a more extensive set of scholarly tools, it has become possible to appreciate the cultural contributions of slaves who left transcribed oral accounts and visual records of their existence. While despite his oppositional stance Douglass's "copy-book" literacy implied a white male model, folklorist Gladys-Marie Fry shows that slave women making quilts for their own families rejected the patterns found in quilting copybooks they had followed when supervised by their mistresses. They used opportunities to make their own quilts as occasions for enjoying their own oral expressiveness and preferred their own cultural aesthetic when it came to making quilts for their own use. My argument is that new

insights into African American literature emerge when texts are read in relation to a continuum of expressivity that includes forms that are oral, visual, tactile, kinesthetic, nonliterate, and extraliterate, as well as literate:

> [S]laves made two types of quilts: those for their personal use, made on their own time; and quilts for the big house, stitched under the supervision of the mistress. . . . The plantation mistress learned some traditional patterns from English copybooks. . . . Slave women, however, learned traditional quilting patterns not only from the mistress but also from each other. . . . Slave women also used original patterns for their personal quilts. . . . Slaves quilted during their "own time." . . . Often during more extended periods of free time, such as Sundays and holidays, authorized quilting parties were held in the quarters for slave women to pass the time making quilts while telling stories and passing along gossip about plantation events. . . . The glue that helped cement the fragile and uncertain existence of slave life was their oral lore. It was an ever-present force—sometimes the main event, as in the slave quilting party—and sometimes the background event while slaves sewed, mended, knitted, and such. But present it was. While the official learning of the master's literate world was denied the slave, it was the slave's oral lore that taught moral lessons, values, attitudes, strategies for survival, rites of passage, and humor! Folklore helped to preserve the slaves' sense of identity, of knowing who they were and how they perceived the world. Folk traditions also served as a buffer between the slaves and a hostile world, both on and off the plantation. For it was in the slave quarters that African traditions first met and intersected with Euro-American cultural forms. What emerged were transformations, adaptations, and reinterpretations. (39, 45–49, 63–64)

9. Perhaps for similar reasons as Douglass, Arna Bontemps also rejects the models of leadership and resistance offered by Vesey and Turner. Desiring to write a novel based on one of the most significant historically documented slave insurrections, Bontemps chose the rebellion led by Gabriel Prosser over the equally doomed plots of Vesey and Turner. While all three conspiracies failed, Prosser's style of leadership seemed preferable to the author. Bontemps wrote in his introduction to the novel, "Gabriel had not opened his mind too fully and hence had not been betrayed as had Vesey. He had by his own dignity and by the esteem in which he was held inspired and maintained loyalty. He had not depended on trance-like mumbo jumbo" (xii, xiii). Yet Prosser's leadership was not devoid of a spiritual or religious component, since he was probably to some degree influenced by his brother Martin, a preacher and co-leader of the insur-

rection. See also Sterling Stuckey's *Slave Culture* and Herbert Aptheker's *American Negro Slave Revolts.*

10. Slave traders and masters deliberately mixed together Africans from diverse ethnolinguistic groups in order to prevent organized escape and rebellion. This uprooting and fragmentation of language and culture indeed destroyed the traditional bonds of kinship (and the kinship-based authority of the African patriarch) that had organized the collective identities of Africans. Although the common experience of the Middle Passage forged bonds among recent captives, many individuals did not begin to identify themselves racially with black people of other "nations" until slaves had forged a common African American culture, while trying to hold together their slave families in their harsh, new environment. Their traditional group identification shattered, such displaced individuals (often adolescents who, like Equiano, were captured before they would have been ritually initiated into their clans) were sometimes easily manipulated by their masters, resulting in the disunity and betrayal of slaves who attempted to escape in groups or conspired to incite insurrection. Douglass's retrospective skepticism about the potency of the phallic root is in part the result of his strong suspicion that his first escape attempt had been betrayed by Sandy, the African-born conjuror. See also *American Negro Slavery.*

11. See Plate 13 (between pp. 88–90) in Lucy R. Lippard's *Mixed Blessings.*

12. Discussing contemporary race relations in the United States, Timothy Simone points hopefully to this imaginative ability of black culture to embrace rather than repulsing otherness:

> Although there is great variation among African societies . . . what is common among them is their ability to make the Other an integral aspect of their cultural and psychological lives. . . . When I ask my students to describe the basic difference between whites and blacks, the most-often-cited factor is the degree to which blacks are willing to extend themselves to the outside, to incorporate new ideas and influences with a minimum of a priori judgment. Minister Neal Massoud of the Nation of Islam: "Our power has been our ability to extend ourselves to that which seems implausible, to that which makes little sense. . . . We have extended ourselves to both the unseen and the visible, to the fruits of our labor and the graves we have dug for them." (57–58)

14

Runaway Tongue

Resistant Orality in *Uncle Tom's Cabin, Our Nig,*
Incidents in the Life of a Slave Girl, and *Beloved.*

The mainstream appeal of Harriet Beecher Stowe's *Uncle Tom's Cabin* cata-
lyzed literary as well as political activity in the nineteenth century. Leaving
aside the numerous attacks, defenses, adaptations, imitations, and parodies
the book inspired among white writers, let us note that Stowe, through the
unprecedented popularity of her sympathetic black characters, had an impact
on black writers so immediate that *Uncle Tom's Cabin* can be regarded as an
important precursor of the African American novel. Through the broad influence of this fictional work, Stowe almost single-handedly turned the interests of black readers and writers to the political, cultural, and economic possibilities of the novel. Recognizing the value of their personal and collective
experience, black writers of both fictional and nonfictional works were influenced by Stowe's exploitation of subliterary genres, her provocative combination of sentimental and slave narrative conventions, and her successful
production of a text at once popular and ideological.[1]

Certainly Stowe provided an enabling textual model, especially for fledg-
ling writers struggling to represent the subjectivity of black women; yet another way of looking at the response of black women writers in the nineteenth century to *Uncle Tom's Cabin* is to notice the different ways their texts
"talk back" to Stowe's novel. Stowe's grafting of the sentimental novel, a literary genre associated with white women and the ideology of female do-
mestication, onto the slave narrative, a genre associated with the literary
production of black men that links literacy with freedom and manhood, is
countered by black women writers who produced texts that question the location of the black woman caught between these two literary models. Stowe
uses the slave narrative as a reservoir of fact, experience, and realism, while
constructing black characters as objects of sentimentality in order to aug-
ment the emotive power and political significance of her text.

Harriet Jacobs, the only black woman author to publish a book-length fugitive slave narrative, and Harriet Wilson, the first published black woman novelist, place the slave narrative and the sentimental genre in dialogue, and often in conflict, in order to suggest the ideological limits of "true womanhood" or bourgeois femininity, while they also call into question Frederick Douglass's paradigmatic equation of literacy, freedom, and manhood in his 1845 *Narrative*. As Harriet Jacobs's text *Incidents in the Life of a Slave Girl* (1861) and numerous dictated narratives of ex-slaves also suggest, slaves countered institutionalized illiteracy with a resistant orality. Not everyone found opportunities to steal literacy or successfully escape slavery as a fugitive, but oral transmission passed on the verbal skills of runaway tongues: the sass, spunk, and infuriating impudence of slaves who individually and collectively refused to know their place.

Nineteenth-century black women writers struggled in their texts to reconcile an oral tradition of resistance with a literary tradition of submission. Jane Tompkins, while arguing in favor of reading sentimental novels for the "cultural work" they accomplished, nevertheless reads them as texts that instruct women to accept their culturally defined roles in order to exercise the power available to bourgeois white women operating within the ideological limits of "true womanhood."[2]

Slave narratives, on the other hand, do not advise submission to a higher authority imagined as benign; they celebrate flight from overt oppression. Having neither the incentive of cultural rewards available to some white women nor the mobility available to some male fugitives, slave women in particular and black women more generally would have found both the slave narrative and the sentimental novel deficient representations of their experience as black women. For this reason the texts of nineteenth-century black women writers concentrate not only on reconciling the contradictions of disparate literary conventions, but also on grafting literacy onto orality. Their texts, by focusing on a continuum of resistance to oppression available to the illiterate as well as the literate, tend to stress orality as a presence over illiteracy as an absence. The oral tradition often permitted a directness of expression (particularly within family networks in less Europeanized slave communities) about matters of sex, violence, and sexual violence that literary convention, particularly the indirection and euphemistic language of sentimental fiction in its concern with modesty and decorum, rendered "unspeakable." It is in the oral tradition (itself preserved through transcription), rather than either the sentimental novel or the male-dominated slave narrative genre, that we find the most insistent representations of strong black women resisting oppression and also passing on, through their oral expression to their daughters, a tradition of resistance to physical and sexual abuse from white women and men.

Illiterate slave women operated within a tradition of resistant orality, or verbal self-defense, which included speech acts variously labeled sassy or saucy, impudent, impertinent, or insolent: the speech of slaves who refused to know their place, who contested their assigned social arid legal inferiority as slaves and as black women.[3] "Impudence" has a sexual connotation: the impudent woman is an outspoken "shameless hussy" whose sexual materiality (pudenda) is exposed. The impudent woman refuses to be modestly silent. Rather, she speaks of the violation and exposure, the sexual, reproductive, and economic exploitation of her body, revealing the implicit contradictions of the sex-gender system that render her paradoxically both vulnerable and threatening. Her speech as well as her sexuality threaten patriarchal order, so that her immodest verbal expression and sexual behavior are continually monitored, controlled, and suppressed. The exposure of the slave woman's body—in the field where she worked, on the auction block, at the public whipping post, along with her sexual vulnerability within the master's household—is at odds with the hidden sexuality and corresponding modesty of the respectable bourgeois white woman, whose body is covered, confined, and sheltered within the patriarchal household designated as her domestic sphere.

The literary tradition that produces the sentimental novel is concerned with the white woman's assumption of her proper place, upon her internalization of the values of propriety and decorum, while the African American oral tradition represents the exposed black woman who uses impudent speech in order to defend her own body against abuse. In some instances the stark materiality of their embodied existence gave black women a clarity of vision about their position as slaves and as women that could occasionally produce the riveting eloquence of an Isabella Baumfree, the former slave woman whose chosen name, Sojourner Truth, encapsulates both her determination to move beyond the static confinement of female existence and the bold self-authorization of an illiterate black woman to enter a discourse from which she had automatically been excluded.

If institutionalized illiteracy was intended to exempt African Americans from access to or participation in the discursive formations of bourgeois society, then to the extent that it succeeded, it also left them outside conventional ideological constructions that played a part in determining white identities. To the degree that undisguised coercion permeated their lives and invaded the interior of their bodies, the self-awareness of such black women was unobscured by ideological constructions of the dominant race and class that shielded the majority of bourgeois white women from sustained consciousness of their own genteel subjugation. Sojourner Truth, memorialized as a body with a voice, packs into a concise "immodest" gesture the ability to shame those who attempt to shame her as a woman. Her power is built upon the paradox of the black woman's possession of a public voice. Because she has endured much worse in slavery, the fear of public humiliation cannot threaten her into silence. She holds up under the gaze of the heckler intent on shaming her off the lecture platform, calmly enduring the scrutiny of an audience demanding the exposure of her body, supposedly to "prove" that she was a woman, but in fact to punish her for daring to speak in public to a "promiscuous" assembly. Freed from slavery as well as the need to embody the dominant, cultural aesthetic of feminine purity, Sojourner Truth could present herself as a black woman unabashed by her body's materiality.

The original edition of Jacob's *Incidents in the Life of a Slave Girl* contains an introduction by Lydia Maria Child. This introduction expresses the concern of white women with a feminine delicacy too easily contaminated by association with the materiality of black women's experience, as much as it suggests a racial division of labor in which white women bore the ideological burden of trying to embody pure womanhood, while black women suffered the harsh materiality of female experience unsoftened by ideology.[4] Child's sponsoring of Jacobs's narrative in order to unveil the "monstrous features" of slavery, especially its component of female sexual slavery, might be read as a response to Stowe's assertion that the successful artist must "draw a veil" over slavery.[5] Child endorses Jacobs in an attempt to divest the white woman reader of the ideological veil that separates her from black women's experience. An unusual instance of a black woman publicly stripping a white woman of her clothing, if not her ideology, occurs in the oral account of the slave woman Cornelia, remembering the spirited resistance of her mother to the physical abuse of a mistress.

> One day my mother's temper ran wild. For some reason Mistress Jennings struck her with a stick. Ma struck back and a fight followed. Mr. Jennings was not at home and the children became frightened and ran upstairs. For half [an] hour they wrestled in the kitchen. Mistress, seeing that she could not get the better of ma, ran out in the road, with ma right on her heels. In the road, my mother flew into her again. The thought seemed to race across my mother's mind to tear mistress' clothing off her body. She suddenly began to tear Mistress Jennings' clothes off. She caught hold, pulled, ripped and tore. Poor mistress was nearly naked when the storekeeper got to them and pulled ma off. "Why, Fannie, what do you mean by that?" he asked. "Why, I'll kill her, I'll kill her dead if she ever strikes me again."[6]

As Sojourner Truth turned the supposed shame of exposing her breasts back onto her brash male accusers and the ladies who were too abashed to look at her body, Fannie's runaway temper turns the slave's degradation back onto her mistress with a gesture intended to shame the white woman who was not too delicate to beat a black woman. The humiliation involved in being publicly stripped seems calculated to deny the white woman the superior status assigned her in the race-gender hierarchy. Fannie's inspired frenzy leads her to attack the white woman's sense of modesty and decorum. This behavior, along with the threat to "kill her dead" if she is beaten again, demonstrates how completely she rejects the idea that her mistress is her superior. Fannie's overt resistance and violent temper initiate a chain reaction of dire consequences affecting her entire family, especially her daughter Cornelia, from whom she is separated after another violent confrontation, this time with the white men hired to punish Fannie with a public flogging.

> Pa heard Mr. Jennings say that Fannie would have to be whipped by law. He told ma. Two mornings afterwards, two men came in at the big gate, one with a long lash in his hand. I was in the yard and I hoped they couldn't find ma. To my surprise, I saw her running around the house, straight in the direction of the men: She must have seen them coming. I should have known that she wouldn't hide. She knew what they were coming for, and she intended to meet them halfway. She swooped upon them like a hawk on chickens. I believe they were afraid of her or thought she was crazy. One man had a long beard which she grabbed with one hand, and the lash with the other. Her body was made strong with madness. She was a good match for them. Mr. Jennings came and pulled her away. I don't know what would have happened if he hadn't come at that moment, for one man had already pulled his gun out. Ma did not see the gun until Mr. Jennings came up. On catching sight of it, she said, "Use your gun, use it and blow my brains out if you will."[7]

Fannie's open defiance makes her too dangerous to remain on the small farm, so she is hired out and sent away. Her determined resistance also nearly results in her committing infanticide when her master threatens, in addition, to separate Fannie from her youngest child.

> "Fannie, leave the baby with Aunt Mary," said Mr. Jennings very quietly. At this, ma took the baby by its feet, a foot in each hand, and with the baby's head swinging downward, she vowed to smash its brains out before she'd leave it. Tears were streaming down her face. It was sel-

dom that ma cried, and everyone knew that she meant every word. Ma took her baby with her.[8]

The mother's subjectivity is underscored by her daughter's oral account, dictated to a Fisk University sociologist around 1929. Through this dictation, Cornelia's memory preserves her mother's small triumphs as a slave, even though both had paid the price of a lengthy separation for Fannie's victories. Indeed, it is only in her mother's absence that Cornelia comes to understand:

> Yes, ma had been right. Slavery was chuck full of cruelty and abuse. I was the oldest child. My mother had three other children by the time I was about six years old. It was at this age that I remember the almost daily talks of my mother on the cruelty of slavery. I would say nothing to her, but I was thinking all the time that slavery did not seem so cruel. Master and Mistress Jennings were not mean to my mother. It was she who was mean to them.[9]

Their forced separation changes Cornelia's opinions about slavery and about her mother. It also transforms her own personality, as she emulates her mother and becomes a fighter. Only in Fannie's absence does she decide to "follow [her] mother's example," and only then does it occur to her that the madwoman who had threatened to murder her baby and had challenged white men to "blow my brains out if you will" was "the smartest black woman" in their community. Stressing her mother's bold intention "to meet [her punishers] halfway," Cornelia is alert to the fugitive "thought [that] seemed to race across [her] mother's mind," as Jacobs's narrative endorses the runaway tongue of slaves her master intended to silence. While the slave narratives employ the trope of writing on the body, with the narrator transformed from a body written upon to a body that writes, Cornelia's illiterate mother Fannie relies upon the spoken word to figuratively brand her child in order to give her some defense against the physical and sexual abuse of slaveholders.

> The one doctrine of my mother's teaching which was branded upon my senses was that I should never let anyone abuse me. "I'll kill you, gal, if you don't stand up for yourself," she would say. "Fight, and if you can't fight, kick; if you can't kick, then bite."[10]

The older woman's language is situated in the violence of slavery, from which she hopes to protect her daughter by instilling in her the spirit to fight back. Cornelia's retrospection also resorts to the violent imagery of branding. Fannie does not threaten to "kill" her daughter in order to teach her docility, but rather to burn her words into her daughter's memory and impress on her the importance of her message. The harsh words of the mother simultaneously teach the daughter what she can expect as a slave and how to resist it. A continuous tradition of resistance also contextualizes the trope of women's bodies and voices as oppositional or supplemental historical texts, motivating the women of Gayl Jones's novel *Corregidora* (1975) to see their bodies as the means to preserve an oral record of atrocities endured in slavery.[11] Within the folk milieu, the African American mother's persistent practice of a labor-intensive oral transmission and her distrust of the labor-saving technologies of writing and print culture are the result of her systematic exclusion from the discourses of educated people, whom she often has reason to count among her oppressors. The reliance on resistant orality results from the placement of slaves, blacks, women, and the poor at the coercive interface of literacy and orality, with the institutionalization of illiteracy as a mode of "silencing" populations rendered "voiceless" so long as their words are not written, published, or disseminated within a master discourse. It is this effect of discursive silencing that the ex-slave narratives and other abolitionist writings attempted to overcome, producing black speaking subjects within a counterhegemonic discursive practice. The textualization of African American subjectivity makes black voices discursively audible and black speakers discursively visible.

While Harriet Jacobs's literacy was a tremendous source of empowerment, it also exposed her to an even more concentrated dose of the ideology of domesticity than the training she received while living and working in the homes of white women and observing their behavior. Frances Smith Foster has made the observation that, in the minds of white women, the black woman's "ability to survive degradation was her downfall . . . since her submission to repeated violations was not in line with the values of sentimental heroines who died rather than be abused." Quoting this, Hazel Carby stresses the role of nineteenth-century literature as a major transmitter of an ideology of womanhood that polarized black womanhood "against white womanhood in the metaphoric system of female sexuality, particularly through the association of black women with overt sexuality and taboo sexual practices."[12]

However, Jacobs is resourceful, almost visionary, in her use of writing to place in dialogue literary and extraliterary resources. From her "loophole of retreat" in the slaveholding South as well as her attic servant's room in the North, she manipulates the ideology of domesticity through successive recombinations of tropes on the home as woman's shelter and prison. In the text, her various confining positions within the sub- and superinteriors of the white household become loopholes in the patriarchal institutions of property, slavery, and marriage, where she gains insight into domestic ideology, allowing her to question and revise the figure of the woman whose interiority is derived from her confinement in domestic space. Thus she is able to link the bondage of slavery with the bonds of marriage and childbearing. Her creative appropriation of literature, which allowed her the latitude to identify herself with Robinson Crusoe the adventurer at the same time that she identified in her bondage with the slave owner Crusoe's native sidekick Friday, suggests that the racial and social ambiguities informing her life developed in her a self-affirming intelligence and a life-affirming empathy, along with a notable capacity for the imaginative transformation and reconstruction of metaphorical and ideological material.[13] Jacobs extends orality to her grandmother and great-grandmother, which is in contrast to Frederick Douglass, who constructs himself as the first member of his slave family to acquire a voice. His darker-skinned family members remain symbolically in the dark while he, the master's unacknowledged son, becomes enlightened.[14] Within his text they are narratively silent, while his literacy bestows upon him the authority of a narrator.

Harriet Jacobs's narrative, which may be seen as ascribing gender to the generic (male) narrative genre, demonstrates that it is possible to appropriate bourgeois ideology to affirm the humanity of slaves and illiterates without resorting to Douglass's rhetorical conflation of literacy, freedom, and manhood, which reinforces rather than challenges the symbolic emasculation of the male slave and the silencing of the female slave. Because she associates the slave's humanity with defiant or subversive speech, resistant behavior, and the ethics of reciprocal relationships, as well as with writing and individual autonomy, Jacobs affirms the humanity of the collectivity of slaves as well as the successful fugitive and literate narrator. In this manner Jacobs implicitly regards her own narrative voice as the continuation of other voices, especially that of her grandmother, whose story she reiterates in the process of telling her own story.

For Jacobs, literacy serves to record for a reading audience a continuity of experience already constructed and preserved within her family through oral accounts. She credits without question the oral history of her family that her grandmother supplies, while Douglass uses orally transmitted information cautiously and is suspicious of any fact not verified by a written document. While Jacobs reproduces and extends the story of her family that she had heard all her life from her grandmother, in Douglass's 1845 text the narrator's acquisition of literacy represents a discontinuity, a definite break with the past, signaling the emergence of a new consciousness. He later states in *My Bondage and My Freedom* that his mother in fact was literate. Yet for the purposes of his first narrative, she represented a force that held him in the dark during her occasional night visits before her death. As a slave she is symbolically with him "in the night" of ignorance and illiteracy.[15] The narrative is the story of a slave son's resistance to the imposed destiny of a slave woman's offspring; it tells of his determination not to follow the condition of his mother, but to seek mastery through the instrumental literacy of his father.

In figuring literacy as radical discontinuity, Douglass foregrounds his own emerging subjectivity within the text against the literal and metaphorical darkness and silence that envelop other slaves, including members of his own family, who remain narratively silent in his depiction of them. Douglass is perhaps unique in the consistency of this figuration. The bond that he forges between freedom and literacy is managed rhetorically by a narrative silencing of the voices of other slaves; yet this insistent tropology has become, paradoxically, the source of the paradigmatic status of this text within the slave narrative genre. Henry Bibb and William Wells Brown, for instance, are much closer to Jacobs in their acquisition and appreciation of literacy, which doesn't overvalue it, and in their use of the narrative voice as an expressive construction of continuity in the face of cultural disruption.[16]

Jacobs's text may be usefully contrasted with Douglass's in her depiction of an instance when the master punishes a slave. In both cases the slave's punishment may be traced back to a sexual transgression committed by the master. Douglass's Aunt Hester, who has apparently replaced his mother Harriet as the object of the master's lustful desires, is beaten when she defiantly visits her black lover on a neighboring plantation. The master indulges himself in an orgiastic flogging, with the young child Frederick an eyewitness to the "horrible exhibition" of Hester's bleeding body. His harrowing description of the first flogging he ever witnessed employs a balanced rhetoric of repetitions and antitheses as a mimetic device. He flails away at the reader with his language, making the scene disturbingly vivid. The flogging is primarily a visual rather than an aural experience, with Hester's voice unable to affect the master. "No words, no tears, no prayers" move him. All are as ineffective as her "most heart-rendering shrieks." If anything, her voice seems to egg him on; screams constitute one side of a ghastly, mostly nonverbal dialogue Douglass represents as an obscene call and response in which language is debased and discourse is reduced to "her shrieks and his horrid oaths."[17]

Jacobs serves as "earwitness" to the beating of a man whose wife is among their master's concubines. Jacobs deals more explicitly with the slave woman's sexual subjugation than Douglass, who is always reluctant, in the 1845 *Narrative*, to rely upon information transmitted orally by slaves, which he generally treats as unsubstantiated gossip or "whisper" opinion, inferior to authenticating (written) documents. This stance perhaps anticipates the skepticism of contemporary historians who are reluctant to state that black women were raped in slavery and who not surprising find scarce documentation of sexual abuse in the journals of slaveholders. In addition, Douglass almost silences his Aunt Hester in the stress he lays on the inability of her voice to affect the master who beats her. Hester's speech is not recorded in his narrative. Jacobs concentrates on her own response to the master's violence rather than on the implacable master, unmoved by the slave's voice and speech.

> When I had been in the family [of doctor Flint] a few weeks, one of the plantation slaves was brought to town, by order of his master. It was near night when he arrived, and Dr. Flint ordered him to be taken to the work house, and tied up to the joist, so that his feet would just escape the ground. In that situation he was to wait till the doctor had taken his tea. I shall never forget that night. Never before, in my life, had I heard hundreds of blows fall, in succession, on a human being. His piteous groans, and his "O, pray don't, massa," rang in my ears for months afterwards.[18]

Her textual strategy does not involve the mimetic rhetoric Douglass employs, but a mimesis of quotation and a narrative constructed from collective testimony. Rather than mirror the master's silencing of the slave, rendering the slave as a silent victim, she represents the slave as a speaker in the text, a more dialogic practice of writing. Jacobs gives a voice to the slave specifically to counter the master's attempt to silence the man and his wife, whose fugitive tongues have "run too far" from his control.

> I went into the work house next morning, and saw the cowhide still wet with blood, and the boards all covered with gore. The poor man lived, and continued to quarrel with his wife. A few months afterwards Dr. Flint handed them both over to a slave-trader. The guilty man put their value into his pocket, and had the satisfaction of knowing that they were out of sight and hearing. When the mother was delivered into the trader's hands, she said, "You *promised* to treat me well." To which he replied, "You have let your tongue run too far, damn you!" She had forgotten that it was a crime for a slave to tell who was the father of her child.[19]

Although Jacobs does reinforce the aural with visual proof, the result of her own investigation, she sifts through "conjecture," relying overtly upon the knowledge and speech of slaves to penetrate beyond the official story of a slave whipped for "stealing corn." Through sight and sound she assembles evidence and documents proof of a different crime, which the guilty slave master tries to cover up by selling the victims "out of sight and hearing." Even more consistently than Brown, Jacobs not only speaks for oppressed slaves but also gives them a voice in her text. Her narrative does not mimic the silencing of those still in bondage but endorses the runaway tongue of the slaveholder's victim.

> There were many conjectures as to the cause of this terrible punishment. Some said master accused him of stealing corn; others said the slave had quarrelled with his wife, in the presence of the overseer, and had accused his master of being the father of her child. They were both black, and the child was very fair.[20]

Jacobs is aware that she is sheltered not only by the community of slaves and free blacks who do what they can to help her, but also by the white community, which protects her indirectly through the voices of gossip and opinion, fueled by rumors among slaves and the "open-mouthed jealousy of Mrs. Flint." The interconnections between blacks and whites in the community, while often, as in the above instance, resulting in tragedy for the slaves, also potentially empower slaves to influence public opinion about their masters. What slaves say among themselves may be powerful when heard and repeated by influential whites. To protect his reputation in the white community, Flint avoids a public whipping of the domestic servants whose lives are so intimately entwined with his family life.

> [Mrs. Flint] would gladly have had me flogged for my supposed false oath; but . . . the doctor never allowed any one to whip me. The old sinner was politic. The application of the lash might have led to remarks that would have exposed him in the eyes of his children and grandchildren. How often did I rejoice that I lived in a town where all the inhabitants knew each other! If I had been on a remote plantation, or lost among the multitude of a crowded city, I should not be a living woman at this day.[21]

Within the stifling intimacy of the master's home, violence is more a shameful secret than a public spectacle. Both as master and as man the slaveholder may hide his sins behind closed doors, while the slave woman whose lover has few opportunities to see her and thus must meet her in the street, lives without privacy, with her emotional life and her sexual behavior and its consequences all in plain sight. Jacobs contrasts his power to conceal both his brutality and his sexual affairs against her own posed vulnerability to his prying eyes and physical abuse. Under the guise of supervising her morality and protecting the value of his property, the master patrols both the public and private behavior of his slave. As he moves freely in the public sphere as a master and head of his household, he controls everyone in sight within the interior of his home. Learning to evade the master's gaze allows Jacobs to conduct a secret affair, which results in her pregnancy by another white man. The slave girl's attempt to empower herself through an affair with her master's social equal backfires when she discovers how much she values her own reputation. Literacy at first paradoxically increases her sexual vulnerability and desirability as her master begins to conduct a perverse courtship consisting of a one-way correspondence in which he writes lewd propositions to her, slipping the notes into her hands as she performs her chores within the suffocating intimacy of the domestic space. Eventually, as Jacobs grasps the instrumentality of her literacy, the production of an ostensibly private correspondence with her grandmother that Jacobs intends her master to read becomes a means for her to outwit her would-be seducer.

While Douglass stresses the definitively heroic and "manly" acts of physically fighting a master and escaping from slavery to become a fugitive headed north to freedom, both oral and written narratives by women concentrate instead on the oral expression of the fugitive thought and the resistant orality of a runaway tongue. Not everyone could physically fight a slaveholder, although the oral tradition offers many examples of slave women resisting masters, and more often mistresses, with physical self-defense. Nor could everyone physically escape from slavery, particularly given the realities of a woman's role as child-bearer and child-care worker, which made escape more difficult.

Douglass himself recognized that literacy, the field of bourgeois knowledge, and the technologies it makes possible, helped white people to define black people as commodities, while providing the means to disseminate a discourse justifying the institution of slavery. But Douglass's text constructs him as an individual acquiring mastery over knowledge as he interiorizes technologies of literacy, while Jacobs's literacy continues to be associated, even in freedom, with the confinement of women and strictures of bourgeois feminine modesty.[22] As a woman, she is caught in the narrative double bind of using her literacy to expose the consequences of her vulnerable sexuality rather than to attain the mastery identified in Douglass's text with the achievement of manhood.

As the salutation of a letter to Amy Post suggests—"My Dear friend I steal this moment to scratch you a few lines"—Jacobs's correspondence with Post and her letters to the newspaper, printed under the heading "fugitive," are in one respect—like the narrative itself—pointedly similar to the letters written for a different purpose in her "loophole of retreat."[23] All her writing, even in the free North, falls under the heading of fugitive writing, accomplished in stolen time by a woman who legally remains a fugitive slave until her Northern mistress purchases her freedom. In her freedom, the time in which she writes is stolen from her sleep rather than from her master, since her writing occurs in her attic servant's room, after a full day of work for her employers.

Like Harriet Wilson's novel *Our Nig,* Jacobs's writing struggles to overcome the compartmentalization of the bourgeois home, with its parlor, kitchen, servant's quarters, and family living space, which tends to reify the existing relations of domination and exploitation between social classes and genders. As Valerie Smith has suggested, these concrete divisions within the patriarchal household provide the material basis for their respective critiques of "true womanhood" and its ideological limits. Linda's "loophole" (which Hortense Spillers calls her "scrawl space") and Frado's "L-chamber" figure the cramped, hidden spaces in which black women's self-expression moved toward literary production.[24] These writers, conscious of the inaccessibility of literacy to the majority of black women, deploy the trope of orality to represent in their texts a "social diversity of speech types" or "heteroglossia."[25] Thus nonstandard dialects may enter the text as something other than literary minstrelsy, even as the authors themselves are required to demonstrate mastery of Standard English. Through their practice of dialogic writing, Jacobs and Wilson (following Stowe and the first black novelist, William Wells Brown) exploit as literary resources discursive conventions familiar to a diversity of speakers, readers, and writers. In Wilson's novel the compartmentalization of the house, which confines the colored servant "in her place" under the supervision of a white mistress who is herself confined to the domestic sphere, produces a compartmentalized language deployed by the white woman, who speaks like an angel in the parlor but like a "she-devil" in the kitchen, where she disciplines "Nig" with a rawhide kept there for the purpose. Wilson exploits both novelistic convention and the resources of oral invective and sassiness through her manipulation of narrative and dialogue. Wilson's acquisition of a literacy sophisticated enough to produce this novel figures critically as an ellipsis somewhere between author and protagonist, between "Nig" and "Frado," between "I" and "she," as autobiographical materials are placed in dialogue with the slave narrative and the sentimental novel and transformed through the textual operations of fiction. The novel's protagonist, Frado, counters the compartmentalized language of the "two-story white house" with a resistant sassiness, while the narrator appropriates the literate, public, and euphemistic language of the sentimental novel and condemns Mrs. Bellmont for the private, abusive speech she uses, as she-devil of the house, to discipline the colored servant confined with her to the domestic sphere. Because Frado's sass challenges the assumption that her body "belongs" in the kitchen rather than the parlor, or elsewhere, it operates very differently from the so-called sauciness of Stowe's Aunt Chloe in *Uncle Tom's Cabin*:

> "Yer mind dat ar great chicken pie I made when we guv de dinner to General Knox? I and Missis, we come pretty near quarrelling about dat ar crust. What does get into ladies sometimes, I don't know; but, sometimes, when a body has de heaviest kind o' 'sponsibility on 'em, as ye may say, and is all kinder '*seris*' and taken up, dey takes dat are time to be hangin' round and kinder interferin'! Now, Missis, she wanted me to do dis way, and she wanted me to do dat way; and, finally, I got kinder sarcy, and, says I, 'Now, Missis, do jist look at dem beautiful white hands o' yourn, with long fingers, and all a sparkling with rings, like my white lilies when de dew's on 'em; and look at my great black stumpin hands. Now, don't ye think dat de Lord must have meant *me* to make de pie-crust, and you to stay in de parlor?' Dar! I was jist so sarcy, Mas'r George."
>
> "And what did mother say?" said George.
>
> "Say—why she kinder larfed in her eyes—dem great handsome eyes o' hern; and, says she, 'Well, Aunt Chloe, I think you are about in the right on 't,' says she; and she went off in de parlor. She oughter cracked me over de head for bein' so sarcy; but dar's whar 't is—I can't do nothin' with ladies in de kitchen!"[26]

Although it can justly be said that the author has depicted an act of "signification" or verbal indirection, Stowe's representation of the black woman's sassiness rings false, since Chloe's speech only confirms that the black woman belongs in the kitchen, just as the mistress in the parlor occupies the proper place of a bourgeois white woman. This rendering of a black woman's speech is not an example of a textual representation of resistant orality, but rather an instance of jocular acquiesce owing more to the conventions of minstrelsy (whites caricaturing blacks who are mocking/"marking" whites) than to African American women's traditional deployment of sass as verbal self-defense. Although the cook indeed knows how to defend herself from the meddling of a well-intentioned mistress, Stowe's evocation of the sassy black woman settles for a comic represent that refuses to construct a complex subjectivity for the black woman who is "a cook . . . in the very bone and center of her soul."[27]

More serious investigations of sass as a form of signification or verbal self-defense may be found within African American oral and literate traditions. These accounts frequently demonstrate the ways black women used speech strategically in potentially violent encounters with white women who sometimes felt anxious about their own authority within the patriarchal household. The possibility of a white woman whipping a slave is raised in Miss Ophelia's disciplining of Topsy for stealing and lying, although Ophelia never actually whips the child. Stowe suggests that Topsy's "wickedness" is the result of her former master's brutality and must be countered by love. Topsy's habit of responding to any accusation with an automatic lie, and perhaps also the verbal inventiveness that made her a popular comic figure, are cured as she is tamed by a Christian education. Similarly, Chloe's comic sassiness in no way challenges the mistress's decorous role as lady of the house.

Stowe's example of spunk and sassiness do not explore the relationship of sass and invective to violence between servants and mistresses. Violence between women, a significant fact reported in slave testimony, is precluded because the mistress is a "true woman" and because Chloe knows and accepts her place within the patriarchal household, where the white man is master and the white woman is overseer. In this case Mrs. Shelby is too genteel to exercise her authority by cracking the black woman over the head as she "ought" to have done to punish her sauciness. Marie St. Clair, no exemplar of true womanhood, declines to discipline impertinent slaves out of laziness rather than scruples. When it comes to applying the rawhide, neither laziness, nor Christian uprightness, nor conformity to the ideals of true womanhood stand in the way of Mrs. Bellmont in Wilson's novel *Our Nig*. She vows incessantly to "strike or scald, or skin" her servant Frado, because of her "impudence."

James sought his mother; told her he "would not excuse or palliate Nig's impudence; but she should not be whipped or be punished at all. You have not treated her, mother, so as to gain her love; she is only exhibiting your remissness in this matter."

She only smothered her resentment until a convenient opportunity offered. The first time she was left alone with Nig, she gave a thorough beating, to bring up arrearages; and threatened, if she ever exposed her to James, she would "cut her tongue out."[28]

Mrs. Bellmont, enraged that her son judges her deficient in the virtues of true womanhood and venting her anger on the most convenient target, seems far closer to the mistress of an actual slave woman, Silvia Dubois, whose dictated narrative appeared in 1883.[29]

> [My mistress] was the very devil himself. Why she'd level me with anything she could get hold of—club, stick of wood, tongs, shovel, knife, ax, hatchet; anything that was handiest; and then she was so damned quick about it, too. I tell you, if I intended [to] sass her, I made sure to be off aways. . . . [O]nce she knocked me till I was so stiff that she thought I was dead; once after that, because I was a little saucy, she leveled me with the fire-shovel and broke my pate. She thought I was dead then, but I wasn't.[30]

In the spiritual tradition of Sojourner Truth and Harriet Tubman, both illiterate women who spoke to God and expected God to hear them, and of Nat Turner, who taught himself to read at an early age, and whose famous slave insurrection was precipitated by Turner's reading of "signs in the heavens," black women preachers demonstrated another way to move out of their assigned place within a racist-sexist hierarchy. Nineteenth-century women who pursued a spiritual vocation as itinerant preachers renounced sass, the verbal self-defense of illiterate slave women, in favor of a visionary literacy based on emotionally charged religious experience that confirms the truth of the Bible and empowers them as speakers and writers. As God's chosen spokespersons, Jarena Lee, Zilpha Elaw, and Julia Foote—through their acquisition of spiritually driven literacy and personal communication with God by means of visionary experience—purify their "impudent" tongues of the "sinful" speech in which, like Wilson's Frado, they had indulged as indentured servant girls, separated from their families and growing up under the discipline of white adults.

The fictional Frado affects a partial conversion to Christianity though she remains ambivalent about a religion professed by her "she-devil" mistress. At first she defiantly pursues spiritual training at least partly because her mistress resents any influence that might loosen her own control over her servant's behavior or cause that servant even temporarily to forget "her place." Just as she wedges Frado's mouth shut with a block of wood, Mrs. Bellmont

zealously blocks her access to literacy and to Bible-centered religious teaching, insisting that her own style of obedience training is all the education a
black child needs. School and church are precisely the institutions that left
lasting impressions on Elaw, Foote, and Lee. Apart from their exuberant embrace of Bible study as an intellectually challenging and pleasurable activity,
they all seem to have been propelled into religious experience in part because it supplied channels of expression and emotional contact with kindred spirits, both of which were denied to them as young servant girls. Their
parents were either dead or unable to rear and educate them because of extreme poverty. These young girls were disciplined at the discretion of their
employers and relied on their own spunk and sass in conflicts with these
powerful adult authorities. When, during her term as an indentured servant,
Foote was beaten by her white mistress for a transgression she never committed, the child responded by taking the rawhide whip out of the house and
cutting it into small pieces, so that it could never be used again.

To such young children, commonly indentured between ages six and twelve,
it must have seemed that the authority of masters and mistresses not only superseded that of their own parents, but also, as they began to be influenced
by Christianity, that such authority must be compounded by the power of
an omniscient God, usually figured as white and male, who could read their
innermost thoughts. Stricken by her conscience after telling her employer
a lie, Jarena Lee relates, "God . . . told me I was a wretched sinner."[31] Such
women had the opportunity to develop both their profound spirituality and
a Bible-based literacy, which enabled them to go beyond exhorting sinners
to convert and fellow worshipers to keep the faith. Ultimately some of them
also claimed the authority of a preacher to "take a text," even when it meant
opposing the Pauline restrictions on women's speech espoused by a male-
dominated church hierarchy.[32]

While attending a "solemn love feast," Zilpha Elaw, whose mother had
died in childbirth after twenty-two pregnancies, took the opportunity to
participate in a free expression of emotion, having found a social space in
which she could define herself as an expansive soul rather than a circum-
scribed body.[33] At an outdoor camp meeting that brought worshipers of different races and classes together for a common purpose, she found herself
moved to speak following a profound spiritual experience which freed her
to begin her life with a new leaf; the social inscription of her black, female
body was erased as she became a blank (white) page to receive God's Word.

[M]y heart and soul were rendered completely spotless—as clean as a
sheet of white paper, and I felt as if I had never sinned in all my life. . . .

When the prayer meeting afterwards commenced, the Lord opened my mouth in public prayer; and while I was thus engaged, it seemed as if I heard my God rustling in the tops of the mulberry-trees. Oh how precious was this day to my soul![34]

As these women reached higher levels of literacy, the study of scripture liberates their "bridled" tongues for preaching and exhorting; through spiritual activity and chaste behavior they attempt to cleanse and purify the black woman's body of the significations acquired through her association in slavery with abusive sexuality. Julia Foote's spiritual autobiography implicitly constructs such a relation between the physical agony of the enslaved mother's body and her daughter's quest for spiritual autonomy and ecstasy. Glorious "heavenly visitations" in which Christ appears to gently strip her body of clothing and wash her in warm water to the accompaniment of "the sweetest music I had ever heard" are spiritual balm for the child who never forgot the story of how her mother had suffered as a slave. Foote's narrative begins significantly with her mother's sexual vulnerability and the painful consequences of her verbal self-defense:

My mother was born a slave, in the State of New York. She had one very cruel master and mistress. This man, whom she was obliged to call master, tied her up and whipped her because she refused to submit herself to him, and reported his conduct to her mistress. After the whipping, he himself washed her quivering back with strong salt water. At the expiration of a week she was sent to change her clothing, which stuck fast to her back. Her mistress seeing that she could not remove it, took hold of the rough tow-linen undergarment and pulled it off over her head with a jerk, which took the skin with it, leaving her back all raw and sore.[35]

Seeking a figure that could combine the secular representation of a blissful black body, emancipated from the negative social inscriptions of slavery, racism, and sexual exploitation, with the spiritual empowerment of the African American prophetic tradition, Toni Morrison invents a character in *Beloved,* Baby Suggs, who is an illiterate black woman preacher whose interest in holiness extends beyond the spirit to the body's wholeness. Her eloquent sermons urge black people to love every part of the bodies that white masters and mistresses abused, overworked, injured, and dehumanized. Implicitly problematizing Douglass's linking of literacy and freedom, *Beloved* and Sherley Anne Williams's novel *Dessa Rose* include a critique of literacy as an

instrumentality of white male domination, represented in both texts by educators: a schoolteacher whose curriculum includes racist pseudoscience and
a social-climbing tutor who covets the material wealth of the slavocracy he
serves.[36]

Yet each also offers an alternative to the binary opposition of predatory
literacy and institutionalized illiteracy: the child who takes dictation from
an illiterate mother in *Dessa Rose,* and the African American schoolteacher
Lady Jones, who teaches the ex-slave's daughter to read in *Beloved.* Morrison's slave community's attempt to process unassimilable experience occurs
within what is still an oral culture. Sethe, Paul D, and Baby Suggs must orient
themselves in a hostile environment without the perceptual apparatus or in-
strumentalities triumphantly claimed by Douglass. Their individual struggles
take place outside the epistemic order of bourgeois society, through processes that Morrison extrapolates by way of her considered appropriation of
the African American expressions "disremember" and "rememory," which
she employs not as corruptions of the standard English words "remember,"
"forget," or "memory," but as cultural neologisms invented to refer to ways
that African Americans retained specific perceptual habits of their African
cultures of origin despite (or because of) their traumatic encounter with an
often brutally applied, certainly exclusionary, instrumental literacy.[37]

The writer's text seeks to undo the amputation or erasure of the ancestor's
voice and presence in the irrevocable break from primary African orality to
institutionalized illiteracy and restore dignity to black speakers of stigmatized dialects. The nonstandard speech of slaves expressed different cultural
perceptions as much as it reflected and often reinforced the power relations of
slavery, which were established and maintained in part by means of a predatory and exclusionary practice of literacy. This exclusive literacy produced a
correspondent black literacy, or what W. E. B. Du Bois called "compulsory
ignorance," as well as "the curiosity born of compulsory ignorance, to know
and test the power of the cabalistic letters of the white man, the longing to
know."[38] The conflation of folklore with ignorance and the persistent, erroneous identification of literacy as the possession of "the white man" are discursive tropes that black writers have always struggled against in their production of literacy texts that incorporate the subjugated knowledge of black folk.

Being neither white nor men, both the possession of literacy and the
mastery of literate discourses have proved especially problematic for black
women. African American women writers have often used their texts to "talk
back" to texts by white men, white women, and black men in which representations of black women are absent or subordinated to other aims. With
her decision to portray the silenced but not speechless black ancestor in

Beloved as an illiterate, pregnant slave woman, Morrison insists on a "herstory" that must be intuited through empathy, as well as a history that can be read, remembered, recorded, and reconstructed by the literate descendants of an illiterate ancestress. Within the oral tradition black women have been anything but silent, unless literally beaten, muzzled, starved, or otherwise suppressed to the point of speechlessness. As for black women writers, if anything, their discursive silencing has been itself a by-product of literacy and their inability to control the sites and conditions of their own textual production or ensure it an appropriate reception. The literal bit, muzzle, and whip used to silence the slave woman gave way to the repressive social structures, discursive silencing, and literary oblivion that continued to mute her emancipated descendants, prolonging the discursive effect of silencing even when black women not only used their voices to speak but had also thoroughly interiorized the technology of writing.

Scholars and critics today are unearthing and reevaluating the works of a number of African American women writers: texts that have finally become marketable commodities, having lain dormant for a century, disqualified from serious study by presuppositions about the tradition of African American writing derived from the study of male-authored texts that dominated the black canon until the 1980s. Suspicious scholars excluded both Wilson and Jacobs from the African American canon because of their self-conscious appropriation of nineteenth-century fictional conventions, which were familiar especially to women readers. Similarly Morrison's novel, which mines the resources of the slave narrative tradition while placing an African American woman at its center, has been scorned by at least one African American critic as "sentimental" and "melodramatic," the unfortunate result of the writer's loss of control over her materials owing to a "failure of feeling" he associates with sentimentality.[39] Morrison's literate ghost story has as much, or more, in common with the Gothic as the sentimental tradition. Unquestionably her work self-consciously excavates popular fictional genres associated with traditions of women's writing and oral narrative, as well as the slave narrative. Her deployment of historically gendered generic codes might be compared to Ishmael Reed's use of vaudeville palter or Charles Johnson's use of the tall tale.

While Morrison privileges the point of view of the illiterate protagonist, it is through the figurative possibilities of a written form, the novel, that Morrison imaginatively constructs and validates the perceptual field of the illiterate. In this manner she offers image after image of a spatiotemporality that is not static, but allows a simultaneity of the present and past, a communication between the dead and the living based on interiorizations of the spoken word: the mother telling a ghost stories that she has never told her living daughter. Sethe's oral transmission of a legacy of struggle and resistance empowers her daughter Denver to overcome a history of silencing and seek instruction from a literate black woman in their community. In the process Sethe also discovers within half-forgotten memory, through the "rememory" of oral narrative, childhood stories of the mother who had killed every child before Sethe, allowing her alone to live, the child not born of rape.

Writing is a literal inscription on the body of Sethe's African mother, the brand on her breast signifying her violent possession through rape and enslavement. For Sethe, writing is a commodity acquired through prostitution—the word gained in exchange for a mother's body.[40] The concreteness of this inscription (the word *Beloved*—her name is not recorded—engraved on the tombstone of the preverbal baby girl) sets the vengeful spirit loose in the haunted house of memory. The ghost is not just embodied but hyperembodied, as it seduces Sethe's lover and becomes pregnant. Beloved emulates the phallic mother's power, as the written word gives a perverse body to the repressed spirit of an oral tradition in which the pain of the child's death and the mother's terror might otherwise be disremembered. Morrison's representation of an illiterate mother, rather than a literate father, implicitly comments on the gaps African American women have discerned, and tried in their own work to bridge, between the male-oriented tradition of the slave narrative genre and the oral folk tradition, which have both been strong influences on the production of African American literature.[41]

The circular, monumental time of primary orality disrupted by slavery and compulsory illiteracy—represented by the ghost in *Beloved*—may be seen on the one hand as covering over all the ruptures and discontinuities that linear historical time, itself a product of writing, is equipped to register. On the other hand, if claims on history implicate the literate slave in the obsessive mastery of linear time, it is through a return to "women's time," which is also "primitive time," that Morrison addresses the power of the pre-Oedipal mother, the power to give or deny life to her child—just as Sherley Anne Williams suggests the power, as mother and as killer, of a woman whose subjectivity is formed outside or at the margins of bourgeois ideological constructions of true womanhood.[42] While slave mothers (as well as their offspring) affirm and stress their power, Morrison chooses to explore the other aspect of women's power over life by constructing a supernatural character that has access to language, yet mimics the child whose "relation to the pre-oedipal, phallic mother is pre-linguistic, unspoken, and unrepresentable," so as to give embodied voice to the voiceless maternal semiotic identified here, as in Julia Kristeva's theoretical writing, with both mother and child.[43] For Kristeva, the maternal semiotic comprises the unorganized, presymbolic bodily impulses of the infant's physical interaction with the mother's body.

In Jacobs's account, the exchange of breast milk in nursing binds both the white and black child in a reciprocal relationship that is betrayed by the white child's entry into the patriarchal symbolic of law, property, and inheritance. For Morrison, the theft by the dominant class of that which would nourish a subjugated class, ritualized in the custom of wet-nursing, graphically demonstrates the interactive workings of the slave woman's exploitation. Sethe is exploited both as breeder and as worker, her body's labor producing both milk and ink.[44] The black woman's milk is stolen and, through institutionalized illiteracy, so is her ability to control her discursive representation within a print culture. Her self-definition as mother and human, her ability to operate as a speaking subject, is contradicted by a body of writings constituting a pseudoscientific discourse that helped to rationalize her enslavement. In *Beloved* the maternal semiotic not only is the physical interactions of the individual mother-child dyad, but also becomes, figuratively, an analogue of the relationship, within African American tradition, of the problematic historical opposition of orality and literacy at the point of linguistic imperialism. African languages were lost to the descendants of captive Africans as access to interiorized epistemological constructions, leaving little more than paralinguistic traces in the rhythms of speech, song, and dance. English, therefore, is associated with the symbolic order of law and the enunciation of the ego in language. The collective racial maternal semiotic of the novel includes a number of associatively related figures: the preliterate African who dies on the slave ship, the non-English-speaking mother with a brand on her breast, as well as the prelinguistic infant. All of these "ghosts" are repressed in the formation of the psyche through insertion into a masculine (white male) symbolic. This process is here made analogous to the slave's internalization of English, literacy, and the symbolic order of Western discursive formations. Yet in any language or semiotic system, something always remains unexpressed—or, in Morrison's own words, "blocked, forgotten, hidden"—whether one operates within primary orality, institutionalized illiteracy, or interiorized literacy.

When Sethe locked the door, the women inside were free at last to be what they liked, see whatever they saw, and say whatever was on their minds.

Almost. Mixed in with the voices surrounding the house, recognizable but undecipherable to Stamp Paid, were the thoughts of the women in 124, unspeakable thoughts, unspoken.[45]

In Morrison's novel the unnamed character variously referred to as a witch, a sexually abused young woman, a "crawling already?" baby girl, a dead and buried child, a vengeful ghost, and Sethe's "Beloved" comes to speak not only on the matter and manner of her individual death, but also as ghost/survivor of the harrowing Middle Passage, that perverse racial birth canal and mass slaughterhouse. A supernatural and multiplex character—indeed, she operates within the text as a sibyl or medium, emblematic of the fragmentation of the unitary self effected in the multiple personality by extreme abuse, or the ultimate shattering of the ego by death itself—Beloved speaks for "Sixty Million and more" silenced black souls estimated to have died in captivity, including all who lost their lives while trying to escape. The child ghost, whose voice blends and merges with the voices of her living mother and sister, is loosed on the household by the act of inscription and called into embodiment by a challenging male voice. She, Beloved, is made to represent the "disremembered" (repressed, unmentionable, nonexistent) offspring who are voiceless because they either died in infancy, or were never born because African American women who were potential child-bearers died while physically resisting slavery, or practiced contraception, abortion, or infanticide to avoid the designated role of breeder. Although the majority of slave women chose to give life, even if it meant that their children would be slaves, Morrison's novel, by stressing the alternative, underscores that motherhood was an active choice, as does Jacobs's narrative.

The slave woman's subjectivity is based upon her self-construction as she who communicates, beyond words, with the dead and the unborn, through her body and through her spiritual commitment to the continuity of generations and the transmission of cultural values. Neither the baby talk of nursing mother to babbling infant, nor the call to and response from a ghost, qualifies as proper discourse within the masculine symbolic order. One is infantile nonsense, a kind of naturalized glossolalia, and the other is evidence of the woman's "hysteria" or the slave's "superstition." The death of the author and the mother's labor in childbirth are conflated in the pregnant child ghost, whose materialization authorizes the collaborative narratives of *Beloved,* in which Morrison puts "his story next to hers."[46] In a writerly yet popular mainstream novel, Morrison merges preoccupations of a Europhaliogocentric literary production with the uterocentric tendencies of African American women writers. The exorcism of the malicious ghost set loose by writing is performed by a chorus of black women producing a sound before or beyond words, an indescribable sound to "break the back of words": perhaps moaning, keening, ululating, or panting as in childbirth, when the woman who has chosen to complete a pregnancy is most aware of her human effort to organize and control the rhythmic involuntary contractions of a body in labor.[47] Kristeva's chora, a space "anterior to naming," associated with the maternal semiotic, may bear a relationship to Morrison's chorus of mothers unnaming the unspeakable desire that precedes language.[48] Like the unborn child, which has not yet entered culture, the chora is a figure of the prelinguistic, yet should not be equated in any simple way with the woman or mother. While conception, pregnancy, childbirth, and lactation continue to be represented as natural events, Maria Mies stresses their importance as cultural activities contributing to a materialist concept of female humanity, which seems particularly appropriate to the slave woman, labeled "breeder," who yet managed to transmit coherent cultural values to her offspring. "[Women] did not simply breed children like cows, but they appropriated their own generative and productive forces, they analyzed and reflected upon their own and former experiences and passed them on to their daughters. This means that they were not helpless victims of their bodies' generative forces, but learned to influence them, including the number of children they wanted to have."[49]

The appropriation of materials from African American oral tradition by black women, as well as their interiorization of writing technologies productive of bourgeois subjectivity, are equally products of analysis and reflection upon their experience and those passed from mothers to daughters. They were not helpless victims of predatory literacy any more than they were passive or silent victims of their bodies' generative forces or of the abuse of masters and mistresses. On the contrary, they have frequently insisted upon a dialogic writing practice that operates against the tendency of the literate to view the illiterate and the oppressed as "voiceless." In telling the story of her own life to her dead daughter, Sethe is able to communicate with her living daughter and at the same time to recover a forgotten connection to her own mother, a captive African who spoke little or no English. The unspoken (unconstructed) history that has silenced Denver, the living daughter, comes to light (is constructed) when Sethe speaks to the ghost, just as Denver loses her paralyzing fear of leaving the haunted house upon hearing the voice of her dead grandmother.

The stories *Beloved* solicits are Morrison's way of imagining an oral, spiritual, and intuitive analogue of the written, material, and empirical history of slavery. In Morrison's text such stories have been pieced together hopefully, like Baby Suggs's color-hungry quilts. For the occasion of writing this novel, haunting tales inspired by the words black women have spoken about their lives have been stitched together as provisional fragments, out of which Morrison constructs stories about a ghost that the text assembles and finally unravels, like Sethe's furtively constructed wedding dress. In such "mammy-made" garments our black foremothers wrapped their human dignity, unable to fit themselves and their histories into the ready-made ideologies of true womanhood. *Beloved* may not be "a story to pass on"—it is neither a folktale nor a text to be lightly dismissed—but Morrison's literate ghost story underlines, through its exploration of opposing, interactive forces of rupture and continuity, how difficult and necessary it is that black women construct and pass on personal and collective "herstories." Like Wilson and Jacobs before her, Morrison insists that the oral traditions of slaves and the popular genres appropriated by women speak and write a mother tongue of resistance.

Notes

1. Eric J. Sundquist, ed., *New Essays on Uncle Tom's Cabin* (Cambridge: Cambridge UP, 1986).

2. Jane Tompkins, *Sensational Designs: The Cultural Work of American Fiction, 1790–1860* (New York: Oxford UP, 1985).

3. Joanne Braxton, "Harriet Jacobs' *Incidents in the Life of a Slave Girl*: The Redefinition of the Slave Narrative Genre," *The Massachusetts Review*, Winter 1986.

4. "I am well aware that many will accuse me of indecorum for presenting these pages to the public: for the experiences of this intelligent and much-injured woman belong to a class which some call delicate subjects, and others indelicate. This peculiar phase of Slavery has generally been kept veiled; but the public ought to be made acquainted with its monstrous features, and I willingly take the responsibility of presenting them with the veil withdrawn. I do this for the sake of my sisters in bondage, who are suffering wrongs so foul, that our ears are too delicate to listen to them." Lydia Marie Child, "Introduction," to Harriet A. Jacobs, *Incidents in the Life of a Slave Girl*, ed. Jean Fagan Yellin (Cambridge, Mass.: Harvard UP, 1987), 3–4 [6]. Originally self-published by Child in Boston, 1861.

5. Harriet Beecher Stowe, *The Key to Uncle Tom's Cabin* (1854; Salem, N.H.: Ayer, 1987), 1. "The writer acknowledges that the book [*Uncle Tom's Cabin*] is a very inadequate representation of slavery; and it is so, necessarily, for this reason—that slavery, in some of its workings, is too dreadful for the purposes of art. A work which should represent it strictly as it is would be a work which could not be read; and all works which ever mean to give pleasure must draw a veil somewhere, or they cannot succeed."

6. Bert James Loewenberg and Ruth Bogin, eds., *Black Women in Nineteenth-Century American Life* (University Park: Pennsylvania State UP, 1976), 50.

7. Ibid., 51.

8. Ibid., 52.

9. Ibid., 50.

10. Ibid., 49.

11. Gayl Jones, *Corregidora* (Boston: Beacon, 1975).

12. Hazel Carby, *Reconstructing Womanhood* (New York: Oxford University Press, 1987), 32. Frances Smith Foster, *Witnessing Slavery: The Development of Ante-bellum Slave Narratives* (Westport, Conn.: Greenwood, 1979), 131.

13. Jacobs, *Incidents,* 115 [92].

14. Frederick Douglass, *Narrative of the Life of Frederick Douglass, an American Slave,* ed. Benjamin Quarles (1845; Cambridge, Mass.: Harvard UP, Belknap Press, 1979).

15. Ibid., 25.

16. Gilbert Osofsky, *Puttin' on Ole Massa: The Slave Narratives of Henry Bibb, William Wells Brown, and Solomon Northrup* (New York: Harper and Row, 1976).

17. Douglass, *Narrative,* 28–30.

18. Jacobs, *Incidents,* 13 [15].

19. Ibid., 13 [15–16].

20. Ibid., 13 [15].

21. Ibid., 35 [31].

22. I have adapted Ong's concept of writing as a technology that restructures consciousness as literacy is "interiorized," along with Lowe's concept of "bourgeois perception," as the dominant mode of subjectivity prevalent in print culture. Walter J. Ong, *Orality and Literacy* (New York: Methuen, 1982). Donald Lowe, *The History of Bourgeois Perception* (Chicago: U of Chicago P, 1982).

23. Jacobs, *Incidents,* 234.

24. Valerie Smith, "Loopholes of Retreat: Architecture and Ideology in Harriet Jacob's *Incidents in the Life of a Slave Girl,*" in *Reading Black, Reading Feminist,* ed. Henry Louis Gates Jr. (New York: Penguin Books/Meridian, 1990), 212–26. Hortense Spillers, "Mama's Baby, Papa's Maybe: An American Grammar Book," *Diacritics* 17 (1987): 65–81.

25. Mikhail Bakhtin, *The Dialogic Imagination,* trans. Caryl Emerson and Michael Holquist, ed. Michael Holquist (Austin: University of Texas Press, 1981), 262–63. See also Mae Gwendolyn Henderson, "Speaking in Tongues: Diologics, Dialectics, and the Black Woman Writer's Literary Tradition," in *Changing Our Own Word,* ed. Cheryl Wall (New Brunswick, N.J.: Rutgers UP, 1989).

26. Harriet Beecher Stowe, *Uncle Tom's Cabin* (1852; New York: Harper & Row/Harper Classics, 1965), 26–27.

27. Ibid., 22.

28. Harriet E. Wilson, *Our Nig; or Sketches from the Life of a Free Black,* ed. Henry Louis Gates Jr. (1859; New York: Vintage Books/Random House, 1983), 72.

29. Ibid., 47.

30. Loewenberg and Bogin, *Black Women,* 45.

31. William L. Andrews, *Sisters of the Spirit: Three Black Women's Autobiographies of the Nineteenth Century* (Bloomington: Indiana UP, 1986), 27.

32. Ibid., 1–22.

33. For Elaw the camp meeting functions similarly to the "Clearing" in Toni Morrison's novel *Beloved.* It is a site of spiritual empowerment for black people, and particularly black women. While Elaw exalts the soul above the despised earthly body, Morrison reinscribes the camp meeting as a scene in which the voice of a black woman and self-described preacher, "Baby Suggs, Holy," rings through the Clearing, powerfully exhorts newly emancipated black men, women, and children to reclaim their broken, unloved, and abused bodies. Toni Morrison, *Beloved* (New York: Plume/New American Library, 1987) 86–89.

34. Andrews, *Sisters of the Sprit,* 67.

35. Ibid., 166.

36. My reading is informed by that of Deborah E. McDowell, "Negotiating Between Tenses: Witnessing Slavery after Freedom—*Dessa Rose,*" in *Slavery and the Literary Imagination,* ed. Deborah E. McDowell and Arnold Rampersad (Baltimore: Johns Hopkins UP, 1989) 144–63.

37. Morrison, *Beloved,* passim.

38. W. E. B. Du Bois, *The Souls of Black Folk,* in *Three Negro Classics,* ed. John Hope Franklin (1903; New York: Discus/Avon Books, 1965) 217.

39. While feminist scholarship has in some instances made possible complex critical readings of sentimental literature as a genre exploited by socially conscious women writers, sentimentality—and for that matter feminism itself—continues to be regarded by both male and female critics as a suspect contaminant by which feminized modes of thinking and writing threaten masculine/universalist norms that have long been implicit in standards of literary criticism and value. In a review of *Beloved,* Stanley Crouch seems to conflate sentimentality and melodrama with feminism in order to censure Toni Morrison. He complains that this novel "is designed to placate sentimental feminist ideology, and to make sure that the vision of black women as the most scorned and rebuked of the victims doesn't weaken. . . . *Beloved* reads largely like a melodrama lashed to the structural conceits of the miniseries. . . . Morrison almost always loses control. She can't resist the temptation of the trite or the sentimental. . . . [T]o render slavery with aesthetic control demands not only talent but the courage to face the ambiguities of the human soul, which transcend race. Had Toni Morrison that kind of courage, had she the passion necessary to liberate her work from the failure of feeling that is sentimentality, there is much that she could

achieve." Stanley Crouch, "Aunt Medea," *Notes of a Hanging Judge* (New York: Oxford UP, 1990) 202-9.

40. African American women novelists Morrison, Sherley Anne Williams, Gloria Naylor, Gayl Jones, Alice Walker, and Octavia Butler have all contemplated the conundrum that the African American literary tradition is, in a sense, founded on the bodies of raped and mutilated ancestors, whose bodies are literally inscribed by the scars of slavery and sexual abuse, or whose illiteracy motivates their offspring to acquire an empowering literacy.

41. The folk tradition itself is sometimes identified primarily with male speech, as in Hurston's novel *Their Eyes Were Watching God,* as opposed to her study of African American folklore, *Mules and Men,* in which women and men participate as equals in the "lying sessions."

42. Julie Kristeva, "Women's Time," in *Feminist Theory,* ed. Nannerl O. Keohane, Michelle Z. Rosaldo, and Barbara C. Gelpi (Chicago: U of Chicago P, 1982), 33–35. See also Julia Kristeva, *Desire in Language: A Semiotic Approach to Literature and Art* (New York: Columbia UP, 1980).

43. Elizabeth Grosz, *Sexual Subversions* (London: Allen and Unwin, 1989) 87.

44. Anne E. Goldman, "'I Made the Ink': (Literary) Production and Reproduction in *Dessa Rose* and *Beloved,*" *Feminist Studies* 16 (Summer 1990): 313–30

45. Morrison, *Beloved,* 199.

46. Ibid., 273.

47. It was Molly Hite, in a 1989 discussion sponsored by the Cornell University Society for the Humanities, who first suggested to me that the sounds made by the chorus of women, all mothers, who participate in the exorcism/psychodrama/communal ritual at the conclusion of *Beloved,* might resemble the extra-linguistic utterances of a woman in labor. This works well with Barthes's notion of the "grain of the voice," which he describes as "the materiality of the body speaking its mother tongue," the intimate associations among mother, body, tongue, voice, and speech constituting the discursive grain of Morrison's text. Roland Barthes, *Image-Music-Text,* trans. Stephen Heath (New York: Hill and Wang, 1977), 182. In their conscious and collaborative manipulation of this collective noise, the women all participate in the unbirthing of Beloved. The ghost child's hysterical pregnancy is terminated as she is spirited back into the unconscious, destined to be forgotten, the memory of her existence repressed by the Christian women who briefly perform the rite of a coven of witches in dispatching her back to the spirit world.

48. Kristeva, *Desire in Language,* 133.

49. Maria Mies, Veronika Bennholdt-Thomsen, and Claudia von Werlhof, *Women, the Last Colony* (London: Zed Books, 1988), 74.

15

Optic White

Blackness and the Production of Whiteness

"You know the best selling paint we got, the one that made this here business?" he asked as I helped him fill a vat with a smelly substance.

"No, I don't."

"Our white, Optic White."

"Why white rather than the others?"

"'Cause we started stressing it from the first. We make the best white paint in the world, I don't give a damn what nobody says. Our white is so white you can paint a chunka coal and you'd have to crack it open with a sledge hammer to prove it wasn't white clear through! . . . Well, you might not believe it, but I helped the Old Man make up that slogan. 'If It's Optic White, It's the Right White,'" he quoted with upraised finger, like a preacher quoting holy writ. "I got me a three-hundred-dollar bonus for helping to think that up."

"'If It's Optic White, It's the Right White,'" I repeated and suddenly had to repress a laugh as a childhood jingle rang through my mind:

"If you're white, you're right," I said.

Ellison 190

Two media reports occurring within about a week of each other caught my attention as one seemed to comment on the other: one, a *Time* magazine cover story documenting with a certain unease what it called "The Browning of America"; and the other, a National Public Radio news broadcast in which George Bush, a man whose family includes Mexican-American grandchildren, reassured Soviet leader Gorbachev that the United States and Soviet Union share common interests because "we are Europeans," thus officially marginalizing the growing number of Americans whose heritage is other than European, as well as significant numbers of increasingly militant non-European Soviets. Bush's rhetoric is an apt demonstration of a floating signifier used in an attempt to heal a history of political antagonism through a not-quite-subliminal appeal to racial bonding. That the international appeal to a common racial heritage ignores racial diversity within the political borders of the respective nations is not surprising, given the traditional orientation of the United States in identifying itself as a white nation allied with other white nations in controlling and policing the globe, as minority populations are routinely controlled and policed within national borders.

The president's insistence that Americans are Europeans, together with the report on America's "browning," suggests to me an interesting connection with the genre of passing literature of which Twain's *Pudd'nhead Wilson* is perhaps the most cynical example. While Bush's statement comments on the contemporary political function of racial identity on a global scale, Twain's problematic and frustrating novel, with all of its shortcomings, is a stinging indictment of a legal tradition that glorifies the freedom of the individual while founding and supporting a race-class-gender system that inexorably reduces individuals to their functions within an economic mode of production. In both cases considerable cultural and political weight is given to the possession of white credentials as a prerequisite for a controlling interest in political and economic transactions. In a nation that has always been at least triracial and that, as *Time* so ruefully reports, is now dazzlingly multicultural and getting browner all the time, Bush presents a vision of a multicolored nation passing as a politically white superpower as it is threatened with diminished influence in a time of global power shifts.

The usual mechanism of passing, which I take as a model for the cultural production of whiteness, requires an active denial of black identity only by the individual who passes from black to white, while the chosen white identity is strengthened in each successive generation by the presumption that white identities are racially pure. Passing on an individual level models the cultural production of whiteness as a means of nation building and as a key to national identity. Just as the white-skinned African American becomes white through a process of silencing and suppression, by denying, "forgetting," ignoring, or erasing evidence of African ancestry, so does the "pure white" family constitute itself by denying kinship with its nonwhite members, as the racially diverse nation claims a white European identity by marginalizing its non-European heritages.

While some Americans who identify themselves as white will admit to, or even boast of, a Native American ancestor, I have yet to meet a white person who acknowledged African ancestry, unless he or she had made a personal decision to become identified racially as black. A few white Southerners will speak openly of sharing a white ancestor with an African American contemporary (which often goes hand in hand with descent from slaveholders imagined as belonging uniformly to a Southern aristocracy), but the possibility that white Americans may be descended from African Americans who became white is rarely discussed, except among African Americans with knowledge of friends or family members who have "passed." Such African

Americans who have used their indistinguishability from white Americans not only to become white through the act of severing their relations with black kin and community, but also, historically, through retrospective validation as ancestors of racially secure white descendants. The very decision of a white-skinned American to identify him or herself as black is usually dependent on preservation of the memory of African ancestors, which rarely occurs in a family that has identified itself as white, since the very conception of whiteness entails the exclusion of blackness.

The deliberate forgetting of ancestors is what Paula Gunn Allen ponders in a chapter of her book *The Sacred Hoop* that asks "Who Is Your Mother?" There she wonders what has been the cultural effect on American identities of the Indian grandmother or great-grandmother silently assimilated into so many white and African American genealogies. It may be African Americans, supposedly those Americans with the sketchiest genealogical records, who have most consistently constructed racial identities for themselves that do not rely on myths of racial purity. African Americans tend to preserve, at the level of family oral history, an acknowledgment that their genetic heritage is the product of different races and that their traditions are syncretisms of interactive cultures. Our elders often preserve oral memory of ancestors with "white blood" or "Indian blood." Although identified as African Americans, poets Jayne Cortez and Ai do not deny, forget, or silence their Filipino and Japanese roots. Robbie McCauley's powerful multimedia performance pieces "Indian Blood" and "My Father and the Wars" painfully explore the territory of racial diversity within a family in which African American men have on the one hand married Native American women and on the other hand participated, as soldiers in a segregated army, in America's genocidal and imperialist wars against other people of color. America's ethnic minorities have remembered what other Americans have chosen to forget.

The literature of passing, particularly within the African American tradition, has as its central concern the American mechanism for the cultural and genetic reproduction of whiteness. In its fictive accounting for the decisions of individuals to reproduce either white or black offspring, this literature constructs a startlingly accurate model of assimilation as "passing": assimilation as the production of whiteness. Of course it is impossible to know how many African Americans actually joined the white race in over three hundred years of racial interaction, since those individuals carefully erased the traces of their passage. Those who have passed or whose ancestors passed from black to white have produced no literature of passing. The very success of their assimilation is a function of their silence about or ignorance of their

African ancestry. Most of the genre of passing literature depicts instances in which an African American ultimately fails to become categorically white, in order to stress the politics of race espoused by authors who insist on an ethics of racial authenticity as a component of identity, however illogical it may be to conclude that a person acknowledged to be at least "half white" (and frequently more than half) is authentically or properly black and that it would be dishonest or duplicitous for such a person to "pass as" or "pass for" white. Passing is criminalized in *Pudd'nhead Wilson* at the same time that a murderer, a slave mother, and slavery itself are all put on trial. Passing is a kind of theft, a grand larceny compared to the petty thievery of the Driscoll slaves; but since it is individual rather than institutional, passing is a crime that pales compared to the everyday business of slavery.

The look-alike babies in *Pudd'nhead Wilson* are both sons of impeccably white gentlemen. One son is born of a white mother of suitable breeding who dies after fulfilling her function of giving birth to a white heir. The other is born of a woman whose slave status designates her function as a breeder rather than a mother. Both offspring must fulfill, above all else, their structural functions as master and slave. Individuality is important only to the extent that it differentiates the white aristocrat, who may function as master, from the descendant of African captives, who must function as slave. The economic system of slavery put white men in control of black labor, just as it required the reproduction of slaves and masters, ensured by white men's control over the reproductive work of black and white women, who functioned respectively as breeders of slaves and as white race breeders. With the abolition of slavery, the maintenance of a color caste system consigned the mass of black people to the lower rungs of a class hierarchy in which they have functioned historically as surplus labor, thus cushioning white workers, to a certain extent, from the worst shocks that inevitably accompany periods of economic stagnation between periods of expanding markets.

In the United States racial difference has been produced in part as an instrument for dividing and segmenting the workforce, leaving black workers, particularly black women, at the bottom. The black woman remains in last place within the color/economic hierarchy, her disadvantaged status reinforcing the already existing prejudice against her. She is always the fly in the buttermilk, imagined as the least likely candidate for cultural assimilation, just as her dark skin would seem to make it less likely that she could reproduce white children or assure them a secure white identity. It is this woman furthest from whiteness who is therefore imagined as being also furthest from all the advantages that whiteness has to offer in a racist-sexist hierarchy of privilege and oppression, in which the privilege of whites and males is based upon and unattainable without the exploitation and oppression of blacks and females. To be white in melting pot America is to be allowed to operate without a limiting ethnic identity—which is precisely what has never yet been granted to African Americans as a group, although the mulatto figure is a way of imagining in microcosm what this kind of social mobility might be like, at the level of the individual.

Assimilation relies upon the genetic reproduction of whiteness and the cultural reproduction of the values of Anglo-Saxons within a genetically illogical racial system requiring that racial identity be reduced essentially to a white/not-white binary, allowing the maintenance of a white center with not-white margins. The literature of passing demonstrates the actual fluidity of ostensibly rigid racial boundaries that define the power relations of margin to center. The center exploits the energy of the margin, augmenting and renewing itself as the racially ambiguous are drawn to the self-validating power of the center to define itself as white and therefore pure, authentic, and "naturally" dominant.

That whiteness is produced through the operation of marginalizing blackness is suggested in a significant episode in Ralph Ellison's *Invisible Man*. The Liberty Paint Company's production of "Optic White" offers a remarkably astute parable of the production of whiteness. During his stint as a worker in the paint factory, the narrator must add ten drops of a "dead black" liquid into each bucket of "Optic White" paint, thus producing "the purest white that can be found," a paint "as white as George Washington's Sunday-go-to-meetin' wig and as sound as the all-mighty dollar" according to his white supervisor Kimbro, who adds, "That's paint that'll cover just about anything." According to the ancient toothless black worker Lucius Brockway, who survives by knowing inside and out the power dynamics of the factory and its machines, Liberty's paint is "so white you can paint a chunka coal and you'd have to crack it open with a sledge hammer to prove it wasn't white clear through!" While Kimbro stresses the all-American purity of the product, daring the narrator to "express a doubt" about the white chosen to paint national monuments, Brockway seems even more impressed by its superior whitewashing ability. His sly understanding of racism earns him a bonus when he composes an advertising jingle to supplement the company slogan, "Keep America Pure with Liberty Paint." The narrator hears an echo of the black oral tradition's comment on American racial hierarchies in Brockway's line: "If It's Optic White It's the Right White." As one of the "machines inside the machine," Brockway has subversive knowledge of the workings of the system, but no political motivation to change it: "These new-fangled advertising folks is been tryin' to work up something about the other colors, talking about rainbows or something, but hell, they caint get nowhere." Although he knows the system exploits him, Brockway continues to keep its machines running. He is grateful to have a job at all, and leery of competitors. Like the mythic black folk hero Shine, whose position in the ship's boiler room allowed him advance notice that the unsinkable Titanic was going down, Brockway is familiar with the fallibility of machines and knows how to save his own skin. He sees through the myth of white America, yet like other Ellisonian tricksters, is not unwilling to accommodate the myth if it can accrue to his advantage. "[T]he Old Man ain't goin' to let nobody come down here messing with me. He knows what a lot of them new fellers don't; he knows that the reason our paint is so good is because of the way Lucius Brockway puts the pressure on them oils and resins before they even leaves the tanks. . . . Ain't a continental thing that happens down here that ain't as iffen I done put my black hands into it! . . . Yes sir! Lucius Brockway hit it square on the head! I dips my fingers in and sweets it!" (Ellison 191).

The American myth may rely for its potency on the interdependent myths of white purity and white superiority, but the invisible ones whose cultural and genetic contributions to the formation of American identity are covered up by Liberty White, those who function as machines inside the machine, know that no pure product of America, including the linguistic, cultural, and genetic heritage of its people, has emerged without being influenced by over three hundred years of multiracial collaboration and conflict.

In the nineteenth century Frances Kemble keenly observed the cunning accommodation of some African Americans to the production of whiteness in an encounter with a slave midwife who seems a prototype of the calculating Brockway, who agrees that Liberty makes "the right white." Knowing nothing of the character of her master's new wife, but certainly hoping to gain any possible influence, the slave woman automatically compliments the master on his recent acquisition, and the mistress on her whiteness.

> "Oh massa!" shrieked out the old creature, in a paroxysm of admiration, "where you get this lilly alabaster baby!"
> For a moment I looked round to see if she was speaking of my baby; but no, my dear, this superlative apostrophe was elicited by the fairness of my skin: so much for degrees of comparison. Now I suppose that if I chose to walk arm in arm with the dingiest mulatto through the streets of Philadelphia, nobody could possibly tell by my complexion

that I was not his sister, so that the mere quality of mistress must have had a most miraculous effect upon my skin in the eyes of poor Rose. (Kemble 66)

Roxana, the slave mother in *Pudd'nhead Wilson*, is a similar figure whose subversive potential, like Brockway's, is cancelled by her conditioned acceptance of a race-class-gender hierarchy she hopes to manipulate to benefit herself and her son. Because the economic system in which she is embedded requires both masters and slaves, the most subversive act Twain can imagine for her is to swap one for the other. Her act results ultimately in the death of a slaveholder, and a farcical trial that rehearses the legal grotesqueries of slavery, but otherwise has no impact on the system itself or its requisite racial hierarchies. This is also the case of Johnson's ex-colored man, who reflects with complex irony on his fate as a successful, if ordinary, white businessman and father of two children who may be confident of their white identity; yet the text forgoes the melodramatic denouement of Charles Chesnutt's *The House Behind the Cedars* or Nella Larsen's *Passing*. In the last sentence of Johnson's novel, the narrator balances the pros and cons of assimilating into white America. "My love for my children makes me glad that I am what I am and keeps me from desiring to be otherwise; and yet . . . I cannot repress the thought that, after all, I have chosen the lesser part, that I have sold my birthright for a mess of pottage" (Johnson 511). His calm assessment of his choice avoids the (his)steric conclusion of Twain's novel, when the temporary birthright of a white scion, won by Roxana's exchange, turns out to be far less wholesome than the biblical Esau's "mess of pottage."

The passing genre is reactionary to the extent that such freedom of choice is limited to the individual, who resolves to practice the rules of the system of racist-sexist oppression, and even to reproduce it by reproducing children whose advantage over others is their whiteness. A different, yet still reactionary, approach is that of George Schuyler's 1931 novel *Black No More*, in which a black inventor and an entrepreneur team up to become millionaires—and in the process change the complexion of American race relations—with a machine that turns black people white. The result is that everyone in the land of the free is left guessing who used to be black. The satire assumes that all African Americans, if given the chance, would choose to be white, although of course whiteness in this instance cannot be separated from its synonyms: freedom, equality, opportunity, privilege.

Nevertheless *Black No More* might be compared usefully with Elijah Mohammed's modern racial myth of Yakub, a black scientist who manufactures "the white man" as a laboratory experiment similar to the brainchild of Dr. Frankenstein. Yakub may be read, perhaps, as a more technologically sophisticated version of Ellison's Lucius Brockway, while Schuyler's Max Disher and Dr. Junius Crookman combine the trickster ethos of Brockway with the technical expertise of Yakub. Schuyler's satire resembles Twain's in its bitter humor, with perhaps a more subversive deployment of irony. At the end of the novel, it is discovered that the former black people are even paler and blonder than the average Anglo-Saxon. The mark of race privilege instantly shifts to a quadroonish tawniness, as the true and pure whites now glory in their high melanin quotient, spend more time than ever working on their tans, and create a huge market for dark cosmetics. Schuyler's shrewd fantasy of an instant assimilation machine was inspired by an advertisement for a hair straightening preparation called Kink-No-More, a purely American product intended to make "the most stubborn Negro hair" conform to the American norm. Yet the idea that black men might control the machines of economic and cultural production, instead of remaining machines within the machine, lies behind such images of technical proficiency as a means of accomplishing the goals of assimilation or of racial self-determination.

The physical fight and literal explosion that end the invisible man's encounter with Brockway may be a convenient resolution of the narrator's anxiety about their analogous positions within the paint factory: the narrator adding the ten drops of "dead black" to each bucket of "Optic White" and Brockway applying "pressure" to the mixture while dipping his black finger into the American melting pot to sweeten it. If dead blacks are an essential ingredient of Liberty's product (corresponding to the "nauseating stench" of the "stinking goo" of which the paint is made, its noxious fumes deadening the narrator's olfactory organs until he "can't smell shit"), then it is with characteristic unease that the narrator's general sense of disgust with the inner workings of the factory focuses on the toothless (castrated) Brockway, whose chief fear is that the narrator will replace him. The narrator hates the old black worker for his pathetic bragging about his influence, his claim to have a finger in the American pie. What can possibly have been gained by Brockway's putative sweetening influence on a system that stinks to heaven? The tree of Liberty is watered with the blood of dead black soldiers who defended a democracy that excludes them, and the "something rotten" in America's production of whiteness is the lynched and castrated corpse of the black man.

Recall that Johnson's ex-colored man opts out of "the race" for an optically white existence after witnessing the spectacle of a black man's burning body surrounded by a cheering white mob. An unresolved contradiction of the text, of course, is that the passing protagonist's marriage to a white woman would seem to place him in a similar position of jeopardy. His method of avoiding the ultimate punishment is to commit the black man's unpardonable offense as a white man. Thus crime is transformed into marital duty, and the wife conveniently dies after reproducing two children to whom she passes on her white credentials.

Brockway's implied sexual/technical prowess (his upraised finger, preacherly yet sweet, suggests a phallus, if a diminished one) is only a revelation of his castration. The narrator implies that what Brockway does in the factory is beneath the dignity of white laborers. He has attained seniority only because his work must be "something too filthy and dangerous for white men." Brockway himself refers to his job as "cooking." The sweetening gesture to which he alludes in his assertion of influence is that of a cook, a feminized position, despite the penetrating finger. The cunning old worker is a racial relic, like the stereotypical plantation cook or mammy. Although he has kept the machines running with the improvisational skills of an untrained engineer, his position is like that of the black cook behind the scenes in the kitchen of a fancy restaurant in which patrons prefer not to see their meals prepared. Despite his lack of political vision, Brockway has something to teach the narrator. The elder worker correctly points to the unacknowledged contribution of black men and women to the production (and reproduction) of white America. The ostensibly sophisticated equipment of the factory is revealed as an elaborate "nigger rig," just as a significant portion of American culture turns out to be "mammy made."

Anxiety about the white man's symbolic phallic power and the black man's symbolic (and occasionally literal) castration may underlie the technological metaphors of production in Ellison, Mohammed, and Schuyler. Women (black and white) are displaced, avoiding biological reproduction and the "problem" of miscegenation. A black partner is most likely to produce assimilably white offspring with a white mate. The technological fantasies feature mechanical production as an asexual reproduction of whiteness, which is not dependent upon the coupling of a black woman with a white man (thus excluding the black male) or upon the coupling of a black man with a white woman (thus risking the castration of the black male). In these technological metaphors/fantasies, miscegenation occurs without sexual reproduction, imagery that continues to be deployed in what I call the production of the media cyborg, which will be discussed later. Assimilation is unimaginable without miscegenation, whether sexual or mechanical-cybernetic: assimilation equals whiteness produced from the resources and raw materials

of blackness. Yet the anxiety provoked by the question of the black man's potential assimilation/mastery through technological rather than reproductive
power persists in Ellison's narrator, and it is fitting that the machinery's explosion is followed by a scene in the factory hospital: a brutal "rebirth" of the
migrant Southerner turned industrial worker, in which the narrator is subjected to yet another traumatizing machine (that he doesn't control) and repeatedly asked, by white doctor-technicians unaware that they are playing
the dozens, "Who is your mother?"

The racial romance often focuses on the black woman whose position as
the white man's concubine resulted in her reproducing the genetic traits of
Anglo-Saxons. Ellison's modernist novel, Schuyler's satire, and Mohammed's
modern racial myth all center on the black male in search of technological
mastery. In the twentieth century such images of mechanical production
increasingly replaced the nineteenth-century romance of the miscegenated
family. For if even the whitest Negroes had difficulty passing, how much less
likely that the consumers of Kink-No-More might be accepted into the great
melting pot as assimilable Americans.

In my reading of the literature of passing, I look at passing as successful
assimilation on the terms allowed to Americans of European descent but
routinely denied to African Americans. I read this literature, in part, as an
exploration of the mechanics of assimilation as a process of identifying oneself culturally and genetically with white Americans, while severing associations with African Americans. Passing is not so much a willful decep-
tion or duplicity as it is an attempt to move from the margin to the center
of American identity. That such movement has been systematically blocked
to the mass of black people is perhaps the primary reason that the ability to
do so is almost invariably interpreted as inauthenticity when managed by
an African American, but as an exemplary instance of cultural assimilation
when accomplished by European immigrants, who shed language, culture,
and tradition in order to become, or allow their offspring to become, true
(white) Americans. This model of assimilation historically has been open
only to those African Americans who were visually indistinguishable from
whites. Rather than "passing for" white, I would say instead that passing individuals actually become white or function as white, which amounts to the
same thing when their participation in the normal activities of mainstream
Americans is enabled by the perception that they are white. The actual passage from black to white may be self-conscious or unconscious, deliberate
or inadvertent, and may operate within spatial or temporal limits. Some individuals maintain a private culturally marginal identity while functioning
as white only for privileged access to employment or public facilities. Oth-

ers may make a decisive break with one identification in order to identify completely with the dominant center, or to allow such complete identification for their offspring.

A person becomes adeptly white when he or she acquires a partner whose white credentials are unquestionable and produces perceptibly white (not "mulatto" or "mixed") offspring. The mechanism of passing is complete when the individual has "passed on" to his or her offspring both the physical features and the social identity of any other assimilated American who is presumed to be (pure) white. This is the fate of the anonymous fictional protagonist of James Weldon Johnson's *The Autobiography of an Ex-Colored Man;* his children, themselves unaware of their African American heritage, are the badge of his own successful passing from black to white, since he is white enough to cast no shadow on their white identity and they are white enough to cast no doubt on his. While Francis Harper's *Iola Leroy* rejects the "opportunity" to enter the white race by successfully reproducing a (legitimate) white child with impeccable social credentials, the morbid anxiety surrounding the possible reproduction of a child too dark to be white pervades the melodrama and repressed sexuality of Nella Larsen's *Passing.* Both novels, along with the biographies of labor activist Lucy Parsons, actress and poet Ada Isaacs Mencken, and stage performer Carrie Highgate Morgan, African Americans who passed from black to white, also suggest how the institution of marriage, which customarily merged a woman's identity with that of her husband, could serve as a practical vehicle for passing women who married white men.

The implication of the sex-gender system in the mechanism of passing is sometimes a submerged discourse within the genre. Johnson's novel shares, with Kate Chopin's "Desiree's Baby" and Langston Hughes's "Passing," an exploration of phallogocentric anxieties about paternity that intersect with anxieties about racial identity. The presumption of women's impurity that rationalizes patriarchal law is operative in Chopin's short story; but in Johnson's novel, it is displaced by the narrator's preoccupation with his own illicit origins. The narrator's patriarchal authority as a white father is stabilized by the erasure of his own black mother as well as by the death of the white woman he marries. The narrator of Hughes's short story is momentarily disturbed by the complications of passing, and he imagines that if his black family left town, this would make his life as a white man easier. His moment of crisis occurs when he passes his mother on the street. They pretend not to know each other because he is out with his white fiancée. The text of the story is his letter to his mother, his written communication "crossing the color-line" to explain the specific instance of "passing you downtown last night and not speaking to you" along with the more pervasive social disciplines of passing, a racial strategy that paradoxically denies the importance of race. Being a white man means never having to think about race, on the one hand, and on the other hand, having the authority to deny paternity and legitimacy to any of his children who look too dark to be white.

> Since I've begun to pass for white, nobody has ever doubted that I am a white man. . . . But, Ma, I felt mighty bad about last night. The first time we'd met in public that way. That's the kind of thing that makes passing hard, having to deny your own family when you see them. . . . I've made up my mind to live in the white world, and have found my place in it (a good place), why think about race any more? I'm glad I don't have to, I know that much. . . . I'm going to marry white and live white, and if any of my kids are born dark I'll swear they aren't mine. I won't get caught in the mire of color again. Not me. I'm free, Ma, free! I'd be glad, though, if I could get away from Chicago . . . somewhere where what happened last night couldn't ever occur again. . . . Maybe it would have been better if you . . . had stayed in Cincinnati and I'd come away alone when we decided to move after the old man died. Or at least, we should have gone to different towns, shouldn't we? (Hughes 49–52)

In Twain's text the question of legitimacy—the question of who is real and who is imitation—ultimately does not matter as much as the requirement that the positions of master and slave be filled by men who have been bred for each role. The requirement for masters and slaves produces an ideology of racial superiority, with its own philosophers, legal scholars, and pseudoscientists to validate it. At a time when genetic and racial theories were emerging as powerful tools of white domination, Twain exploits the ambiguity in the common use of "breeding" to signify cultural as well as, or instead of, individual or genetic endowments, as well as the conflict between democratic impulses and notions that human virtue and vice are inbred, hereditary, and racial attributes. Twain's preoccupation in *Pudd'nhead Wilson* with the plight of "imitation niggers" is reminiscent of Harriet Beecher Stowe's odd note on reverse passing in her *Key to Uncle Tom's Cabin*. Stowe warns that a system in which white-skinned African Americans are bought and sold would sooner or later allow some enterprising speculator to profit by selling white orphans to unsuspecting masters as fair-skinned octoroons. Twain's concern with passing, as a metaphor for black assimilation, perhaps registers the dismay with which white Americans during and after Reconstruction viewed the strivings of freedmen and the upward mobility of the black middle class.
     The story of an assimilating African American required to part with kin-

dred in order to establish a new identity could not be more typically American, and as such, it is fitting that the family romance of what Susan Gillman calls "race melodrama" and the literature of passing are present in embryonic form in the slave narrative, where explications of the gendering of race and racialization of gender also have their beginning. The slave narratives themselves are, like Stowe's *Uncle Tom's Cabin,* miscegenated texts that until recently have been disowned by patriarchs of American literature.

Harriet Jacobs's *Incidents in the Life of a Slave Girl* provides one of the earliest representations of racial passing in an African American text, with the story of Jacobs's uncle, who in the tradition of their family is depicted as a "slave who dared to feel like a man." This uncle, called Benjamin in the text, is close to the narrator in age, but his sex and color give him options unavailable to his olive-skinned kinswoman. He apparently chooses to pass as white, although the narrator only obliquely acknowledges this possibility, in her account of his successive escape attempts following a fight with his master. "He was a bright, handsome lad, nearly white; for he inherited the complexion my grandmother had derived from Anglo-Saxon ancestors" (Jacobs 342). The fact of his white complexion, mentioned prominently in her initial description of him, is reiterated, along with his dangerous, almost suicidal insistence on acting like a man, which results in his imprisonment and his sale at a reduced price to a speculator. "Long confinement had made his face too pale, his form too thin; moreover, the trader had heard something of his character, and it did not strike him as suitable for a slave. He said he would give any price if the handsome lad was a girl. We thanked God that he was not" (Jacobs 357).

Jacobs underlines the contrast between her own fate and that of her uncle, whose gender allows him mobility and whose white complexion is a chance inheritance the slave receives from white male ancestors. This individual who passes may consider his color as a kind of property or asset, as an inadvertent birthright and a way to freedom requiring only that he separate himself from those who know him as a slave—his family in particular. Racism reifies whiteness to the extent that it is known or presumed to be unmixed with blackness. "Pure" whiteness is imagined as something that is both external and internal, while the white complexion of the mulatto, quadroon, or octoroon is imagined as something superficial, only skin deep, the black blood passing on to the body an inherited impurity. "Pure" whiteness has actual value, like legal tender, while the white-skinned African American is like a counterfeit bill that is passed into circulation, but may be withdrawn at any point if discovered to be bogus. The inherited whiteness is a kind of capital, which may yield the dividend of freedom. This color capital is as much an asset for the man prepared to use it as it would be a liability to the slave woman who does not wish to be a sexual commodity. The slave woman's color capital may enrich her master, as the white woman's husband controls her inheritance. The white-skinned slave may sell at a higher price for the aesthetic value of her pink or tan complexion, and some women managed to negotiate their own and/or their children's freedom, as Jacobs herself eventually did, but this required the cooperation of a master willing to manumit them. A woman could not pass herself into society, since even a marriageable white debutante had to be formally "introduced" to society and "given" in marriage. Property, including color capital (the only capital available to poor whites), may pass through women (as Benjamin's white complexion, inherited from white ancestors, passes to him through his mother—along with her slave status), but women themselves do not control it or determine its value. Aside from their different positions within the shared role of displaying or embodying the wealth of white men, the function of bourgeois white women is to marry and reproduce heirs, while the function of slave women is to be sexually available to black and white men and reproduce slaves. "If God has bestowed beauty upon her, it will prove her greatest curse. That which commands admiration in the white woman only hastens the degradation of the female slave" (Jacobs 357).

A slave woman as white and attractive-looking as her uncle could be sold for "any price," but the "handsome lad" is sold at a discount because he is a slave who, "no longer a boy," acts like a man. The slave woman may be "broke in" through her role as sexual chattel and as child-bearer—an assault upon her body's interiority, in addition to the usual means—while the corporal punishment of the male slave (Douglass comes to mind) is a more exterior means of breaking the spirit of resistance.

> Benjamin's master had sent for him, and he did not immediately obey the summons. When he did, his master was angry, and began to whip him. He resisted. Master and slave fought, and finally the master was thrown. . . . "I have come," said Benjamin, "to tell you good by. I am going away. . . . To the north." He said he was no longer a boy, and every day made his yoke more galling. He had raised his hand against his master, and was to be publicly whipped for the offence (Jacobs 354).

Within the community of "favored" slaves who work as artisans or in domestic service, confinement in jail may replace the public flogging, making her uncle's jail term similar in some respects to her own imprisonment in the master's house, to which "The felon's home in a penitentiary is preferable"

(Jacobs 363). While her own flight only takes her as far as the super-interior of her grandmother's house, where she remains accessible to the adult members of her family in her "loophole of retreat," this uncle "vanished from our sight," in harrowing voyages taking him first toward New York, and later "over the blue billows, bound for Baltimore." Each time, however, he was "pursued, captured, and carried back to his master. . . . I saw him led through the streets in chains, to jail. His face was ghastly pale, yet full of determination" (Jacobs 355).

At the same time that she contrasts his physical mobility with her own confinement (as well as the decision of her other uncle to remain with their mother, her grandmother), she stresses implicitly that her own determination is equal to that of the mobile fugitive. By emphasizing the goal of freedom, which may be approached by various means, she honors all forms of resistance to slavery and also suggests that freedom as well as oppression may be stratified by gender and color. She does not condemn her uncle's decision to "part with all [his] kindred," although the fact that her text resorts to evasively elliptical, metaphorical language in its depiction of his last, successful escape indicates a degree of ambivalence on the narrator's part toward his particular route to freedom.

Almost subliminally, Jacobs prepares the reader for his passing, with images contrasting his paling face and waning body to his fierce determination to be free by any means, which both suggest and evade this resolution. This uncle's eventual decision to fade into the white race, a symbolic death and rebirth that, in its figuration of movement from the confinement of blackness to the freedom of whiteness, anticipates James Weldon Johnson's ex-colored man, who chooses this means of escaping the agonizing dilemma of black manhood. In his second "effort for freedom" when he is "bound for Baltimore," Benjamin uses his color to his advantage. Daring to "act like a man," the slave passes the test of self-confident movement ascribed to the white male traveler, and thus is presumed white and free by those who are unaware of his slave status. He allows himself to betray none of the previous "embarrassment" that had marked him as a suspected fugitive on his earlier passage to New York. "For once his white face did him a kindly service. They had no suspicion that it belonged to a slave; otherwise, the law would have been followed out to the letter, and the thing rendered back to slavery" (Jacobs, *Incidents* 358).

The logic of passing is intrinsic in the logic of slavery, which defines the black as a facsimile or counterfeit of the white in order to deny the rights and privileges of whiteness. The male slave can merely "feel like a man." Only by passing from black to white is he able to be a man in the full sense of the legal entitlement of manhood. Better to be treated as a man than as a thing, and better a free white man than a slave—if he must become white to be treated as the man he is. "Death is better than slavery," a recurring refrain in Jacobs's and other slave narratives, acquires an ironic significance when Benjamin dies as a slave, vanishing into the white race in his third and final escape. Throughout his ordeal of two failed escape attempts and a lengthy jail term, he is described as growing thinner, paler, and ghostlier, yet more fiercely determined to be free, until finally, after an emotional farewell, he fades from their lives altogether. He ceases to exist as a slave—or as a black man—apparently blending into the white population. To his family, who never see him again, it is as if he were dead. "[Phillip] furnished him with clothes, and gave him what money he had. They parted with moistened eyes; and as Benjamin turned away, he said, 'Phil, I part with all my kindred.' And so it proved. We never heard from him again" (Jacobs 360).

Jacobs's grandmother Molly Horniblow is a real Roxana who lost her son as he found a route to freedom. While Jacobs represents her grandmother, a former slave, as an alternative prototype of "true womanhood," contrasting her virtue to the treachery of white mistresses, it could be argued that the image of the black woman as a supermaternal figure in this text is augmented by her dual function as mother to both white and black children. The grandmother (called "Martha" in the text) bears five living children in slavery, breastfeeding her own (when she could) as well as the child of her mistress (when required). Among the generations that follow her is a son whose white complexion enables him to pass from black to white on the way to freedom; as well as a grandson, also very pale, who joins the gold rush in California, and also loses contact with his black kin; and a great-grandson who is presumed to be white until his Northern schoolmates learn of his African American identity, in an incident similar to an early episode in the fictional life of Johnson's ex-colored man. Like Twain's Roxana, Martha reproduces and mothers "black" and "white" children, although the white children born of their enslaved bodies can function as white only through deformations of white patriarchal law. Even Sojourner Truth relied, for some of her authority with audiences, on her virtue as a supermother who had suckled black and white infants. Roxana carefully separates her mother/breeder functions, which are split in twain by the conflicting requirements of rearing a master and training a disciplined slave. The self-division of Roxana also suggests the child's splitting of the maternal figure into the good and the bad mother, complicated by the shared maternal functions of black and white women in the South. The black woman as a conflicted site of the (re) production of whiteness is figured in Roxana's meticulous distinction, beginning in infancy, between the functions of slave and master; while the dialect-speaking white character Twain invented exemplifies the fears expressed even by such a liberal observer as the English actress Frances Kemble that the speech of white Southerners had been "corrupted" by the influence of black dialect speakers who cared for them as nursemaids and nannies.

> I am amused, but by no means pleased, at an entirely new mode of pronouncing which S[ally] has adopted. Apparently the Negro jargon has commended itself as euphonious to her infantile ears, and she is now treating me to the most ludicrous and accurate imitations of it every time she opens her mouth. Of course I shall not allow this, comical as it is, to become a habit. This is the way the Southern ladies acquire the thick and inelegant pronunciation which distinguishes their utterances from the Northern snuffle, and I have no desire that S[ally] should adorn her mother tongue with either peculiarity. (Kemble 280–81)

The legal (white) heir's acquisition of Roxy's black speech, in this case because no white mother is there to prevent it, raises a question about the true mother tongue of Americans nourished on the milk of black mothers, who, like Lucius Brockway inside the machine and umpteen black cooks, have dipped their fingers into the pot to sweeten it. The industrial image of the melting pot, which produces a uniformly white dominant America, has its counterpart in the legislation passed by white males to ensure their jurisdiction over the reproductive work of white and nonwhite women and thus to assert quality control over the production of whiteness and the reproduction of white patriarchy.

The American tradition to which Twain belongs is clearly that of the miscegenated texts of the slave narratives. It is the illicit issue of an oral tradition, often figured as the voice of a maternal slave, mated with a written tradition, figured in Frederick Douglass's narrative as forbidden white texts: "the master's copy-book" as well as dangerous abolitionist pamphlets. In *Pudd'nhead Wilson* the two traditions are at bitter war with each other, and the tools of the master, the legal and scientific discourses of judges and attorneys, are used like an iron bit to mute the resistant slave woman's mother tongue. The young master—or the white author—may acquire Roxana's blackened language, but he may inherit his privileged position only as the legitimate offspring of a white patriarch with a "lilly alabaster" white race breeder.

After the nineteenth century the use of the black image to represent repressed elements of what has been constructed ideologically and semiotically as a "white psyche" becomes more pervasive, as well as more easily subsumed within technical and aesthetic operations. The very means of expression are tied to technologies highly susceptible to regressive and repressive ideological formations, as Jim Pines's analysis of the interlocking racism and increasingly proficient technologies of Hollywood film empires might suggest. Pines argues, for instance, that Al Jolson's groundbreaking "talkie" films *The Jazz Singer* and *The Singing Fool* utilized the sentimental, emotive power of the blackface image in a way that suggests a great deal about the construction of the white male as a (universal) human image. The attenuated humanity of the controlled, repressed, rational, ambitious white male has to be augmented by the animal/child/woman/black who stand in relation to it as dependent/inferior. The white male paternalistically reincorporates the values consigned to the Other, investing the Other with what is repressed and devalued in himself, so that the Other has to exist as reservoir and supplement, expressing for the dominant male the values and emotions that, because of his position of rational authority, he cannot afford to express himself.

> Jolson's particular use of blackface in both *The Jazz Singer* and *The Singing Fool* . . . shows an interesting deviation from the traditional use of the artifice employed by whites. . . . It is clear from Jolson 'splay of feature that the primary function of his blackface guise is to inflate the emotional content of the scene, of the (white) character's moral dilemma. His agony, in other words, is symbolized and enhanced by the minstrel image, an image that evokes pity. . . . Clearly, the overall effect of the scene is achieved through the emotive visual content of the tragic minstrel image. . . . Jolson's white character (his "normal" role) always conveys tough, self-confident determination, whereas his blackface "alter ego" is most certainly a bundle of tearful sentimentalism. In both *The Jazz Singer* and *The Singing Fool* the white Jolson is portrayed as an ambitious type working positively toward some form of quasi-rational solution. At some stage in his development he takes an excursion into simplistic emotionalism via the blackface "alter ego" figure. Exploiting this as a kind of "soulful" reservoir the Jolson character is thus able to exorcise intense and generally repressed feelings—such as sorrow and guilt—without actually having to disrupt the basically white rational world the white "ego" is striving to succeed in. The pathos of the blackface Jolson character is markedly an attempt to inject a sense of spiritual substance into the white character's ambitions

and dilemmas; and by so doing facilitate the audience's experience of the white protagonist's development as a popular humanizing figure. (Pines 17–19)

The black begins to be seen less as the dark body contrasted with the enlightened mind and more as the repressed and emotional soul of a white social-cultural-political-economic body. As Du Bois had done in *The Souls of Black Folk*, Martin Luther King Jr. and other twentieth century civil rights activists drew upon such imagery in figuring black people as the sign of an incompletely realized ideal, the rumbling conscience of America, and guardians of an endangered ethical tradition. As the imagery has become increasingly secularized, its metaphysical implications are both transformed and made graphic via the technological possibilities of electronic media, cropping up in contemporary film and advertising, with black expressivity now encoded in countless images: as black back-up singers in white rock groups (or, for that matter, the miscegenated history of rock and roll itself, with black musical ancestors producing soulful white offspring through the in vitro fertilization of radio and phonograph); as the Motown soundtrack of the film *The Big Chill*, in which black music nostalgically evokes the turbulent youth of the aging cohort of baby boomers—a generation metonymically signified on screen by an all-white clique, as voice-over lyrics sung by unseen black performers on television commercial soundtracks accompany hip white images.

Abolitionist literature—particularly the slave narrative—with its interracial collaborative textual production made possible by the sharing of the technology of writing, despite legal codes prohibiting literacy for slaves with the intent and effect of legislating institutionalized illiteracy, anticipates the technological grafting of white body and black soul through the mechanical synchronization of filmic image and soundtrack. In the narrator-amanuensis dyad, the white hand writes for the black voice, turning speech into text and, in many cases, nonstandard dialects into standard English. (More than anything, the technology of the tape recorder contributes to the desire to transcribe dialects in their nonstandard form, setting the WPA narratives apart from nineteenth-century narratives.) Or the white editor solicits, corrects, tidies, and introduces the black text. The miscegenated text of abolitionist literature constructs the African American subject as a black body with a white soul (an interiority comprehensible to white readers—with the blushing of white skin as the underlying trope of emotional readability). William Blake's image of the black whose skin is a cloud that obscures a bright soul or a consciousness susceptible to enlightenment ("I am black, but oh, my soul is white") is deployed with varying degrees of irony or pathos by African American writers. Northup, for example, feels compelled to use whiteness as the standard of humanity in order to make white readers understand that he loves his children as much as they love theirs. "Their presence was my delight; and I clasped them to my bosom with as warm and tender love as if their clouded skins had been as white as snow" (Northup, *POM* 233).

Harriet Wilson, in *Our Nig,* has a black character defend his honor by declaring, "I's black outside, I know, but I's got a white heart inside. Which you rather have, a black heart in a white skin, or a white heart in a black one?" Jacobs tropes on the color coding of body and interiority to castigate the hypocritical white Christian, with her angry image of the town constable as a "white-faced, black-hearted brother," a Methodist class leader "who whipped his brethren and sisters of the church at the public whipping post" and who was "ready to perform that Christian office any where for fifty cents." Her inversion of the conventional trope leaves blackness as a negative signifier at the same time that it invalidates whiteness as a positive signifier.

A more complex response than taking up the trope of the black body with a white soul in order to humanize the black, or the simple inversion of the trope, with a white body negated by a black interiority, is the passage below, from Henry Bibb's narrative, in which there is an attempt to problematize and distinguish among the conventional tropes linking African descent, black skin, and darkness as negative signifiers. Bibb signifies, in the African American tradition, on the privileged position of the white race as well as its conflation of whiteness and "white" skin with goodness and light. Placing himself in the role of actor-trickster whose deceptions are meant to redress the evil of enslavement, Bibb moves deliberately and carefully from literal light and shadow to the symbolic use of light and dark as indicators of moral value to shade of skin, which in his case is not much darker than that of an Anglo-Saxon. Moreover, notwithstanding the social usefulness of a light skin, especially in deceiving slave catchers, he does not negate the value of the "dark complexion" of which he has been "almost entirely robbed" through the white slaveholder's sexual enslavement of black women.

> I crowded myself back from the light among the deck passengers, where it would be difficult to distinguish me from a white man. Every time during the night that the mate came round with a light after the hands, I was afraid he would see I was a colored man, and take me up; hence I kept from the light as much as possible. Some men love darkness rather than light, because their deeds are evil; but this was not the case with myself; it was to avoid detection in doing right. This was

one of the instances of my adventures that my affinity with the Anglo-Saxon race, and even slaveholders, worked well for my escape. But no thanks to them for it. While in their midst they have not only robbed me of my labor and liberty, but they have almost entirely robbed me of my dark complexion. Being so near the color of a slaveholder, they could not, or did not find me out that night among the white passengers. (Bibb, *POM* 84)

The collaborative literary production re-enacting textually the actual genetic miscegenation embodied by a Frederick Douglass, Henry Bibb, William Wells Brown, or Harriet Jacobs—who were all products of racial mixing—was the nineteenth-century equivalent of today's crossover hit song moving from "black charts" to "mainstream pop," or the latest successful buddy film with the big box office demographic casting coup of a commercially compatible salt-and-pepper team. However, the nineteenth-century textual production of a black body with a white soul gives way in the twentieth century to its inversion, as the soul of black folks is extracted from the black body through textual exteriorizations of black interiority, and rhythmic expressions in traditions of dance, music, and orality in commodified forms of entertainment and media technologies that privilege exteriority over interiority—the body over the soul—draw upon the figure of the black as an icon of expressivity.

The contemporary electronic version of the miscegenated text uses a different model of integration: a media cyborg constructed as a white body with black soul. This production model has become so iconically suggestive and such a pervasive image of racial integration—achieved, if nowhere else, through an audio-visual medium—that its message is almost subliminal. A technology encodes racial ideology so powerfully that it accomplishes an otherwise unachieved racial integration through a synthesized synchronicity of images and voices drawn from disparate sources, the media equivalent of gene splicing. (Gene splicing: a biotechnological metaphor derived from audio and film technology, suggesting the pervasiveness of information models due to the proliferation of information technologies. DNA is regarded as genetic information, while information has long since been transformed into both commodity and capital. The dominance of the information model results in life itself being regarded as simply another form of information storage and retrieval.) Despite the appearance of a merger, a segregated or ghettoized music industry continues to be commercially viable. The split and merged sound-image has itself been made the content as well as the form of one television commercial that explicitly articulates this figuration of a white body with a black soul through its depiction of a white teenager alone in her room, with headphones, lip-synching lyrics recorded by Aretha Franklin, illustrating the advertising slogan, "Be the music." This advertisement uses film editing conventions of the music video while parodying the lip-synching common not only to music video (which often goes to great lengths to separate the music and lyric of the song from the visual narrative of the video) but also to early television programs formatted for promotion of recorded rock and roll music, such as *American Bandstand,* and the earlier movie musicals which allowed nonsingers to appear in singing roles with performances dubbed by professional vocalists. This parodic use of a very visible process makes perceptible, rather than subliminal, the technique of grafting or splicing together the sound and image, the white body with a black voice and soul, by cross-cutting the color film image of the white teenager with vintage black-and-white footage of Franklin singing what might be regarded as her personal anthem—"Respect." Here the technical solution for dramatizing the slogan, "Be the music," demonstrates how even the film stock itself may be used ideologically.

The technical resources of film signifying the division and separation of black and white (black-and-white film evokes legalized Jim Crow segregation and the "race records" predating music crossover, civil rights, Black Power, and "Black is beautiful") are shown to underlie the merging of black and white in the miscegenated colored image of a media cyborg: the white body with black soul, black-and-white film representing the nostalgic/turbulent past just as the soulful crossover soundtrack of *The Big Chill* evokes yuppie nostalgia. It is as if the visual media of film and television had thoroughly digested the black image, anatomizing and redistributing its energy so that the plasticization of the kinetic visual icon is no longer strictly required, the re-editing of synchronous sound and image (read as the empowerment rather than the silencing of the white lip-syncher, whose voice is omitted) producing something like a contemporary whiteface minstrelsy.

This movement has been accompanied by a corresponding shift in the representation of essential blackness from body ("African" skin, hair, and features) to (soulful) voice or movement, while the use of a white dancer as body double for the African American actress Jennifer Beals in the film *Flashdance* suggests that the media cyborg may be constructed paradoxically by splicing in for the dance sequences a soulful white body to provide the rhythm all God's children haven't got. Yet, because she lives alone, works with whites, and dates an affluent white man, the deracinated black character (or generic white American) that Beals plays is probably presumed to be white by movie audiences who don't read *Ebony* or *Jet*. Aside from the surgical strategies, hair weaves, and "commercial voices" of performers like

Michael Jackson, Diana Ross, or Whitney Houston, who embody in their public personae a bankable merger of "black" and "white" styles, the racial composition of the media cyborg more typically works by grafting black soul as supplement to a white body, effectively placing the black body off-stage, behind the scenes, or in the recording studio as back-up. Whites covering black material: the invention of rock music. Berry Gordy's gold mine: the "sophisticated soul" of Motown and millions of crossover dollars. Who covers? Who crosses over? These are questions anticipated in *The Autobiography of an Ex-Colored Man,* a text that disseminates the ethical problem of passing beyond the individual decision of one man to reproduce black or white offspring, to satirize "passing" as a national mechanism for forgetting a history that links African Americans with other Americans in kinship, a mechanism for the production of whiteness and suppression of blackness. The unnamed narrator lets his white skin cover his African heritage as he crosses over into the freedom of mainstream America through a strategy of self-denial; this is a loss of soul, but he finds this preferable to the loss of life of the black man burned alive, whose horrific public execution by a white mob determines the narrator's decision to pass into the white race in order to escape the stigma of blackness. Johnson's musician protagonist is a passable mulatto whose sense of belonging essentially to a black race (acquired rather late in life to begin with) is associated metonymically with the voice of his African American mother. Her repertoire included black spirituals, those same sorrow songs that inspired the writings of Douglass and Du Bois:

> Sometimes on other evenings, when she was not sewing, she would play simple accompaniments to some old Southern songs which she sang. In these songs she was freer, because she played them by ear. Those evenings on which she opened the little piano were the happiest hours of my childhood. . . . I used to stand by her side and often interrupt and annoy her by chiming in with strange harmonies which I found on either the high keys of the treble or the low keys of the bass. I remember that I had a particular fondness for the black keys. Always on such evenings, when the music was over, my mother would sit with me in her arms, often for a very long time. She would hold me close, softly crooning some old melody without words, all the while gently stroking her face against my head; many and many a night I thus fell asleep. I can see her now, her great dark eyes looking into the fire, to where? No one knew but her. The memory of that picture has more than once kept me from straying too far from the place of purity and safety in which her arms held me. (Johnson 395–96)

As the sorrow songs provide the content of black soul for Du Bois, the voice of the black mother or grandmother figures the transmission of a distinctly African American culture for Johnson, as well as Brown, Bibb, Jacobs, and others—if not for Douglass, whose mother and grandmother are represented as virtually silent in the 1845 narrative. The soulful singing voice, representative of the repressed or appropriated cultural contribution of the descendants of African slaves, becomes an aural rather than visual conveyor of emotional expressivity, or "soul." The white visual image absorbs the plastic iconicity and emotive content of the black through the expedient of a black soul technologically grafted to a by now thoroughly materialized white body. The inscrutable interiority of the African American, having by now been pried out of the shell of the body and made comprehensible in its expressiveness, is purveyed in various media representations as a "black" voice that has become the essence of consumable soul.

The commercial potential of black soul to sell everything from raisins ("I heard it through the grapevine") to plastic wrap ("It don't mean a thing if it ain't got that cling") has been proven time and again. It is illustrated spectacularly in a Pepsi Cola advertisement's cyborganic production of Tina Turner as a cross between an 8x10 glossy photo of a conventionally attractive blond white woman and a soft drink accidentally spilled in a high-tech dream machine by mad scientist David Bowie. This absent-minded scientist is himself transformed from klutzy nerd to hip rocker as the plain vanilla erotic appeal of the white woman of his wildest dreams is raised to the tenth power by a racier partner for Bowie's walk on the wild side, to the tune of his hit rock song "Modern Love." Reading the mini-narrative of the commercial alongside Johnson's novel suggests different possibilities, within the twentieth century, for incorporating race into a narrative of (re)production: from the early 1900s when Johnson's novel first appeared anonymously, to the 1980s cola commercial, a shift from repression to expression, from anonymity to celebrity, from blackness as the sign of illicit sexuality to blackness as the sign of sexual freedom. Repression is figured in the novel as a cultural production and racial reproduction of whiteness, a movement from black to white that allows and is reinforced by a corresponding movement from illicit sexuality to marriage. In the advertisement, expression of desire and fulfillment of fantasy lead to a racial integration produced technically with the invention of the cybernetic mulatta as the ideal partner for "modern love"—sex without reproduction. The mechanical production of the sexy cyborg out of the mating of Pepsi and pin-up girl by the scientist taking a cola break replaces the sexual reproduction of the mulatto driven by a puritan work ethic who, once he has become a successful white businessman—concerned with supporting his white offspring, protecting his white identity, and concealing his (black and illegitimate) origins—presumably can no longer afford to waste time or risk recognition by visiting his old haunts, the dives and gambling dens of his youth, marginal sites where blacks and whites met and mingled illicitly.

The "love" without marriage that brought a white Southern aristocrat and his family's colored servant together to produce Johnson's narrator—a musical prodigy who trades his cultural birthright as an African American for white assimilation, giving up his dream of composing an American classical music based on African American folksong and ragtime in order to pass as a safe, successfully average white businessman—has been superseded by the "modern love" made possible by technologies that improve on fantasy. The interracial marriage of black rhythm to white melody produces rock and roll, a music that can no longer be seen as a bastard child but has to be acknowledged as big business as well as one of the most successful products the United States exports to other countries. While Johnson's text models itself on the slave narrative and pushes to its logical conclusion its construction as a miscegenated or mulatto text striving to pass the test of humanity measured as whiteness, the Pepsi commercial is a contemporary descendant of Mary Shelley's Frankenstein, with fears of technology, sexual expression, and the irrational or unconscious drives associated with blackness tamed—so that the scientist and his soulful creation make a stylish couple rather than deadly antagonists.

The discursive formation of black soul in the slave narratives, as Douglass sees it, is a textual production somewhat equivalent and parallel to the oral production of spirituals and folksongs, an oral production itself characterized as equivalent to "whole volumes of philosophy." Douglass asserts it is "[t]o those songs I trace my first glimmering conception of the dehumanizing character of slavery." In their exteriorization of the slave's interiority, both have the paradoxical effect of constructing an expressive humanity for African Americans at the same time that they begin to construct white audiences for cultural productions in which black soul may be a more lucrative commodity than black bodies ever were.

16

Phantom Pain

Nathaniel Mackey's *Bedouin Hornbook*

> There has been much lost in Africa. As in the case of a lost loved one, the loss is neither to be accepted, rejected, or simply compensated for. The loss of traditional value reveals the madness of that which the tradition promised, i.e., the circumvention of loss—what tradition must promise but which no tradition can deliver. Tradition's loss propels those who valued it into resigning themselves to the impossibility of a coherent universe.[1]

In contemporary fictional texts such as Octavia Butler's *Kindred,* Gayl Jones's *Corregidora,* Charles Johnson's *Oxherding Tale,* Ishmael Reed's *Flight to Canada,* Alice Walker's *Meridian,* and Nathaniel Mackey's *Bedouin Hornbook,* the historical fact of slavery is associated explicitly or implicitly with constraints on the freedom of the contemporary African American artist as well as the artist's relation to a syncretic tradition. Amputation and castration, conflated in memory's trace as ritual punishment for runaway slaves and other "bad niggers," powerfully suggest, in Mackey's *Bedouin Hornbook,* both the heroism and the psychic danger of the black artist's radical individuality. With its insistent yet gracefully improvisational reclamation of the fragmented, dispersed, and syncretic elements of black diaspora aesthetic traditions, Mackey's novel plumbs the "ontology of loss." It is the textual equivalent of Ed Love's evocative Vodou Loa sculptures made of shiny chrome auto bumpers salvaged from junkyards and dedicated to African American jazz musicians. Mackey's novel also shares similarities with Mel Edwards' series of "Lynch Fragments," which are sculptures that pointedly resemble wall trophies at the same time they ironically comment on a tradition of sculpture that celebrates the phallic object. Edwards' densely compact metal assemblages serve as tragic and dreadful emblems of threatened black masculinity. Their harsh, burnished strength and aesthetic potency belie the vulnerability and fear that sustain the construct of masculine sexuality and dominance. Composed of assorted hardware—scrap metal welded to links of chain, railroad spikes, knives, scissors, and other blades or bladelike objects—these broken tools allude to the exploitation of black male workers as, in Ellison's words, "the machines inside the machine," and to the historical fact of literal as well as symbolic castration.

That a careless word can kill or maim is a primary consideration of Richard Wright's *Black Boy*, in which the narrator is schooled by kindred and enemies alike to adopt a properly submissive verbal restraint or risk destruction. The accumulated images of castration/amputation in *Bedouin Hornbook* are related to the persistent association of African Americans with both coerced silence and strategic inarticulateness, although what Mackey investigates is the relative stress placed on either articulation or disarticulation as oppositional values within and between cultures. The discursive representation of the African as *alogos* in Western culture becomes, for Mackey, the background for a series of meditations on music, myth, mastery, and masculinity. Just as the individual who seeks to distinguish himself through literacy from the "voiceless" mass learns the value of secrecy and indirection, like Wright's black boy, and his prototype, the ex-slave Frederick Douglass, so also the need, within traditional black communities, to shroud African spirituality in secrecy has contributed to the elusiveness, evasiveness, and enigmatic quality of African cultural practices in regard to a Western context of misunderstanding, oppression, and often deliberate distortion.

> [T]he various elements of religious life in Brazil have shown varying degrees of resistance to change or oblivion. The rites have held out much more tenaciously than the myths. Of course, just because we know little about a certain area, we cannot conclude that certain elements in a religious complex do not exist. At present few Afro-Brazilian myths are known to us, but this does not necessarily mean that there are none. . . . Our lack of knowledge may . . . have something to do with the law of secrecy. All ethnographers who have studied *candomble* life have been struck by the important function of "the secret" in protecting the cult against the whites. The priests are reluctant to explain the profound meaning of rites, even public ones, to people inspired only by curiosity. They are afraid that this knowledge might be used against them or ridiculed as "superstition."[2]

This defensive adaptation, born of the need to insulate Afro-diasporic spirituality from hostile outsiders, may have shaped its characteristic traits, allowing orality, flexibility, and syncretic energy to prevail over tendencies toward orthodoxy, authority, and textualization. "Vodou seldom halts its kinesthetic and sensory drama to force its wisdom into concept or precept; proverbs, anecdotes, ancestral tales, and songs are the only vehicles subtle and flexible enough to cradle the messages when the truths of vodou are put into words."[3]

While Reed's *Mumbo Jumbo* tantalizingly suggests that "Jes Grew's text" is both the possible reconstitution of an ancient body of knowledge that is lost, stolen, or strayed, as well as the always awaited potential text yet to be written by today's or tomorrow's "carriers" of Afro-diasporic culture, Luisah Teish echoes the concerns of the spiritually adept that esoteric knowledge, once textualized, might be misused: "While direct possession is ultimately desirable, I feel it would be irresponsible to put such instructions in a book."[4] Both oral and literate traditions essentialize the spoken word, although the authority that resides in the book is more readily preserved, maintained, and circulated than the knowledge transmitted to initiates through direct contact with spiritual technicians. Mackey plays with and against the logocentrism intrinsic to oral as well as literate traditions; in his text the word made flesh is the aesthetic creation of the jazz musician, whose music produces a visceral effect on its audience.

Both visual artists and writers in the African American tradition have looked to the example of jazz musicians when staking out an aesthetic claim to a universally acknowledged cultural achievement of black artists. Mackey's work opens up aesthetic space for his own textual improvisations by taking serious liberties with the notion that musicians "speak" with their instruments; thus words and music become interchangeable as his text performs itself as a verbal composition, an idiosyncratic yet culturally resonant transliteration of the music he loves to hear. Although many musicians "in the tradition" of black music have been classically trained performers who could read and compose music, blues and jazz also emerged from illiterate performers, the African American equivalent of Homeric bards. The Eurocentric idea that African languages and cultures are "mumbo jumbo," largely based on their privileging of orality and on the invasion and domination of Africa by Europe, has been redirected by writers such as Amiri Baraka and Ishmael Reed. The supposed lack of precision associated with aesthetic and spiritual traditions of the African diaspora is transformed into a positive value, rather than a deficit. What might sound like faulty grammar or a blurred pronunciation of Standard English is, for Baraka, exact, precise, and accurate in its signification of a profound difference in worldview.

For Mackey, music serves as the model for what Baraka calls "expressive language," while Reed's formulation, "Jes Grew seeking its text," activates a positive interpretation of the African diaspora's aesthetic and therapeutic use of disarticulation for the evocation of spiritual and emotional states of being. Timothy Simone identifies characteristics of African cultural systems with the aesthetic techniques of postmodern writing.

> In traditional African cultures, the surfaces, depths, and beyonds were barely distinguishable from each other. Oscillating the demarcations with his own movements, man was simultaneously located in every di-

mension. Imprecision, fuzziness, and incomprehension were the very conditions which made it possible to develop a viable knowledge of social relations. Instead of these conditions being a problem to solve by resolute knowledge, they were viewed as the necessary limits to knowledge itself, determined by the value with which such knowledge was held, and the attitudes taken toward it.

There were choices among readings to be made. People looked for the best way to read things. That chosen as the best was not viewed as inherently the best to the exclusion of other readings. The best was one that added resiliency, validation, or sustenance to the act of reading. Africans did consider every surface as a surface to be read. Each reading was to add something else that could be said, neither to the detriment, exclusion, or undoing of any other reading. Not all surfaces were visible.

The position of being an individual with a capacity to articulate freely is expressed by the Songhai of Mali as: "I am a voice from elsewhere free to say exactly what they want." . . . Because he voices the thoughts of others, the speaker is not implicated, constrained, or held back in the speaking. His freedom to speak is not contingent upon what he has to say. He can make something happen—invent, undermine, posit, play—without it seeming that he is the one doing it. The speaker is not to be located in the situation he represents or creates with his speech and its concomitant assumptions and ideas. Some part of the speaker is always some place else. Therefore, no matter what happens as a result of the speaking, he is never fully captured, analyzed, apprehended, or pinned down by the listeners. Although this notion sounds like a Western deconstructive position toward identity in general, the difference in the Songhai context is that this notion is consciously recognized as the precondition for speaking in general and descriptive of the psychological orientation assumed toward speaking. (Simone 153–154)

According to anthropologist Karen McCarthy Brown, the positive value placed on disarticulation as a precondition for articulation allows for a greater sense of communal interaction and participation in Vodou ritual. The individual possessed by certain Afro-Haitian spirits, for example, may produce inarticulate sounds that nevertheless are subject to interpretation by other participants. The very openness of signification that such enigmatic expressions allow serves to generate the creative interpretive energies of the collectivity.

Whatever the form, [the Loa's] inarticulate sounds gain meaning in a vodou ceremony only through her body language and the interpretive efforts of the gathered community. . . . [The Loa's] inability to speak emphasizes something that is true of all the vodou spirits: their messages are enigmatic. Terse, multireferential language works in similar ways with other spirits. Whether a given spirit uses articulate speech or not, the participants, individually and collectively, interpret and apply what is said. Yodou spirits do not often make authoritative pronouncements. Their presence in the thick social weave of a ritual is a catalyst activating group wisdom and group resources. Yodou ceremonies are accurately described as group healing sessions in which both individual and collective problems surface and are addressed. The community is therefore both the subject and the product of vodou ritualizing. (Brown 230)

In the absence of any such "thick social weave" of communal ritual, Mackey's academically educated, hyperliterate, and ultrahip jazz musician "N." substitutes the esoteric discipline and lore of the music itself, which builds improvised temporary communities wherever the performers find an audience willing to listen. In a play on recent debates about "essence," elements of African aesthetic and spiritual systems are the "broken bottle" from which "traces of perfume still emanate." These shards of a broken whole are embedded in the psyche of Mackey's protagonist, who sometimes associates them with fragments of broken glass or cowrie shells and at other times with the "African teeth" of an Ndembu healing ritual described by Victor Turner, whose ethnographic account has been reinterpreted provocatively by Mackey, and subsequently by Michael Taussig in *The Nervous System*. These fragments disturb the psychic equilibrium of N. while also making him a more sensitive receptor of spiritual energy, thus allowing him to find secular parallels in black communities for the spiritual practices and traditions of the black diaspora. For instance, the enigmatic quality of the spirit's voice in the Vodou ceremony migrates to the oracular scribblings of the urban graffiti writer who, for reasons Paulo Freire would comprehend, resists the school curriculum, and therefore remains uneducated in the conventional sense.

The writer/composer uses words as music to heal the phantom pain of a social body torn asunder and music as a presence to heal the absence associated with the "'space' we're all immigrants from," as the text puts it (a spatiotemporal conflation of Africa and the womb as tropes of origin. In this manner the writer/composer sets out "to reconstruct—with all the comely

lost illusion of lore—to reassemble a Way, as though this were 'his' (he himself realized the presumption) to do anything with." Like his African ancestors, N. learns to heal psychic disturbances through the efficacy of music, and
by extension, through language bent as the musician bends notes to make
inanimate objects produce "human" sound.

Mackey's lyrical epistolary prose work begins with the inspired musician's
utopian desire to communicate the incommunicable: "You should have heard
me in the dream last night." It goes on to assemble, out of oral lore as well
as textual artifacts of high literacy, a series of hyperarticulate conversations
among the musical instruments through which his characters speak, literally, a music "'composed' of our disagreements." The precision and ambiguity
of the word meet the emotive nonreferentiality of music, with the semantic play of Mackey's poetic prose a promising antidote to phallogocentricity
as a mode of domination. As a seriously playful interrogation of the phallo-
centrism embodied in a masculinist jazz tradition, Mackey offers a "Mystic Horn Society" in which women musicians challenge the seminal idiom
of their male colleagues' performance ethic, itself an articulate response to
the exclusion of African American men from institutional patriarchal structures. To the extent that it conditions the present, the slave past problematizes the acquisition of mastery, whether of standard English, literacy, postmodernist discourse, or the jazz tradition itself: "The wretched of the earth
can hardly be accused of elitism." Negation, deferral, interruption, contradiction, equivocation, qualification, and modulation continually complicate
or preclude any categorical statement.

The esoteric meditations of an artist-initiate (the divinely eccentric jazz
man of Mackey's text who seeks a rite of passage to an alterative source of
cultural empowerment) construct a network of associations that ally penis/
horn as the player's "third leg," or unauthorized phallus with the trickster
power of Yoruba-Dahomean deity of crossroads, Eshu-Elegba, who is said to
stutter or to walk with a limp, and who is associated in the African American tradition with the blues musician's initiation into the life of playing "devil's music." Through the recurring figure of the "phantom limb" (a trope
for the liminality of the African American, the artist, and the postmodern
condition itself), condensed and displaced symbolizations of amputation/
castration extend the jazzy, dream-like improvisations of the sometimes hal-
lucinatory text into a discourse on the innovative artist as an individual figuratively cut off from an already marginalized or mythologized collectivity.

Beginning where the modernist *Invisible Man* leaves off, with the emergence of the alienated black artist from cultural hibernation underground,
the existence of black music itself, toward which Ellison's text gestures, is,

Mackey suggests, a starting point for a postmodern literary expression, "a dense form of writing" as rich and complex as black music already is. In Al Young's short story, "Chicken Hawk's Dream," a drug-addicted urban youth, mistaking dream for reality, is unable to produce with a saxophone the sounds he hears in his head. In *Bedouin Hornbook,* however, N.'s dream of standing outside a manhole as a whole man and picking up the pieces of a broken horn—reminiscent of folk artist Lonnie Holley's sculpture-collage, "The Music Lives after the Instruments Is Destroyed"—leads to discipline, apprenticeship, creative composition, and a form of intellectual community, as he develops his "chops." Edwards' statement about his "Lynch Fragments" might apply equally to N.'s heady dispatches to the Angel of Dust: "They are powerful and they are ours, and they are mine, and they are not made by our oppressor."[5]

Knowing a tradition inside and out; knowing that every tradition is shaped as much from outside as from inside, that gathering and dispersal and systole and diastole are complementary and interactive rather than opposed processes, Mackey seeks to overcome the reductive effect of binary systems, which are merely the warp and woof on which this text weaves its "percussive cloth." The artist's esoteric knowledge and mastery of an instrument that blows East as well as West allow an epistemological shift so that both articulation and disarticulation may signify as forms of human expression. That the artist is arrested for "indecent exposure" is only one of many ironies this text lays bare.

Notes

1. Timothy Maliqalim Simone, *About Face: Race in Postmodern America* (Brooklyn: Autonomedia, 1989), p. 149.

2. Roger Bastide, *The African Religions of Brazil,* trans. Helen Sebba (Baltimore: Johns Hopkins UP, 1978), pp. 240–41.

3. Karen McCarthy Brown, *Mama Lola: A Vodou Priestess in Brooklyn* (Berkeley: U of California P, 1991), p. 106.

4. Luisah Teish, *Jambalaya* (San Francisco: Harper and Row, 1985), p. 91.

5. Lucy Lippard, *Mixed Blessings: New Art in a Multicultural America* (New York: Pantheon, 1990), p. 61.

17

A Collective Force of Burning Ink

Will Alexander's *Asia & Haiti*

A homegrown if not "organic" intellectual, Will Alexander is an African American writer from South Central Los Angeles whose surrealist poetry is global, even cosmic, in scope, encyclopedic in its display of esoteric knowledge and arcane vocabularies, and visionary in its apocalyptic intensity. The author of numerous works of poetry, fiction, drama, and essays, of which only a fraction has been published, Alexander has been largely ignored by black as well as mainstream readers, scholars, and critics, despite regular appearances of his poetry and prose in *Sulfur* and *Hambone,* literary journals friendly to avant-garde poetics, edited respectively by Clayton Eshleman and Nathaniel Mackey. Beyond convenient labels such as "African American surrealist" or "North America's Aimé Césaire," Alexander is difficult to categorize aesthetically as well as ideologically. However, the political landscapes of *Asia & Haiti,* published by Douglas Messerli's Sun & Moon Press, could bring Alexander to the attention of a wider audience, including more black readers.

Born into the early cohort of the post-war "baby boom" generation, Alexander is a child of the Cold War era, which in part defined the aspiring revolutions and liberation struggles of so-called Third World nations, which in turn inspired the civil rights movement and black nationalist struggles in the United States. Alexander's father, born in New Orleans and a World War II veteran, married a Texan and left the South for California following a military tour that took him, among other places, on a brief visit to the Caribbean. There, the elder Alexander was impressed to see black people in positions of power, and his story of that experience left a distinct impression on his son, who counts among his cultural heroes Césaire of Martinique and Wifredo Lam of Cuba. *Asia & Haiti* deals with relatively recent historical events—shifts in power that began during the poet's childhood—that also represent the changing role of the Third World in the latter half of the twentieth century. Not only do Cold War ideologies provide subjects for Alexander's poetry in *Asia & Haiti*, the era also supplies metaphors for his poetics, as seen in his essay, "Poetry: Alchemical Anguish and Fire":

> Poetics which reduce, which didactically inform, take on the infected measures of the gulag. During the earlier part of the 1950's we see the poet Césaire in sustained resistance against this gulag. He takes on the "Communist" party boss Aragon and the latter's demand for plain spoken diacritics, for abject poverty of description. (16)

Published together as a book titled *Asia & Haiti*, the two poems "Asia" and "Haiti" exist in a kind of dialogic or interactive relationship to each other, so that together they imply a more comprehensive statement about Third World politics and global oppression in a post-Cold War world no longer divided into two superpowers. Pairing these poems together allows the poet to explore correspondences between the political weakness and spiritual strength of the inhabitants of two countries, Tibet and Haiti, the one overwhelmed by communists and the other by capitalists. Crucial to the perspective of this work (and perhaps to Alexander's marginalization as a black writer) is the absence of any "white oppressor" in "Asia" or "Haiti." Alexander is careful to point out, in response to this observation, that the majority of the world's population is not white and that people who are not white govern this global majority. The power of so-called Third World people, and not only their oppression, should be a topic for serious discussion and analysis by black intellectuals.

Asia & Haiti brings to mind some of the difficulties of writing and evaluating poetry within a political framework. The political messages of poetry written about recent or ongoing events are interpreted differently than those concerning events that for the reader have receded into distant history. In the former case, the political message tends to be foregrounded; in the latter case, the literary and historical value of the work becomes the more important concern for most readers. To the extent that these poems articulate a political position, it could be said that *Asia & Haiti* seems crude and inadequate at one level and complexly sophisticated at another level. As political analysis, *Asia & Haiti* might seem to some readers primitive, ineffectual, and naive. However, it might also be argued that as symbolic verbal acts, these poems are aesthetically complex, imaginatively sophisticated, and intellectually stimulating, while aspiring to karmic balance. The rhetoric of these poems owes more to corrective magic and therapeutic ritual than to politics. The writer's alchemy turns the base materials of fear, hatred, terror, and vengeance into a fierce and complex poetry of empathetic witness. The poems themselves represent an interesting syncretism of spiritual practice, cultural ritual, and political critique.

Each poem has a collective narrator. In "Asia," the speakers are Tibetan Buddhist monks forced out of their monasteries when Mao's Communist army invaded Tibet in 1950. In Alexander's poem, the monks are heroic shamans inhabiting a spiritual realm, hovering "in invisibility, vertically ex-iled, in an impalpable spheroid, virescently tinged, subtly flecked with scar-let, conducting astral warfare against the Chinese invasion and occupation of Tibet" (9). The collective voice of "Haiti" is that of "les Morts," the "anony-mous dead" of Haiti, macheted, shot, and tortured to death at the hands of the Tonton Macoutes during the brutal regime of Francois "Papa Doc" Duva-lier, who came to power in 1957. Speaking for the exiled monks and the mur-dered Haitians, the poet apparently identifies his voice with theirs, including himself in their first person plural: "we / of the old certitude of mantras / of lucid spell" (59); "who summon forces / rapid & oracular with menace" (68); "we who speak / with a sun of splinters spewing from our heart . . . we / the first gatherers of wool" (72); "we speak / as the referential poltergeist / as the living comprehension" (117).

Including himself in this "we," the poet counts himself among those whose power is more spiritual and magical than material or political. In both cases, the "rebellious" and "vertically exiled" monks as well as "les Morts," rest-less souls in limbo, are disembodied entities, existing outside the physical realm, thus unable to act directly against their enemies. The Tibetan Buddhist monks appear to exist in some liminal state between death and rebirth, de-laying their reincarnation or their achievement of Nirvana, or nonexistence, in order to stick around and do spiritual battle against the Chinese commu-nists. The monks in their "liminal exile" (67) claim "the power of Padma Sabhava / who subjected local demons to the power of the faithful" (17).

For the Tibetan Buddhists of "Asia," defense against the military inva-sion of Communist China relies not on armed response, nor even nonvio-lent political struggle, but on rituals of exorcism. The poem (which perhaps includes the reader as well as the poet in the "we" of the collective speak-ing personae) evokes, with the voices of the spiritually endowed Buddhist monks, their magical word spells intended to drive out secular "demons." The poem itself partakes in the ritual of spiritual self-defense, as the reader is invited to empathize with displaced Tibetans attempting to chant their way to freedom. As a verbal, rhetorical, and aesthetic construct, the poem advocates no particular political action but instead participates, along with the rebellious monks, in a collective spiritual act.

The pacifist monks see themselves as spiritual sorcerers for whom "life follows a syllabus of omens" and whose weapons are "muttering spells" (63), while the enraged dead of Haiti, like reverse zombies, call on Petro *Vodou* power to avenge themselves and curse their oppressors and murderers, the Duvaliers. Tibetans "pushed . . . to the 'verge of famine'" as they resist China's forceful reannexation of their country respond with the powers of the weak: "we 'spat at them' / 'sang rude songs about them' / hit them with 'knots' 'tied' in our prayer 'shawls'" (14, 15). The "undistinguished dead," the abject poor killed by the hundreds during the Duvalier regime, "haunt the gargoyle couple with a puncturing kind of guilt" (84). These collective personae, displaced by death and/or exile from life in their homelands, rely instead on the spiritual and magical powers of words: as prayer, as critique, as invective, as condemnation, as the deliverance of a curse, as a verbal blow against an enemy that they cannot strike directly. The poet's position is analogous to that of these disembodied souls: "we who exist as voice," (83) "a collective force of burning ink" (119).

In "Haiti" justice is reduced to a primal vengeance, a "utopian Armageddon" (93) in which the oppressed change places with their oppressors, as in the Biblical story of Lazarus and Dives. In the imaginary realm of the poem, those who were hacked and tortured to death by Duvalier's Tonton Macoutes now relish the torture of their enemies. The despised Duvaliers, addressed familiarly as Francois and Simone, are "forced to watch" themselves as their vile bodies writhe in a painful pornographic embrace beneath the unflinching gaze of the murdered multitudes (76). Their souls now resting in limbo as their enemies are caged in hell, the people of Haiti democratically resolve to punish the Duvaliers: "so we've granted ourselves this law / that we watch the gargoyle couple from our vector / as we vote & restructure new methods of torture" (81). The pornographic horror of Duvalier's rape of Haiti throughout his regime of torture is literalized in the grotesque torture devised for "the gargoyle couple" by "les Morts," the anonymous victims of the corrupt Duvaliers. Francois is condemned by "les Morts" to be locked in an eternal pornographic rape of his wife Simone (96).

This "forced and eternal coupling without letup" (95) might be regarded as a less than appropriate penalty for his rapacious rule of Haiti, as it would appear that his wife is punished more severely than the dictator himself. From the perspective of the poem's collective personae, there seems to be no indication that this lurid punishment inadequately addresses the crimes of Papa Doc against the Haitian people. It is designed to satisfy the victims' primal desire for retaliation, if only in the visualization of horrific detail: "if we want your flesh to slither / or have your eyes extracted in fragments / it is the measure of our bedazzlement with anger" (88). Although the oppressor changes places with the oppressed, this is not the joyful subversion of carnival. Certainly there is nothing in it of Christian forgiveness, nor is it the exact symmetry of Old Testament justice—an eye for an eye, a tooth for a tooth. Nevertheless it is perhaps fitting that the miscreants receive zombie vengeance dispensed by a jury of dead Haitian citizens given the Duvaliers' reputed transactions with the "left hand" powers of Baron Samedi, a cigar-smoking graveyard trickster from the Vodou pantheon of Petro Loa. The poem's image of righteous punishment is the syncretic melding of the fierce rage of the Petro Loa combined with the eternal damnation of a fire-and-brimstone Catholic hell. The collective vengeance of the poor and powerless against their wealthy oppressors, in any case, is not literal but occurs entirely at the level of the imaginary. It is disturbing, although perhaps appropriate, that the sympathetic reader who persists in reading this scathing poem, swept up within the poem's "we" along with the poet, is also "forced to watch," to recall hideous crimes while imagining a loathsome punishment, as one more witness to the scatological and pornographic horror of the Duvaliers.

In the vitriolic poems of *Asia & Haiti,* the overlap of geopolitical and spiritual worlds, along with the scatological, pornographic, and surrealistic imagery, creates a critical dissonance. In neither case is action in the real world the primary focus. The exorcism of demons in "Asia" and the vengeance visualized in "Haiti" as the tortured confront and torment their torturers both occur on an imaginary or spiritual plane of nonexistence or limbo. *Asia & Haiti* confirms the observation of Marxist critics that literature offers imaginary solutions to real problems. Both poems address the terrible imbalance of power that allows totalitarians and dictators to destroy the lives of the poor and the weak. Like the "curse prayer" collected by folklorist and novelist Zora Neale Hurston, which Alice Walker incorporated into her short story "The Revenge of Hannah Kemhuff," *Asia & Haiti* locates the powers of the poor and the weak in the realms of spirit and magic rather than reality and politics.

While Ishmael Reed has written several poems and novels in which Haitian Vodou and North American "Hoodoo" become metaphors for black creativity, and Ntozake Shange's novel *Sassafrass, Cypress & Indigo* also explores the realms of magic, dreams, and visions that inspire artists, Shange's *Spell #7,* included in her *Three Pieces,* specifically comments on the relative effectiveness of what might be called "Third World technologies" of magic and ritual. Her theater piece *Spell #7* is presented as an upbeat "magic trance manual for technologically stressed third world people" (1). Shange offers protective incantations for people of color living under the sometimes destructive influence of industrial and postindustrial technologies and with the toxic effects of racism. In this sense, magic might be equated with therapeutic tools for reinforcing psychological well-being through affirmation and visualization. Significantly, the show begins with a monologue that is sometimes anthologized as a poem, "My Father Is a Retired Magician." Here the speaker recalls a failure of the parent's magic to deal with a child's low self-esteem and internalized racism. For the black child who asked a magician "to be made white," *Spell #7* offers the alternative of learning to "love it / bein colored" (7, 8).

Asia & Haiti can be read quite seriously as an eccentric political analysis of Tibetan Buddhist exorcism and Haitian *Vodou* revenge, or as a manual of spiritual and psychic martial arts. These poems follow the cultural logic of the respective religious traditions of Tibet and Haiti. Their rhetorical strategy is a Third World syncretism of political critique with demonology and exorcism. Among other things, Alexander's poem investigates some of the political implications of Third World religious beliefs and traditions of collective identity. In this sense, *Asia & Haiti* bears some resemblance to the work of Bessie Head, particularly her novel *A Question of Power*. Garrett Caples makes a strong argument for Alexander's custom blend of political awareness and aesthetic complexity: "The tension between the poetic and the polemical in Alexander's work contributes to its success as it yields a poetry irreducible to trite answers and sentiments and yet expressive of outrage in the face of very real, historically-specific injustice. . . . That the poet manages to exploit these historical materials while steadfastly refusing to lecture his audience in any obvious or banal way—using cadences of argumentation while allowing his poem to remain 'open'—is a testament to both his skill and discretion" (74–76).

The strategy of curse and exorcism in *Asia & Haiti*, a strategy of creative vengeance through ritual condemnation and magical speech acts, parallels the therapeutic climax of *When Rabbit Howls*, the memoir of Truddi Chase, a woman diagnosed with multiple personality disorder whose psychic upheaval can be traced to a history of traumatic abuse beginning in early childhood. Like the Tibetan Buddhist monks driven into exile and the abject poor of Haiti, Chase seeks vengeance in the realm of the imaginary rather than reality. Her fantasy of murdering the stepfather who had physically and sexually abused her remains a fantasy. Instead of killing him, she assembles a collective memory of the abuses he committed and creates a fictional narrative of his destruction, a story written collaboratively by "the troops," her name for the collection of personalities representing her fragmented self. Among the troops that protect Chase, a white female, is a tough black male version of herself. Like Alexander's collective personae, his "plankton armies," Chase dispatches her enemy by symbolic means, through the collaborative writing of her troops, her own collective force of burning ink. It is the difference between burning an enemy alive and burning him in effigy. The latter indicates a higher level of spiritual awareness. Still, readers of *Asia & Haiti* might wonder whether the habit of magical thinking condemns the oppressed to a failure of political action. Of course, it might be argued that political action is itself symbolic, if not magical.

As to their style and form, Alexander's poems are both unpunctuated, so it is difficult to know for sure how to parse them, but given their expanding structure, it seems as if each might be read as a single very long, very complex sentence. Readers might apprehend "Asia" and "Haiti" each as one sentence or many, or perhaps as a potentially unbounded structure of dependent and independent clauses. Describing the cascading rhetoric of the Alexandrian sentence in a blurb for *Above the Human Nerve Domain,* Norma Cole wrote, "The reader is dazzled by expanding forms of predictory anaphora." The rhetorical, grammatical, and syntactical structure constitutes each poem as one or more hypotactic (or hyperhypotactic) sentences. Each poem is a complex sentence-machine turning out elaborate grammatical parallelisms, extensive series of epic catalogues, and an open-ended syntax of discordant clauses and appended prepositional phrases. While Ron Silliman, Charles Bernstein, and Bob Perelman as well as other contemporary poets and theorists have emphasized parataxis as an aesthetically and ideologically oppositional strategy for a "new sentence" intended to break down some of the hierarchical effects of language, Alexander's style lies at the other end of the continuum. Although there is nothing intrinsically ideological about syntactical structure per se, it can be argued that any aspect of the verbal construct may be deployed oppositionally within a given context or set of conventions: for example, within syntax and grammar as well as in the more obvious weapons of rhetoric and lexical selection.

Alexander's preference for hypotaxis rather than parataxis possibly has something to do with the "cadences of argument" that Caples notes, as well as the diverse fields of knowledge to which the poet has access. Because hypotaxis accommodates lavishly expansive sentence construction, while parataxis is suitable for the tersely concise statement, it might follow that the latter would have difficulty incorporating the load of information and history to which these poems allude. In *Asia & Haiti* the poet is interested in classification and hierarchy, maybe because of personal proclivities but also because of the social organization of the two oppressed cultures: the Tibetan Buddhists, the collective personae of "Asia," on the one hand, and on the other hand, the dead multitudes of the poor who speak in "Haiti," "plankton armies / empowered by anger with a special knowledge of torture" (76). Through enumeration, classification, hierarchy, and grammatical parallelism, poetic correspondences and oppositions are articulated. The classification of different grades of tea parallels the hierarchy of social classes in Tibet (23), while the "objective" enumeration of physical and natural features of the benign or neutral Haitian landscape (125–26), whether geological or horticultural, implicitly contrasts the enumeration of disgusting and unnatural physical attributes associated with the corrupt Duvaliers.

The sentence structure of Alexander's surrealist poetry is specifically contrasted with the paratactical "new sentence" of Ron Silliman and other Language writers in Keith Tuma's review of *The Stratospheric Canticles*. Before this review, the few critical discussions of Alexander's work were more concerned with the eclectic breadth of his poetic diction and word choice, the wide-ranging vocabularies and at times arcane lexicons found in his work. In contrast to other critics, Tuma believes: "The energy of this poetry is not wholly or even importantly an effect of its pyrotechnic particulars. . . . I'm struck instead by the agglutination of parts in Alexander's poems, and more problematically by the way in which an expressivist force distills all the poem's matter to the ONE MATTER to the cosmos which is also the self-pressurized, turbulent, eruptive" (171).

Eliot Weinberger calls Alexander "an ecstatic surrealist on imaginal hyperdrive"—a fair description, although Weinberger guesses incorrectly that he is "probably the only African American poet to take Aimé Césaire as a spiritual father (and behind Césaire, Artaud and Lautreamont)" (182). Jayne Cortez is also inspired by French, Caribbean, and African surrealists. She has spoken particularly of her connection to Césaire, as well as to Leon Damas and Leopold Senghor. These poets of the Negritude Movement are invoked in her poem "At a Certain Moment in History," which celebrates a moment when the poet's political consciousness begins the process of decolonization: "When Césaire arrived home to / clarify the contradictions / of too much French wine in / the wee wee of Martinique" (92-93). Surrealism has also influenced the work of other African American poets, notably Ted Joans, whose "Nadja Rendezvous" in *Black Pow-Wow* and *Flying Piranha* collaboration are products of his creative engagement with the work of André Breton. Like Alexander, Joans sees surrealism as a potentially liberating aesthetic, which both poets view as particularly appropriate to their identity as black artists working in a variety of media. Joans once declared, "Without surrealism I would have been incapable of surviving the abject vicissitudes and racial violence which the white man in America imposed on me every day. Surrealism became the weapon I used to defend myself, and it has been and always will be my own style of life" (Fabre 313). Alexander values Césaire as a writer whose interests are global, while invoking Breton, Artaud, and Lautreamont along with Rimbaud, Lorca, and Caribbean painter Wifredo Lam, who participated in the Surrealist and Cubist movements, as creative inspirations.

"Poetry commences by the force of biographical intensity, by the force of its interior brews, by the sum of its sub-conscious oscillations," Alexander writes in "Poetry: Alchemical Anguish and Fire," an essay on poetics that is rhetorically similar to his poetry. "It is like a netling piranha spurring the voice with condensed alchemical pain." Of his word searches through weighty books of knowledge, he writes, "the language of botany, or medicine, or law, takes on a transmogrified dictation, where their particulars blend into a higher poetic service, in which they cease to know themselves as they were, thereby embarking upon a startling, unprecedented existence." Alexander even anticipates the critical response his work has barely begun to accumulate: "Of course the scholars would appraise me with their niggling sort of glimpses, they would examine my footnotes, and even in their minuses give me credit for a poetic action or two" (15). So far, his various works have been read, blurbed, published, and reviewed by writers, virtually all of them poets as well as critics, editors, or scholars, who honor Alexander's alchemical gold card with extended credit.

Although Alexander resists discussions of the technical aspects of writing, it would be useful to have a fuller account of his process of lexical selection and combination; to understand how his reading habits and writing practices overlap in the intertextuality and diverse vocabularies incorporated into his poetry; and to appreciate how certain rare, unusual, specialized, foreign, or archaic words are used in the poem for their precise denotative meaning, connotative meaning, metaphorical resonance, aural or phonemic qualities, or all of the above. Committed to the surrealist's practice of automatic writing, Alexander tries to achieve a state of trance, possession, or uninhibited flow of language. He also engages in aleatorical procedures of random access as he skips through the pages of his dictionary. Of further interest are the poet's spontaneous generation of neologisms, his preference for British (or otherwise variant) spelling, and his insistence that his English is similar in its rhythms to Spanish or Italian—perhaps because of his Latinate vocabulary and his unconventional syntactical and grammatical constructions, as well as his surrealist aesthetic. Alexander's privileging of the unconscious as the locus of surrealist activity, as well as his interest in alchemy, necromancy, shamanism, Vodou, and other magical practices and beliefs, have their corresponding expression in the incantatory quality of his writing. Treating the dictionary as if it were the *I Ching,* while splicing one esoteric system of knowledge to another, Alexander writes like an adept Aladdin who has discovered the recombinant genie of language.

What Mark Scroggins calls the poet's "logolatry" includes not just an entrancing litany of polysyllabic and arcane words but also a fondness for utterances of humbler origin. For instance, might the phrase "a collective force of burning ink" (119) be a distant echo of the paronomastic blues line, "a churning urn of burning funk"? While stirring his custom blend of surrealist chant rant and strutting his dictionary skills, Alexander is not above indulging in serious wordplay, resulting in such double-take puns as "stabbed in the eyes with crystallized assault" (81). The polysemous significance of "we / the first gatherers of wool" (72) suggests images of African people as the first dreamers and thinkers, as well as the first herders, spinners, and weavers, and also the first to retrieve human hair for use as a powerfully symbolic ingredient in magical charms and talismans.

Also of interest is how the reader's experience of lucid intervals and moments of clarity and comprehension interact with the linguistic equivalent of dizzy spells, blackouts, blind spots, and moments of incomprehension, when the poem veers away from the comprehensible toward glossolalia, word salad, dub freestyle, jazz scat, speaking in tongues: the aesthetic equivalent of spirit possession. The poem alternates lucid intervals of declarative statement, political witness, historical chronicle, enumeration, and description with off-road excursions into a surrealist ectopia where words are set free of the need to represent anything other than themselves.

In *Black Chant: Languages of African-American Postmodernism,* Aldon Nielsen argues "the case for a black vernacular base for African-American surrealism, a jazz and blues-based surrealism," such as one encounters in the poetry of *Dasein* poet Joseph White, "that would find its culmination in such works as the densely compacted writings of Los Angeles poet Will Alexander two decades later. . . . Thus a methodology of the avant-garde is provided with a traditional genealogy, and surrealism becomes the working means of black poetic saturation" (70). In relation to a tradition of African American vernacular orality, as well as to contemporary mainstream and avant-garde American poetic traditions, Alexander regards himself as "a psychic maroon." Certainly, as Nielsen suggests, Alexander is one of the poets whose peripheral relationship to the recently established canon of African American literature points to the existence of alternative genealogies for black writers.

With a different critical emphasis, Nathaniel Mackey's *Discrepant Engagement* also investigates "dissonance, cross-culturality, and experimental writing" in the work of a number of poets of diverse cultural backgrounds, including African American, Caribbean, and European American poets familiar to the avant-garde. For Mackey, "creative kinship and the lines of affinity it effects are much more complex, jagged, and indissociable than the totalizing pretensions of canon formation tend to acknowledge" (3). Like the work of a number of African American poets, including Mackey himself, along with Jay Wright, Ed Roberson, Clarence Major, Lorenzo Thomas, Julie Patton, C. S. Giscombe, Claudia Rankine, Mark McMorris, Akilah Oliver, and Erica Hunt, Alexander's work challenges conventional or reductive descriptions of "black poetry," "black language," and "black orality," while confronting head-on the conventional splitting of identity politics from aesthetic practices, innovations, and influences of literary avant-gardes. Although speech and voice are frequently invoked in *Asia & Haiti,* the hyperhypotactic structures and bookish vocabularies of these poems are more indicative of the written sentence than the spoken utterance. These poems are less invested in "talking the talk" than in writing the rite as a means of righting the wrong.

Alexander's preference for the British rather than American spelling of words such as "colour," "vapours," and "manoeuvred" begs the question of whether he is even writing in American English, much less what is called Black English. Alexander's most cherished influences wrote poetry in languages other than English. Clearly his interests, as a reader and as a writer, are global. His literary influences connect him to an international avant-garde, just as his experience as an African American connects him to a black diaspora and to the political struggles of Third World peoples. In Alexander's work, the reader finds an expansive vision accompanied by an equally expansive vocabulary, as the poet avails himself of the opportunity to travel without boundaries while comfortably settled in the library, and he demonstrates how to conduct "astral warfare" without killing a soul.

Notes

My thanks to Will Alexander for providing critical information and to La'Tonya Rease Miles for assistance with research.

18
Incessant Elusives

The Oppositional Poetics of Erica Hunt and Will Alexander

With the long-awaited publication of the *Norton Anthology of African American Literature*, teachers, readers, and writers now have access to a widely available text and easily accessible pedagogical tool that constitutes, for the moment, a scholarly consensus about a collection of works selected for what is virtually an officially institutionalized African American literary canon. At the same time, critics including Nathaniel Mackey in *Discrepant Engagement: Dissonance, Cross-Culturality and Experimental Writing* and Aldon Nielsen in *Black Chant: Languages of African American Postmodernism* have challenged the criteria by which such a canon has been constituted, while pointing to many significant, interesting, imaginative, and challenging works that this recently constituted canon excludes.

Two intellectually engaging and aesthetically unconventional African American poets not included in the Norton Anthology, Erica Hunt, of New York, and Will Alexander, of Los Angeles, represent a post-canonical attitude toward the literary production of black writers in the United States. While Hunt is associated with the so-called "Language Poets," a loose network of avant-garde and politically conscious writers whose work is deeply engaged with critical theory, and Alexander's work is obviously influenced by French, Afro-Caribbean, and African Surrealists, in practice each writer might be regarded as what Alexander calls a "psychic maroon." Both poets exist on the boundaries of mainstream aesthetics, black aesthetics, and the aesthetics of a restless avant-garde, and they both engage each of these aesthetic formations and their respective writing practices with what Hunt has called "oppositional poetics." Hunt, born in 1955, has published two books of poetry: *Local History* (1993) and *Arcade* (1996). Alexander, born in 1948, has published six books, ranging from poetry and fiction to philosophical essays:

Vertical Rainbow Climber (1987), *Arcane Lavender Morals* (1994), *The Stratospheric Cantides* (1995), *Asia & Haiti* (1995), *Towards the Primeval Lightning Field* (1998), and *Above the Human Nerve Domain* (1999).

Hunt and Alexander are useful poets to examine in light of Ron Silliman's observation in his book *The New Sentence* of a tendency of readers and critics to separate poetry associated with "the codes of oppressed peoples" from what is regarded as "purely aesthetic" poetry (31). Whether one's perspective is more aligned with the white-dominated mainstream of United States poetry or the white-dominated avant-garde, whose American members see themselves as part of a historically international aesthetic tendency, the work of black poets tends to be excluded or marginalized in relation to other practices of poetry that are regarded as more purely concerned with aesthetic matters. Although Silliman himself shows this to be a false opposition, it is a remarkably persistent idea that continues to affect the critical reception of black poetry. In the imposed dichotomy that pits "codes of oppressed peoples" against "purely aesthetic" schools of poetry, African American poets are normally presumed to be allied with the former as poets for whom the poetic function of language must be subordinated to a felt obligation to represent the racial, socioeconomic, cultural, and linguistic difference of black individuals and communities. A number of other assumptions are implicated in this assumption, including the assumption that the poetics of an African American writer differs significantly from that of any other writer, and that the aesthetic value of the work is at least partly determined by subject matter. These assumptions may skew the reception of any poet's work to the extent that social identity often overdetermines the critical response to the work of black and other minority writers, at the same time that it may be an under-acknowledged aspect of poets whose work is celebrated for the supposed purity of its aesthetic preoccupation. Similarly, the aesthetic principles intrinsic to the "oppositional poetics" of minority writers may be lost on readers who assume that a socially engaged and ideologically conscious poetic discourse is incompatible with the highest values of aesthetic practice.

The work of Erica Hunt and Will Alexander seems specifically designed to render inoperative such assumptions. Their work challenges conventional or reductive descriptions of "black poetry" and "black identity," while confronting head-on the conventional splitting of identity politics and black literary production from aesthetic practices, innovations, and influences of literary avant-garde movements typically identified with Europe. While they certainly differ from each other in style, ideological position, and aesthetic influences, both poets allow themselves a broad range of subject matter. Alexander is especially eclectic and inclusive when it comes to choosing topics for writing, from alchemy, philosophy, and religion to the history of visual art. Hunt's poetry brings to the page a recognizably urban female persona that eludes common racial stereotypes, while Alexander's hermeticism and surrealism signal the continuing influence of a historically international avant-garde.

Differences in style, subject matter, and rhetorical stance may contribute to the marginalization of black poetry, separating it from what is regarded as mainstream. The Black Arts poets of the 1960s and 1970s attempted to redefine the meaning of aesthetics in accordance with the political slogan, "Black is beautiful." In this formulation, a poem that reflected or celebrated the beauty and struggle of black people was regarded as an aesthetically as well as politically powerful work of art. This radical departure from mainstream poetics gave a positive value to the separation and distinctiveness of black poetry from the aesthetic and cultural values of the mainstream. Such a radical redefinition of aesthetics in fact allowed a great many black poets to emerge, contributing to the further development of a potentially radical poetry and poetics. The emergence of a new black poetry attracted the attention of a predominantly white avant-garde that also defined itself aesthetically, and sometimes politically, against the mainstream. These avant-gardists were interested in black poetry's expression of radical ideologies, but often perceived the work to be less engaged with their own ideas of radical aesthetics.

The poetry of Hunt and Alexander is oppositional in the sense that Hunt uses the term in her essay "Notes for an Oppositional Poetics." For Hunt, a black woman associated with the contemporary avant-garde of "Language Poets," neither a commitment to a black aesthetic nor an avant-garde stance sufficiently describes her position as a poet. Hunt seems opposed to the sometimes doctrinaire and exclusive aspects of either at its most extreme. As a formally intrepid poet who also works as a progressive political activist, Hunt is aware that the boundaries so carefully drawn between aesthetic innovation and ideological engagement cannot maintain their separation. For her, the term "oppositional poetics" encompasses the possibility of a radical politics aligned with a radical aesthetic practice, with each reinforcing the radical potential of the other. Ideally such reinforcement would also help bring into affiance communities with different histories of marginalization from the dominant culture.

While his ideological position is more difficult to locate, Alexander also is wary of identifying completely with the cultural nationalist agenda of a black aesthetic or with the devotion to ceaseless aesthetic innovation espoused by the avant-garde. Alexander's commitment is to surrealism as an aesthetic legacy and practice (shared by European, African, Caribbean, and American writers, including African American poets Bob Kaufman, Ted Joans and Jayne Cortea), within which he feels free to explore a variety of issues and conflicts arising from the disjunctive culture clash of modernity and postmodernity. The *New York Review of Books' Reader's Catalog* describes his works as: "Long poems which are at once surreal and historical, characterized by extraordinary flights of verbal invention." Alexander's phrase "incessant elusives" might articulate his own position as a poet who wishes to steer between radical politics on the one hand and radical aestheticism on the other. The historical conflicts that the poetry engages, in which individual expression has frequently been an early casualty, apparently inform Alexander's wariness of political and social movements.

Of the two poets I am comparing, Hunt's poetry is in some ways easier to place within a progressive ideological framework. Her writing, with its moments of visionary possibility, always seems located in the arcades and archives of an actual social world, however eroded or alienated. In contrast, Alexander's apocalyptic cosmological visions and ecstatic spiritual expeditions—historically based though they might be—often send the poet and his readers into a "stratospheric" realm "above the human . . . domain," like the otherworldly limbos inhabited by Tibetan Buddhist monks and "les Morts" in *Asia & Haiti* or the deep orbit from which the reader is addressed in a poem from *Above the Human Nerve Domain,* "The Iridescent Enigma":

In this smokeless harrier desolation
I have surmounted inscrutable errata
under two electric polar moons
shifting between colours of slate-blue and magenta

I

the Andean Hill Star
hovering in these Martian x-ray wastes
the iridescent enigma
my centripetal wings
against the soul of cartographical surcease
its enervated distension
with its migrating sun loss
the triple atmosphere corroded

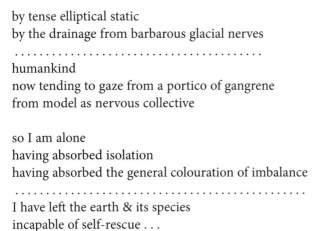

by tense elliptical static
by the drainage from barbarous glacial nerves
. . . .
humankind
now tending to gaze from a portico of gangrene
from model as nervous collective

so I am alone
having absorbed isolation
having absorbed the general colouration of imbalance
. . . .
I have left the earth & its species
incapable of self-rescue . . .

The remoteness of the speaker in this poem increases space, subject, and aesthetic language through the distance of the Andean Hillstar, with the poet persona speaking as a member of an endangered South American hummingbird species. Alexander's verse poems are unpunctuated, their expanding structure suggesting that each might be read as a single very long, very complex sentence. Readers might apprehend each poem as one sentence or many, or perhaps as a potentially unbounded structure of dependent and independent clauses. Describing the cascading rhetoric of the Alexandrian sentence in a blurb for *Above the Human Nerve Domain*, Norma Cole wrote: "The reader is dazzled by expanding forms of predictory anaphora." The rhetorical, grammatical, and syntactical structure constitutes each poem as one or more hypotactic (or hyperhypotactic) sentences. Each poem is a complex sentence-machine turning out elaborate grammatical parallelisms, extensive series of epic catalogues, and an open-ended syntax of discordant clauses and appended prepositional phrases.

While Ron Silliman, Charles Bernstein, and Bob Perelman, as well as other contemporary poets and theorists, have emphasized parataxis as an aesthetically and ideologically oppositional strategy for a "new sentence" intended to break down some of the hierarchical effects of language, Alexander's style lies at the other end of the continuum. Although there is nothing intrinsically ideological about syntactical structure per se, it can be argued that any aspect of the verbal construct may be deployed oppositionally within a given context or set of conventions: syntax and grammar may be used in this manner as well as more obvious weapons such as diction and rhetoric. Alexander and Hunt share an unsettling disjunctive grammar: her humankind work is disjunctive and paratactic, while his is disjunctive and hypotactic. Alexander's preference for hypotaxis rather than parataxis possibly has something to do with the diverse fields of knowledge to which the poet has access. Because hypotaxis accommodates lavishly expansive sentence construction, while parataxis is suitable for the tersely concise statement, it might follow that the latter would have difficulty incorporating the load of information and history to which his poems allude.

In *Black Chant: Languages of African-American Postmodernism*, Aldon Nielsen argues "the case for a black vernacular base for African American surrealism, a jazz and blues-based surrealism," such as one encounters in the poetry of *Dasein*-poet Joseph White, "that would find its culmination in such works as the densely compacted writings of Los Angeles poet Will Alexander two decades later. . . . Thus a methodology of the avant-garde is provided with a traditional genealogy, and surrealism becomes the working means of black poetic saturation" (70). In relation to the African American tradition of vernacular orality, as well as to the contemporary mainstream and avant-garde American poetic traditions, Alexander regards himself as "a psychic maroon." Certainly, as Nielsen suggests, Alexander is one of the poets whose peripheral relationship to the recently established canon of African American literature points to the existence of alternative genealogies for black writers. For Alexander, Caribbean and European artists and writers—including Wifredo Lam, Aimé Cesairé, Lautréamont and André Breton—are closer aesthetic kin than most of his contemporaries in the United States.

While Alexander, a West Coast poet whose parents migrated to California from Texas and Louisiana, has chosen Caribbean writers and artists as aesthetic ancestors, an often elided site of difference within black communities is the Caribbean ancestry of African American poets such as Hunt. The response of such poets to the domination of the English language and Anglophone literature may be oppositional and yet may differ from the response of other African Americans. Hunt's poetry often takes language and subjectivity themselves as topics for exploration rather than accepting them as given:

> I was thinking that if the ceiling were mirrored we would have to watch what we say about what we feel. ("Preface," *Local History*, 9)
> The left brain turns the other cheek. The right brain can't imagine it. ("Coronary Artist [1]," *Arcade*, 13)
> All the great heroes slept late . . . look at myself in the mirror and see the person I might have been had I gotten more sleep. ("Coronary Artist [1]," *Arcade*, 13)

> I have resisted the power of spelling and broken the spell of pronouns in-
> venting continuity where persons and personalities change sides. ("Coro-
> nary Artist [2]," *Arcade*, 15)

Hunt's poetry evokes not nostalgia for oral tradition, but rather a critical dialogue within the self-reflexive discursive universe of writing, print, and electronic media. A disjunctive parataxis gives many of her sentences the pithy
eloquence of a literary aphorism wedded to the postmodern irony of an advertising slogan aimed at Generation X. *Local History,* with prose poems that
draw on the conventions of letter and diary writing, explicitly frames the
work as a writer's address to a reader. *Arcade,* perhaps with a nod to the bourgeois Paris of Walter Benjamin, locates the New York poet within an urban
space that is as cold as commerce, a city of decayed arcades where "We wear
our indifference with dignity" (*Arcade* 27). Her poem "Coronary Artist (2)"
contains explicit and self-reflexive references to writing, grammar, and punctuation, aspects of language that the speaker in the poem imagines that she
embodies in a literal way as her body becomes a signifier: "my palms turning into asterisks, my bent arms into commas," as a black speaker of standard English provides a salient example of one who is perceived to be "alien
in [one's] own language" (*Arcade* 15–16). That Hunt declines in this poem to
write in what is called "Black English" or "black vernacular," that she declines
further to use either euphonious lyrical lines or normative speech-like sentences constituting what is called an "authentic voice," leaves this work outside the mainstream American canon as well as outside the currently constructed canon of African American literature—a canon constituted around
the central idea of textualized orality, or "the speakerly text."

My understanding of Hunt's use of the term "oppositional poetics" is influenced by my reading of Hank Lazer's *Opposing Poetries.* Here Lazer observes a clash of writing practices that divide poets in an ongoing "debate
over the transparency versus the materiality of the word" (9). As an advocate
of the material word and the innovative poet, he diagnoses a crisis in American poetry and offers a prognosis for its recovery through the rethinking of
what counts as diversity and the reconnection of poetry to its historical engagement with intellectual, philosophical, and political discourses. Lazer locates the crisis in mainstream poetry in the professionalization of academic
creative writing programs and in the ascendancy of what some disparage as
"workshop poetry." This poetry of personal revelation, therapeutic insight,
and everyday epiphany models itself on the mainstream poetry that is vali-
dated by what Charles Bernstein identifies as "official verse culture." According to Lazer, this official verse culture is stifling itself through its refusal

to examine critically its writing practices, aesthetic values, and ideological premises in light of contemporary intellectual discussions of representation, language, and subjectivity, while justifying its own aesthetics in the name of clarity, authenticity, and excellence.

In Lazer's view, the recent addition of writers of color to the mainstream canon has largely resulted in more of the same, as contemporary minority poets are themselves as likely as anyone to acquire their training in the same workshops. Lazer points to recent multicultural anthologies in which he finds "significant selections of multiculturalist poetry but an extraordinarily narrow range of modes of representation" with few exceptions to "the mostly flat poetry of plainspoken experience" (128). Lazer even suggests that the formal experimentation of a literary avant-garde may challenge and disturb the mainstream more profoundly than the conventionally representational "speakerly texts" of black writers, or at least those black writers whose work is included in major anthologies of American literature:

> As an oppositional literary practice, Language Writing questions the tendencies of mainstream poetry, including its evasion of modernism's formal challenges, its resultant devotion to the plainspoken lyric, its correlative hostility to philosophy and critical theory. Language Writing specifically takes seriously those theories of the sign and those issues of representation that mainstream poetry repudiates. Language Writing also proposes and makes necessary new methods of reading that force us to reconsider the political dimensions of literary activity. (37)

Alexander and Hunt are both poets whose work problematizes subjectivity and racial identification while deviating from the dominant mode of representation in poetry. Hunt's discussion of "oppositional poetics" and her own work as a poet can be read as a different take on the situation Lazer describes, in which mainstream poetry is challenged by questions of racial and cultural difference, or "identity politics," as well as by aesthetically radical practices of formal innovation. Implicitly Hunt questions, on the one hand, the assumption of poets like Amiri Baraka of an intrinsic link between social and aesthetic marginality, between black culture and stylistic innovation, and, on the other hand, Ron Silliman's assumption that people of color are less likely to indulge in experimental writing, preferring realistic modes of representation in the interest of "authenticity" and the need to make sure their stories are told in accessible forms and comprehensible language.

Hunt is alert to the kinds of stagnation that can occur when a minority community emphasizes tradition, consonance, and identity to the detriment of the vital stimulation provided by innovation, dissonance, and diversity. She is also aware that marginality based on identity and marginality based on aesthetic practice are more analogous than equivalent in their consequences for the respective marginalized communities. Rather than automatically link minority identity with political dissidence and aesthetic innovation, Hunt allows room for discussion of how such linkage might actually occur in practice as marginalized groups activate the potential of their analogous, but not identical, oppositions to the ideological and aesthetic values of the dominant culture. Thus, she is able to consider how reciprocal understandings based in such analogy or contiguity can bring about meaningful syntheses as the strengths of various oppositional positions can be combined through mutual commitment to work in solidarity for a shared social vision.

The appearance of poets like Hunt and Alexander affirms the expansive diversity and complexity of black identity and helps reveal submerged literary genealogies of practitioners of innovative black poetry. I think it is not coincidental, but entirely to be expected that an emerging critical discourse has begun to focus on black writers considered marginal to, or outside of, the quite recently institutionalized African American canon. The struggle to include representative works by black and other minority writers and women in the canon of American literature, along with the scholarly and critical activity necessary to construct alternative canons and curricula, has taken place only within the last three decades. I see this recent success of African American literary criticism as perhaps the necessary precondition for the shifting of attention to what the black canon might have excluded.

III
Interviews

"The Solo Mysterioso Blues"

An Interview with Harryette Mullen by Calvin Bedient

This interview with Harryette Mullen about her collection of poems Muse & Drudge *took place on April 14, 1996. The interviewer is her colleague in the English Department at UCLA.*

CALVIN BEDIENT: What do you think growing up in Fort Worth, Texas, has meant for your poetry?

HARRYETTE MULLEN: It means partly that my notion of who I was had to do with being in a Southern state—but in another way, Texas isn't Southern: it's southwestern or western. So it's being in and actually on the edge of a Southern black culture. Texas, when I was young, was a segregated state. I remember the colored and white signs on the rest rooms and water fountains, and I remember the first time we tested integration by going to a drive-in restaurant where they refused to serve us, and we left after waiting there for about thirty minutes for our hamburgers that never arrived. We were the first black family in our neighborhood, and our neighbors moved out; the next door neighbors packed overnight bags and went to a motel so that they would not have to spend a single night next to us. Another neighbor used to let his German Shepherd dog out to chase my sister and me while we rode our bicycles to the Book Mobile, and it took us about three trips before we realized that he was doing it deliberately when we saw him actually get up from his porch and open the gate and let the dog out.

So that's part of what growing up in Texas meant to me. And the black community was a part of it, but we had a different perspective on it because my family had come from Pennsylvania and we spoke English somewhat differently. My mother was a schoolteacher, my grandfather was a Baptist minister, and we were considered to be very proper speakers of English compared to most of the people we lived around, who spoke definite black English and felt that our English was seditty or dicty or proper.

Living in Fort Worth also meant hearing Spanish spoken whenever I was outside of my neighborhood, say downtown or on buses, and wanting to know what people were saying in that language. Actually, where I heard Spanish spoken frequently was in my grandmother's neighborhood, a black community with one Mexican-American family. We used to practice our few words of Spanish with them. We always exchanged greetings in Spanish with the Cisneros family, her next door neighbors.

BEDIENT: You use some Spanish in *Muse & Drudge*. Did you have any particular purpose in mind?

MULLEN: I always thought Spanish was a beautiful language, and whenever I had the opportunity to study it, I did. One of my elementary school teachers when I was still in a little segregated black school was a man from Panama, who was a native Spanish speaker, bilingual, so I identified Spanish also with black people as well as with Mexican Americans. The Spanish is there partly because I think it's a beautiful language and partly because I associate it with people who were a part of my life. I use it in a political way, because I think we should all have more than one language. I think it's crazy that in this country it's considered better to be monolingual than to be bilingual or multilingual. People in Africa routinely speak three or more languages. It's not unusual at all for people to speak three, four, or five languages. Even not very well-educated people speak several languages.

BEDIENT: The language in your poem has, of course, a mongrel aspect. There are different registers of English. Do you think of it as a white/black text in some ways?

MULLEN: A lot has been said of how American culture is a miscegenated culture, how it is a product of a mixing and mingling of diverse races and cultures and languages, and I would agree with that. I would say that, yes, my text is deliberately a multi-voiced text, a text that tries to express the actual diversity of my own experience living here, exposed to different cultures. *Mongrel* comes from "among." Among others. We are among; we are not alone. We are all mongrels.

BEDIENT: On page 32 of *Muse & Drudge*, you speak of "white covers of black material."

MULLEN: That was a comment on the history of music in this country. What's done by black people and then redone by white people, and white people are the ones who became the millionaires.

BEDIENT: You have another quatrain with white and dark in it: "History written with whitening / darkened reels and jigs / perform a mix of wiggle /

slouch fright and essence of enigma" (45). "Mix of wiggle" is a pretty good description of your book. Do white and dark in that quatrain refer to races?

MULLEN: Literally I was working with a quotation from President Woodrow Wilson about the film *Birth of a Nation*. He said it was history written with lightning. That's often quoted when people are discussing *Birth of a Nation*. People talk about that film's technical genius and then they try to avoid in some discussions the actual racial content of the movie. This whole page is about the movie industry, American films and their depiction of race. The stereotypes we still live with came from the minstrel tradition right into film and have been distributed globally. "Slouch fright" is the depiction of African Americans in Hollywood films, and as for "essence of enigma" I think there is always something in excess of what the Hollywood stereotype intends, and I think that comes because a real person is playing that role. There's also obviously a pun in "enigma"—not only the "n-word" but also a black dance called "essence of Virginia."

BEDIENT: The speaker of this poem has a large stake in self-determination, which, in Lyotard's perhaps too-strong statement in *Just Gaming*, "is the end of tradition." She doesn't want to be submerged in a people, as if the people were a single thing, anyway, to begin with.

MULLEN: A people is many individuals.

BEDIENT: Her concern with self-determination as an individual takes the poetic form of experimentation.

MULLEN: Sure.

BEDIENT: And the form of the poem itself seems to foster, in fact to depend entirely on, self-determination. That is to say, the form is not "inevitable," developmental. A few consecutive quatrains may dwell on the same subject—for example, the movie industry that we were just referring to—but not necessarily in an argumentatively developmental way. The poem as a whole is like repetitive music, in that what matters is the beat, a beat that does not, so to speak, accumulate time. Traditional form recognizes time and development. This form does not rely on memory; yes, the quatrain form is remembered, and that's a kind of automatism, but at the same time continual invention is being asked of you, constant renewals of self-determination, an accumulation of atemporal contents.

MULLEN: I would say the self-determination applies not just to the poet or the voice or voices within the poem but to all the people. All the people have access to means of self-determination.

BEDIENT: As Lyotard says, to every poetics there corresponds a politics.

MULLEN: Also the self or the selves in the poem come from a tradition; there's a recycling of tradition in the making of the self. The making of the voice in the poem is the recycling of tradition. So these things are not independent of each other. One feeds the other. Any time "I" is used in this poem, it's practically always quotation: it comes from a blues song, or it comes from a line of Sappho; it comes from—wherever it comes from. The "I" in the poem is almost always someone other than myself, and often it's an anonymous "I," a generic "I," a traditional "I," the "I" of the blues, that person who in reference to any individual experience also speaks for the tradition, speaks for the community, and the community recognizes the individuality of the speaker and also claims something in common.

BEDIENT: Do you begin the poem with the familiar blues subject of disappointed love in order to establish the relation of the poem to the blues tradition?

MULLEN: Yes.

BEDIENT: The references in the poem to the troubles that women have with men don't seem particularly personal. Do they come from the blues tradition?

MULLEN: They do come from the blues tradition. The poem reflects the full range of that tradition: sexual relationships, but also relationships with community, spirits, tradition, and circumstances in one's life. It's the individual confronting all the circumstances that may open or close down the chances for that person to thrive and develop. I tried to suggest this multiplicity of experience in my book.

There's the blues on the one hand and lyric poetry on the other hand, and where they intersect or overlap. Thinking of this poem as the place where Sappho meets the blues at the crossroads, I imagined Sappho becoming Sapphire and singing the blues. There's that range of possible ways of the self being spoken in the blues and in the lyric. The writing of the poem is influenced by compositional strategies of the blues, because blues verses are actually shuffled and rearranged by the performer, so new blues can be composed on the spot essentially by using different material in different orders. Quatrains can be free standing and shuffled in and out of the work in the way that blues verses are shuffled in and out in any particular performance—that is one way that the echo of the blues enters the structure of the poem.

You were talking about the poem as not having a kind of trajectory or arc of development. I thought about the book, and the quatrain form also, as ways of dealing with ideas about continuity and discontinuity. The quatrain allows a structural continuity in the work, but the thematic texture of the work does not require it to go to any place in particular. It can visit many sites along the way, but there is a kind of texture of recurrence and repetition, things coming back, and variations on things such as hair, head, and hat, and how one thinks and how one dreams. Those are all eventually connected, I believe, simply by virtue of being repeated in different variations.

BEDIENT: Do you have a stake in how the quatrains are ordered?

MULLEN: Because it is a book and because they're written on pages, I had to eventually determine an order. I tried to find in some cases thematic strands that could bind them together, or in some cases I may have written three or four together in one sitting that had some relationship to each other. Also, the form of the book required that I sit down and make a sequence. I might have used another form, you know, there are poets who have used what look like recipe card poems, as Robert Grenier has poems on cards that the reader can shuffle. My poem might have had that kind of form. But because I had to set it in a book, I tried to think about ways that things could go together, so there could be rhythm or flow or some kind of dynamic movement, even though it's not progressive or narrative. I think I just tried to feel, intuit, how the quatrains might be ordered. In some cases, there's a local order that may continue for a page, usually not longer than a page.

BEDIENT: To continue with the "among" aspect of the poem: the poem mixes together certain African American song forms, primarily the blues but also other folk forms, with vanguardism, with what's never been seen or heard on land or sea before. Sensibility research, or something like that, in the form of language. If this is postmodernist work, and in some sense it certainly seems to be that, it's postmodernism with a memory. That was a very important concern for you?

MULLEN: Yes.

BEDIENT: I'm thinking of Donald Davie's probably not very representative view, because it's so British and so conservative, of postmodernism as an eclipse of historical memory and thus problematically similar to consumerism, which doesn't require any fidelity to truth or any other sort of faith. In postmodernism as Davie understands it, value is measured by the stick of experimentation alone, by the distortion inflicted on the materials. But, again, if *Muse & Drudge* is postmodernism, it's postmodernism with a memory.

MULLEN: I think African American tradition has relied more on memory because of the literal proscription on writing during slavery, when the law said one could not learn to read or write. And then the de facto proscription on literacy of going to poorly equipped, substandard schools, in some cases, or simply the fact of one's history being erased or never recorded, one's culture not acknowledged as a culture, so that memory had to take the place in some cases of the recording of information in books. Now that's beginning to change since we have more scholars who are digging for artifacts and historical documents and reconstructing the history that has actually been in the repository of memory and folklore, people passing down stories that could not necessarily be verified. Frederick Douglass talks about how he didn't know when he was born, although actually in a certain sense he did know, because slaves had a different way of thinking about time; it seems that they marked time through a particular event or season, cherry picking season or what have you, but that they didn't really have a date. So that's two different ways of thinking about time, depending on whether one's in an oral culture or a literate culture. Are things recorded or are they remembered? And if you have one, you don't necessarily have to have the other.

I have writing and memory, and I'm trying to use both.

BEDIENT: Right. Are there kinds of hybridity that are important to you in the poem that you'd like to talk about?

MULLEN: I've been concerned about the "amongness" within a black African-based culture. Coming from the South, and coming from a Baptist Christian tradition, a family that had a particular . . . I mean even that is already disrupted, because we're Southern and northern at the same time and so certain things I thought of as being traditionally black because that was the example of my community, my family didn't necessarily do all those things, because they came from another region and spoke the language differently and had different customs and so forth; so there's already this kind of disruption in the notion of a black identity or a black subject. This book is partly trying to enlarge what the black culture or the black tradition might be. So there's that sense of black people having various cultural references and different languages that are spoken and different geographical regions and different communities, different religious practices. I think the sixties were about constructing a unified, almost monolithic black culture and I think that we're now more engaged in seeing the differences within, and that leads to multiple cultural references that are part of the input.

BEDIENT: From what you've said already about a few of the quatrains, I take it that the poem is extremely dense with allusions to a great many things. Probably every quatrain has several allusions in it.

MULLEN: Yes.

BEDIENT: Does it matter to you whether or not these allusions are detected by many readers?

MULLEN: I know they won't be detected by many readers. Some readers will get some, and other readers will get others, and that's fine; that's as it probably should be.

BEDIENT: Why is the allusive method important to you?

MULLEN: It's important to me because I wanted the poem to be interesting and complex, as I think experience is, language is; language has that capacity. I was interested in concentrating, distilling, and condensing aspects of orality and literacy. Because when you have an oral tradition and you also have writing, you don't have to put the oral tradition on the page as transcription. I think that maybe in Sterling Brown, Langston Hughes, Dunbar, there's a way in which the oral tradition is—though this is not completely true, because there's obviously transformation in what they're doing—but they're closer to a practice of transcribing the oral onto the page. I am more interested in a transformation of the oral into something that draws together different allusive possibilities in one utterance, which is something that writing can do better than speech. I'm interested in taking a speech-based tradition and transforming it through the techniques that are available to me in writing.

BEDIENT: Ultimately in the interest of self-determination, or perhaps of making the history of culture useful to you and present to you?

MULLEN: Primarily in the interest of making the poetry swing and also of making it richly allusive and complicated. But also, yes, those things that you mentioned. I want to push my work, and those are ways that I have found to push it beyond transcription, beyond the mimetic reproduction of speech or the oral tradition. I'm trying to transform the materials of orality into text and into a very dense and complexly allusive writing practice. You can also heighten paradox and contradiction when you compress together things that come from very different registers or different lexicons; they jostle each other so there's more tension. Yet there's more elasticity in the utterance.

BEDIENT: And so the result is complexity, density, and a sort of freedom, "rumba with the chains removed" (9). You don't want to be held hostage by any tradition.

MULLEN: [Laughter] You got me.

BEDIENT: My temptation as a reader ignorant of much that you're alluding to is to see a great many of the lines as self-reflexive, as providing tags or metaphors that describe the work itself and the aim of the work.

MULLEN: Yes.

BEDIENT: So that when I read "If I had my rage / I'd tear the blueprint up" (13), I want to read that as a hyperbolic statement of Harryette Mullen's relation to traditional form or to any sort of enchaining order.

MULLEN: That, by the way, is from a very traditional song about Samson in the Old Testament: "If I had my way I'd tear this building down."

BEDIENT: It's extraordinary how dense this poem is with allusion. The line "hum some blues in technicolor" (14) on the next page again seems self-descriptive.

MULLEN: Yes.

BEDIENT: But some of the lines I took as self-descriptions, lines you've already commented on, turn out to be about something else, such as those on the movie industry. So I see the need to be cautious about such lines as "write on the vagina / of virgin lamb paper," if not of "hand-me-down dance of ample / style stance and substance" (40) or "not her hard life / cramped hot stages / only her approach / ahead of the beat" (20). Some of the possible self-descriptions seem slightly off, mostly hyperbolically so, so that a kind of bracketing of the poem's actual activity is going on, like "soulless divaism" (15), for instance. To go back to Donald Davie's antagonistic stance toward postmodernism: one of his complaints was that postmodern work—he is thinking of John Ashbery, for example, and the English poet Jeremy Prynne—is that it is unfeeling. One of the things that he meant by that is that it's not concerned with great, intense moments and crises in life. I think it's fair to say that he meant, in part, the familiar pathos that we think of as deep and serious and tragic. Your work seems to me essentially sassy and jubilant. That has a political implication.

MULLEN: "We shall overcome."

BEDIENT: But I don't see it as unfeeling.

MULLEN: Feeling is important. It's a human quality that I value. But the construction of subjectivity is problematical these days and I reflect the problematics of my own subjectivity in this work.

BEDIENT: Some of the quatrains refer to conflict between men and women. A few of them seem to imply that your poetics is a woman's poetics. Once or twice you seem to be challenging the men who write poetry. What do you see as womanly or feminine about the method itself? Or is that the way you look at it?

MULLEN: I'm not sure that that's how I look at it. I know that some of the poets that have been meaningful to me, inspirational, have been male as well as female poets. I was a student of Nate Mackey; he was on my dissertation committee at UC Santa Cruz. Gwendolyn Brooks and Lorenzo Thomas have been important to my work. I don't know that I'm setting up a specifically female or feminine poetics. I think that there's a feminine or feminist content throughout the work. There's a feminist attitude, let's say.

BEDIENT: There's attitude. It's a little rocky. I think you're alluding to it in "you have the girl you paid for / now lie on her / rocky garden" (22).

MULLEN: Yes.

BEDIENT: And "on her own jive / player and instrument / all the way live / the way a woman might use it" (22).

MULLEN: Yes.

BEDIENT: So that there's an uppity, sassy edge to a lot of the tone and in some of the content.

MULLEN: Yes. I was thinking about this poem in terms of musical tradition, blues and jazz, and women's voices have been very important in blues and jazz. It's been interesting because the female vocal singer has been more important than the female instrumentalist. This connects with the poem; for instance, in the beginning there's "Sapphire's lyre" and then "styles / plucked eyebrows," so that there's an association of the woman's body with her instrument. Then at the end there's something about who she's playing for. The woman's body is her instrument; in the jazz tradition, at least, the instrument she's playing is her own voice, so there the woman's voice is very important and women are very important in the construction of the blues. You know the old blues man said, "If it weren't for women we wouldn't have the blues." When the blues get transformed into jazz, the woman's contribution is limited to the vocal. You could say limited in one way, that she's a human element in the mix of instruments; but there's a good deal of anthropomorphizing of instruments that goes on in jazz tradition, too. Nate Mackey's work exploits the trope. His fictional jazz combo includes two female musicians, but they need to find a drummer and end up searching for a woman drummer. However, in certain African traditions women were not supposed to touch drums. So there's a reflection on these traditions in which women's voices are important but their musical expression is also limited in certain respects, where men are given instruments that women are not supposed to play.

BEDIENT: The first quatrain identifies the female artist with her body and with her sexiness, and there are many references in the poem to female sexiness—sexiness and sexuality. For example, on the second page: "that snapping turtle pussy / won't let go until thunder comes." Is that an allusion to a particular blues lyric?

MULLEN: I have heard people talk about this as a legendary aspect of women. I've been interested in mythic constructions of the sexual prowess of males and females. It comes from outside and inside black tradition. People brag about their conquests or their abilities in blues songs; the men and the women do this. In rap also. Then there's the kind of stereotyping of black people as sexual entities without maybe anything else added to that. I wouldn't want to erase the sexual in order to emphasize other aspects, but only to add more to the picture.

BEDIENT: Is there, in your view, a sort of governing or running personality in the poem, if not exactly a persona—at least a set of attitudes that advertise the "self-made woman," to quote your phrase from page 36? And if that's true, then is a certain sexual confidence and even come-on quality part of this personality, this aesthetic personality—this sort of collective spirit of the attitudes? Just the very mention of sex is sexy, to be sure; but does the theme of the sexy woman in the poem make a feminist statement?

MULLEN: Partly what the poem is doing is reclaiming the black woman's body, so that the body is hers, something that she can enjoy, because so many people have tried to define and limit and imprison her body and her sexuality. The idea is that she can be in charge: she can play her own instrument, and she can play the tune that she wants on the instrument.

BEDIENT: Yes, she's "the essence lady" in "her irregular uniform, . . . syncopation suit" (35).

And she can say: "ain't your fancy / handsome gal / feets too big / my hair don't twirl" (38).

MULLEN: And even that "virgin lamb paper" refers to an actual magical practice. I believe that virgin lamb paper is (or was) made from the tender parts of lambs and is used in certain voodoo spells that require writing people's names on parchment.

BEDIENT: So it's dangerous tender skin. Do the lines "some fat on that rack / might make her more tasty" (41) have for you a self-reflexive quality? Do they refer to the rather spare quatrain form that you use?

MULLEN: Well, there's the epigraph from Callimachus at the beginning of the poem: "Fatten your animal for sacrifice, poet, / but keep your muse slender." He's suggesting something about the economy of poetry.

BEDIENT: Yes, "sue for slender" (8).

MULLEN: Then there's the body image of black women. Some surveys suggest that young black women have a better body image and better self-image than white women of the same age. They're less likely to be anorexic and more likely to see their own relatives as models of beauty as opposed to some model in a magazine or some actress on television. These attitudes are very healthy, and I think that we're in danger of losing that kind of self-esteem as people become more involved with the dominant culture and its images. But traditionally in black culture a woman with meat on her bones appears in a lot of blues songs. You know, "Every time I shake some skinny gal loses her home."

BEDIENT: "Built for comfort, not for speed."

MULLEN: Exactly. That quatrain refers to some of that as well as to Callimachus. There's a range of representations from the diva to the debased woman—the muse, the drudge. Those are the polarities. Those are the extreme oppositions that we see in representations of black women in the media. Either the fabulous diva or the mother using crack, the prostitute. The super-skinny black model versus Aunt Jemima. I was interested in more of a continuum, filling in or troubling those kinds of oppositional constructions of black women.

BEDIENT: To bring it back to the poem as a way of proceeding, a way of sounding. Your muse is slender. The poem doesn't have drudgery in it; obviously, you've concealed any drudgery that went into the composition of it. So, there isn't a lot of meat on the bones, or what meat is there is terribly compounded. Do you see the quatrain as a cut-back blues form?

MULLEN: There is a relationship that I saw between the quatrain form and the blues form, and forms that are part of the folk tradition that are familiar and accessible. Some of those quatrains are actually couplets that are broken up and some of them may be actual lines from blues, without the kind of repetition that one finds in blues.

BEDIENT: With some rhyme to nail things down. Tack things down, because of course the whole poem moves forward ripping up whatever has been put down before. So the quatrain form, as such, with its compression, is very close to the classical epigram.

MULLEN: Yes.

BEDIENT: It's traditional in that way. I mean what could be more traditional than a quatrain that has some rhyme in it?

MULLEN: Yes. A lot of folk poetry is in the form of couplets or quatrains.

BEDIENT: It's the discontinuousness among the stanzas that feels modernist or postmodernist. Even within them: often the third line begins a new thought.

MULLEN: And there are quatrains that are actually lists.

BEDIENT: Yes. Some are lists, some are phonemic games, like the one on Isis.

MULLEN: Yes, "divine sunrises / Osiris's irises / his splendid mistress / is his sis Isis" (64).

BEDIENT: So there's quite a diversity in the poem, ranging from stanzas that seem to be sort of gaming on sound, or "prattle," in Barthes's sense in *The Pleasure of the Text,* or the text as bliss . . .

MULLEN: Scat singing.

BEDIENT: . . . to stanzas that really are commentaries, that make discursive statements about things.

MULLEN: Yes, in some cases, they participate in a commentary.

BEDIENT: A complicated, allusive commentary. You may be referring to your own method when you speak of "occult iconic crows." Does the line "add some practice to your theory" refer to postmodernist theory as against the practice that you yourself are performing?

MULLEN: It might, it could, definitely. In the political sense, we think of theory as not existing for its own sake but as a way of thinking toward action and how we actually exist in the world after we've thought about things. Thinking should change that.

BEDIENT: The line "recite the fatal bet," which obviously puns on "alphabet," represents your rejection of fatality through free play, though it's not exactly free—there are certain rules that you're observing. I'm thinking of Lyotard's idea that the postmodern artist presents difficulties because she resorts to ruse; that's to say, she has to make up the rules as she goes along, and her audience has to catch up. You do use the word "ruse" . . .

MULLEN: "ruses of the lunatic muse" (21).

BEDIENT: I don't know whether you were thinking of Lyotard or not, but there are certain rules, most obviously the constant use of the quatrain. What comes to be an expectable discontinuity is another one. There's perhaps a rule of allusion, which is present in virtually every quatrain, perhaps in every quatrain.

MULLEN: Right. Also a hybrid blending of diverse resources in a single quatrain. Allusions to different spheres of knowledge in a single quatrain, in some cases. You've mentioned the linguistic play that goes on in some of the quatrains; some of them are more playful, while others are more commentary-like. There's movement back and forth between play and commentary or observation or more straightforward response to current events, news.

BEDIENT: The movement is random but it becomes expectable—one of the looser rules.

MULLEN: Change is one of the rules.

BEDIENT: Do you allude to Stephen Hawking in "Hawkins was talking / while I kept on walking" (53)? The scientist?

MULLEN: Oh, that's interesting.

BEDIENT: "stepping back on my abstract" sounds like relativity theory or something. I'm sorry about that.

MULLEN: No, I like what you're saying, but actually, in that case, that's not what I was thinking. "Hawkins" is the wind; in Chicago they refer to "the hawk." There's a play in those four quatrains on birds, on the names of birds. I think it just became a riff on birds. But "standing in my tracks / stepping back on my abstract" is an exact verbatim quotation from Zora Neale Hurston's *Mules and Men*. So that's directly taken from the folk tradition.

BEDIENT: Like Joyce you'll have the scholars working for umpteen years: "park your quark in a hard aardvark" across the page (52) catches my eye.

MULLEN: Those four quatrains are all about my mother.

BEDIENT: Ah, "tomboy girl with cowboy boots." Is she somehow the quark in the hard aardvark?

MULLEN: That refers to her diction. She loved the Boston accent; she loved the Kennedys partly because of their Boston accent. So "park the car in Harvard yard" is a homophone.

BEDIENT: Is there a lot of homophonic play in the book?

MULLEN: There are quite a few of those, like "stark strangled banjo" (18).

BEDIENT: Do you see that as a metaphor for your poem?

MULLEN: Oh, yeah. That allows some readers to hear two lines at once, so that's a form of compression. When you can hear two lines at once, that contributes to the density of the poem and the possible meanings of the poem. You can hear "star spangled banner" and "stark strangled banjo" at the same time, and you can think about the relationship between the two of them. And park your car in Harvard yard, which is one of those elocution lessons such as Eliza Doolittle had to practice, has to do with my mother being a teacher and correcting our diction. We sounded dicty so we were said to be proper speakers of English and sometimes insulted because of that. And then "park your quark" has to do with my mother's energy. My mother has amazing energy; she's a middle-class schoolteacher who could have been who knows what? But that's what she was allowed to be. The "hard aardvark" is just an allusion to the armadillo. It's about my Mom being in Texas and becoming (for her Pennsylvania cousins) a kind of cowgirl.

BEDIENT: Going back to your relation to various traditions, primarily literary and ethnic: there are several references in the poem to restoring and curing. Do you see your effort as in some way an attempt to be restorative, curative? Or are these not self-reflexive at all?

MULLEN: Well, they might be. I'm not the first to associate the poet with the conjurer or the root worker. There are community healers traditionally who helped people come to terms with their experience, and I think that's what I'm doing as a writer: I'm coming to terms with my own experience and, if I do it well, then perhaps it can serve a somewhat similar function for other people.

BEDIENT: Lyotard further says ruse becomes the artist's primary activity in work that has no assigned addressee. Modern literature addressed the people or the folk, he said—modernist literature is evidently not what he had in mind!—but postmodern work, again, has no assigned addressee. The last line of your poem refers to the addressee, "what stray companion" (80). The word "stray" suggests that you as a poet have no certain idea of who your addressee is.

MULLEN: That's true.

BEDIENT: Is your addressee anyone who's interested in poetry that pushes the limits of what's already been done?

MULLEN: That would be one of the possible addressees. But I wrote this book to bring the various readers of my work together. In the work that I have done, the three books that preceded this one, *Tree Tall Woman* had probably a larger black audience than *Trimmings* and *S*PeRM**K*T* had, and this book was my attempt to continue the innovative technique that emerged in the writing of *Trimmings* and *S*PeRM**K*T,* and to use a recognizable cultural content, while at the same time expanding that beyond a fairly simple or reductive notion of what black culture is. I was trying to make a text that did address various audiences, and so the various registers and different lexicons and different allusive potentials had to do with that diverse audience that I want as my readers. So I address black audiences and audiences that are not black as well. I hope that different people reading this book will respond to something in it. I'm not always able to predict what one reader or another will comprehend and respond to, but I tried to put lots of different things in there for people to respond to or recognize. So for me the audience is made by the text.

BEDIENT: Did you think about including notes to the poem? Even though they might require as many pages as the poem itself?

MULLEN: No, I didn't think about that. I thought that the music of the poem would carry any reader through the poem. And whether they understood every line or not is not really essential to me. I want them to hear it as poetry; I want them to get flashes and glimpses of recognition that come from their own experience and connect with parts of the poem that are familiar. One reader said it sounded like listening to old people who talk in cryptic ways, and then when you ask them to explain they just repeat what they said before. There are certain traditional forms such as riddles and proverbs that are compressed and cryptic. I'm interested in aspects of the oral tradition that are enigmatic and cryptic formulations, open to various interpretations.

BEDIENT: After the phrase "hand-held interview," you have the "steady voice over view" (59). That's not really a concern of yours in the poem, is it, the steady voice over view or overview? There's no outside to the poem where you could stand and photograph the whole poem, in a sense.

MULLEN: Right. There's mobility, rather than a fixed position.

BEDIENT: There's a great deal of mobility. There's no scheme; it's not a planet on the table; it improvises and metamorphoses.

MULLEN: It grows like Topsy.

BEDIENT: You have a reference to Topsy in connection with Liberia: "today's dread would awe / Topsy undead her missionary / exposition in what Liberia / could she find freedom to study her story" (45). Will you comment on that?

MULLEN: There's a pun on library and Liberia, which means freedom. The former slaves that went to Liberia established basically an oligarchy there, and the violence that's occurring in Liberia now has to do with the reaction of the people who are not the Americo-Liberians, the former slaves who were a colonial presence in Liberia. The former slaves oppressed the people who were there. Now, it's completely deteriorated; who knows what they're fighting about now? So partly the quatrain is a comment on Liberia today, which is far from the promise that it meant for someone going there in the 19th century, for someone like Topsy in *Uncle Tom's Cabin* to be sent there.

BEDIENT: Was Topsy a believer in religious mojo? I'm thinking of the quatrain, "Joe Moore never / worked for me—oh moaner / you shall be free / by degrees and pedigrees" (58). That's a serious political statement, isn't it? It's a belief that freedom will come by degrees?

MULLEN: That's what we've always been told. I heard someone on the radio saying recently: "Well, you know, people are always going to want more freedom and if they just wait long enough, they'll get it." But I kept thinking as I listened, "Doesn't this person know African Americans have been here as long as any pilgrim or immigrant?" Black people were with Columbus. Van Sertima says Africans beat Columbus to the New World.

BEDIENT: So this is not your credo that you're stating.

MULLEN: No, I think that freedom should be what everyone has simply at birth, simply because you're human. But there's the notion that some people are not ready to be free. The freedom that we do have has come by degrees and pedigrees. And education obviously comes with degrees.

BEDIENT: Is the "I" of the poem never Harryette Mullen?

MULLEN: I won't say that, exactly. There are places in the poem that are very personal to me, that really have to do with my own particular experience. Even then, I can abstract from it and make it generic, so it actually fits into a blues conception of the individual, a subject that speaks but not simply as oneself.

BEDIENT: "massa had a yeller / macaroon a fetter / in his claptrap"—I do get the allusion there, but "of couth that shrub rat" (58)?

MULLEN: That's an anagram: "that touch of tar brush," with "that" and "of" remaining unchanged.

BEDIENT: Can you explain why certain words and images became motifs in your poem, the word *hat*, for instance, which you're playfully skirting here—"a feather in his cap"?

MULLEN: They were things that kept coming up, and eventually I decided that they were meaningful and began to think about how they were connected. The references to hair, to heads, to hats, to umbrellas, which unite the head and the sky, are all connected; all have to do with consciousness, and also have to do with one's notion of self, because from what I've read, there's a widespread Afro disaporic tradition of adornment of the hair and the head. The head is seen as the location of one's subjectivity and one's uniqueness as an individual. The umbrella is the extension of the head. The royal umbrella or parasol that's used for the king, usually held by someone else over the head of the king—and in Dahomey the elaborately embroidered umbrellas of appliqué designs. I also think of certain images of black women with umbrellas, with hats and parasols going to church. In Julie Dash's film *Daughters of the Dust* there are very evocative images of black women wearing hats and carrying parasols. So they're just recurrent images that to me are evocative of the self, of black women's, black people's sense of ourselves.

BEDIENT: "Dick's hatband" (66)—is that a reference to the male sexual organ?

MULLEN: That was actually a surprise to me as I was writing this. I didn't realize that this expression that I've heard forever from my mother and my grandmother, "tighter than Dick's hat band," alludes to a condom. As soon as I wrote it, I realized that.

BEDIENT: You refer to a scarecrow a number of times in the book. Do you have a particular sense of how that figure fits in?

MULLEN: There's the scarecrow and the crow. There's the iconic crow that flies out to the other side of far, a phrase from *Mules and Men*. That I associated with the avant-garde or innovative aspects of the work, which I also associate with jazz musicians, people like Thelonious Monk as a kind of "iconic crow" (40). And also as "solo mysterioso" (40). "Mysterious," according to Clarence Major [*Juba to Jive: A Dictionary of African-American Slang*], refers to the avant-garde musical tradition, something that's way out. The terms "in the tradition" and "mysterious" have a relationship to each other: the things that are familiar and comprehensible within the notion of what the black tradition is and the "mysterious," which is outside of that or which pushes the boundaries of that. So the crow for me is mystery flying out. The scarecrow is staked to the ground. The scarecrow is there to scare away the crow, but the crow is really not scared of the scarecrow. The bird sits on top of scarecrow's head a while. Then flies out.

BEDIENT: Do you play with the image of mules in your poem because of *Mules and Men,* a title re-echoed, in a warped way, in the title *Muse & Drudge*?

MULLEN: Yes. Who are the mules and who are the men? If you think about black and white, then the black people are the mules and the white people are men. If you think about the black community, then the women are the mules and the men are the men. In *Their Eyes Were Watching God*, the grandmother says the black woman is the mule of the world. I changed that to muse of the world.

BEDIENT: And "mules and drugs" (74)?

MULLEN: That refers very literally to the frisking and strip-searching of black women in airports, because they're supposed to fit the profile of the drug courier, or mule. I've talked to black women who've had terrible humiliating experiences. To themselves, they look like executives carrying briefcases, but to someone in the airport they look like the profile of the drug courier.

BEDIENT: Which question would you like to have asked about your book?

MULLEN: I don't know, I guess one of the things that has been a concern for me about this work is the matter of reception and comprehension. I say, in a confident manner, that I think the poetry carries the reader along. But I am concerned about audience reception and the dense allusiveness. One of the texts that has been inspiring to me is the work of Melvin Tolson, *The Harlem Gallery*. Tolson is seen as a belated and derivative modernist by some people, because he comes after Pound and Eliot and so forth, and he seemed to be responding to them and wanting to make his work reflect what they were doing in poetry. He saw possibilities that he hadn't thought about before, so he went about very systematically changing how he wrote and making it allusive and very complex. And one of the results is that Tolson's work is not being taught or read very much. So one of the questions or problems for me is the kind of aesthetic turf that exists for black writers, and how black writers who do not fit into the notion of what black turf is can sometimes be overlooked or forgotten or go unread, because people require interpretive strategies related to their notion of the black canon, or what it means to be outside of the black canon. There are certain examples, like Bob Kaufman, Melvin Tolson, or LeRoi Jones (before he became Baraka) or Stephen Jonas. Robert Hayden, even. Robert Hayden usually does get included in anthologies, but people sometimes talk about Robert Hayden as being in some sense on the edge of a black tradition, because the black tradition is being constructed as based in orality, and as concerned with a black subjectivity in language that is speech-like. Some of my concerns about my work have to do with a fear of writing myself out of the tradition, which I don't intend to do. There are cautionary figures. I think that Baraka saw that possibility and averted it. Gwendolyn Brooks changed the way she wrote in response to the

Black Arts, Black Aesthetic Movement. I don't want the oral tradition to be a prescription. I mean I have access to it and I think it's a rich reservoir of possibility, but also the written tradition is a rich reservoir of possibility. I feel myself wanting, especially in this poem, to use both possibilities. I think that other people do that as well, but sometimes the discussion suggests that one is producing either a writerly text or a speakerly text. We have the possibility of speaking and writing informing the text. And that's what I'm trying to do.

BEDIENT: Maybe that's the work of your generation. Movements do have their necessity and natural life span and then something else has to come along. Speaking of new developments, did you once say to me that you think of your poem as being like hypertext?

MULLEN: Hypertext, as I understand it, and I'm technologically behind, allows the shuffling of virtual pages or cards; the computer does that. In some respects I could use hypertext as a metaphor for the way shuffling is going on within the poem, the shuffling of sources or phrases or different fragments from the literary and oral traditions and from media as well.

BEDIENT: When you use the word "shuffle" in the text, are you thinking along those lines?

MULLEN: Oh, yeah, but there's always at least some punning going on with "shuffling," because it's not a neutral term when you're talking about images of black people. And shuffling also has to do with some of the dances that were done by slaves in coffles: "rumba with the chains removed" is a literal reference to a dance that was done by slaves in coffles. Slaves wearing shackles. Rumba comes from that initial constraint on the movement of the body.

So I've been thinking about hypertext virtual shuffling as a technological metaphor for how I've written the poem. I've thought about it more, I guess, because of recent work in a feminist collaborative art project, connecting our different contributions with hot spots that you can point and click on when you have a particular page, and that page sends you to another page, to a layering of pages; I've been thinking about allusion as a hot spot, the allusion leading you to another page and another page. Before we had the computer, we had scholarly ways of digesting texts, to take various materials and work them over, footnotes, and ways of moving around within a text. I think that I'm similarly trying to compress information in these quatrains. I think of the quatrains as being playful and poetic, but I also think of them as containing bits of information. If readers spent time, there is information about Afro-diasporic culture that is collected in these fragments. Each one of the fragments could lead you into another area of study. All of these things come from my own study and my own reading, as well as other kinds of experience.

When I was studying at the University of Texas, Roger Abrahams was the white folklorist there who taught Afro-American folklore, and I was in his class, the one black person in the room. When he asked me what HNIC is, I had no idea what he was talking about, and I thought "Oh gosh, does this mean I am not an authentic black person?" I think that if I hadn't been in the room, he wouldn't have had to ask me to say what HNIC is. It means "head nigger in charge." We didn't tend to use the n-word in our household, and I'd never heard this expression; but I thought "Oh, this is a piece of Afro Americana that I should know." He eventually wrote it up on the board so that he still would not have to say the n-word aloud. It was a crisis for me. Here I am, the one black person in the room, in the Afro-American folklore class being taught by the white male authority figure, who then selects me as a native informant and I'm unable to perform as a native informant, because I had to be in the class in the first place to learn what my oral tradition is. Parts of that oral tradition were not accessible to me, coming from where I came from and being in a very religious household. There were aspects of the blues that I never got until I was an adult, because that was considered basically gutbucket, lowdown music in our household. We heard a lot of religious music. I collected my culture from books, from media, and to a certain extent from an actual oral tradition that I do participate in, but there were things missing that I have since gathered and collected. So I think of hypertext as virtual index cards. When you asked "How do you know all this stuff?" it's because I've been searching. We feel incomplete, and we search to make ourselves, our knowledge, more complete. I have been collecting these virtual index cards for a long time. Not wanting to be that person who does not know her own culture and must learn it from the white male authority figure, although I figure that once I get it, it's mine, regardless of how I got it. This poem is a performance of that knowledge. It's a very hard-won knowledge that I treasure, because I did not want to be ignorant of my culture.

20

An Interview with Harryette Mullen
by Daniel Kane

Harryette Mullen was born in Florence, Alabama, and raised in Fort Worth, Texas. A city with a rich musical tradition, Fort Worth was home to W. C. Handy, self-proclaimed "father of the blues"; Townes Van Zandt; Willie "Prince" Lasha (whose daughters lived across the street from the Mullens); and noted free-jazz innovator Ornette Coleman (Coleman's music, like Mullen's poetry, often suggests or quotes from childhood nursery songs and playground rhymes.) Mullen's love of words was instilled at a very early age by reading family copies of the Bible, an unabridged *Webster's Dictionary, Roget's Thesaurus, The Complete Works of Shakespeare,* and the *World Book Encyclopedia.* One of her favorite memories is sitting on her grandfather's lap while he read nursery rhymes from a large illustrated Mother Goose. "In some mysterious way," Mullen says, "all of this has something to do with my growing up to be a poet." She has worn many hats: waiting tables in a bar, typing itemized bills in a law office, working as a receptionist at Goodwill, taking orders at a Jack-in-the-Box, sweeping the floor of a florist shop, and assisting a grouchy caterer. Most of Mullen's professional career, however, has been in the field of teaching and writing. Mullen received a B.A. in English from the University of Texas and a Ph.D. from the University of California, Santa Cruz. She is currently a professor of English and African American Studies at the University of California, Los Angeles.

Mullen's poetry draws upon "popular" culture—pop music, cartoons, and children's games. In Mullen's case, the earliest poems and lyrics that influenced her were *Mother Goose,* jump rope rhymes, and "the dozens." Mullen's childhood was also enlivened by church hymns, R&B and pop songs on the radio, Gilbert and Sullivan operettas, folk songs, Gershwin's *Porgy and Bess,* and jazz divas Sarah Vaughan and Nancy Wilson. One can find echoes of, allusions to, and quotations from these sources—along with church, folk, and blues music by Odetta, Leadbelly, Pete Seeger, and music anthologized on the Alan Lomax folklore recordings—throughout Mullen's work. Mullen also recalls the importance of memorizing Langston Hughes's "Mother to Son" and James Weldon Johnson's "The Creation."

Mullen's volumes of poetry include *Sleeping with the Dictionary* (University of California Press, 2002), *Muse & Drudge* (Singing Horse, 1995), *S*PeRM**K*T* (Singing Horse, 1992), and *Trimmings* (Tender Buttons, 1991). The first book I read of Mullen's was *S*PeRM**K*T*—the fragmented, hilarious, intellectual, and moving references to contemporary consumer culture were absolutely fascinating to me. *Muse & Drudge* might be a good place to start as well, since the meter is clearly indebted to hip hop rhythms. To find out about *Sleeping with the Dictionary* read our interview!

Dim Lady
My honeybunch's peepers are nothing like neon. Today's special at Red Lobster is redder than her kisser. If Liquid Paper is white, her racks are institutional beige. If her mop were Slinkys, dishwater Slinkys would grow on her noggin. I have seen table-cloths in Shakey's Pizza Parlors, red and white, but no such picnic colors do I see in her mug. And in some minty-fresh mouthwashes there is more sweetness than in the garlic breeze my main squeeze wheezes. I love to hear her rap, yet I'm aware that Muzak has a hipper beat. I don't know any Marilyn Monroes. My ball and chain is plain from head to toe. And yet, by gosh, my scrumptious Twinkie has as much sex appeal for me as any lanky model or platinum movie idol who's hyped beyond belief.

Variations on a Theme Park
My Mickey Mouse ears are nothing like sonar. Colorado is far less rusty than Walt's lyric riddles. If sorrow is wintergreen, well then Walt's breakdancers are dunderheads. If hoecakes are Wonder Bras, blond Wonder Bras grow on Walt's hornytoad. I have seen roadkill damaged, riddled and wintergreen, but no such roadkill see I in Walt's checkbook. And in some purchases there is more deliberation than in the bargains that my Mickey Mouse redeems. I love to herd Walt's sheep, yet well I know that muskrats have a far more platonic sonogram. I grant I never saw a googolplex groan. My Mickey Mouse, when Walt waddles, trips on garbanzos. And yet, by halogen-light, I think my loneliness as reckless as any souvenir bought with free coupons.

Daniel Kane: My college students, who are generally not versed in avant-gardist work, really "got" your book *Muse & Drudge*—maybe due to the fact that it seems influenced by hip hop, has an abundance of popular and race-specific references, and consistently rhymes! Could you talk about what influenced the book?

Harryette Mullen: As much as I claim Jean Toomer, Langston Hughes, Gwendolyn Brooks, Melvin Tolson, Bob Kaufman, Margaret Walker, and the poets of the Black Arts movement as literary ancestors, Language-oriented poets are important influences on my work, from the paratactic prose poetry of my books *Trimmings* and *S*PeRM**K*T* to my desire, in *Muse & Drudge,* to write a poem that encourages collaborative reading across cultural boundaries. I might add that my connection to the Language poets of the Bay Area was through Nathaniel Mackey and Gloria Watkins, and my link to the poetry of the New York School, Umbra, and Black Arts movement was through Lorenzo Thomas.

Muse & Drudge, like Toni Morrison's *Jazz* with its multiple narrators, employs not one but a chorus of possible "speakers" or "singers." They include, among others, lyric poet Sappho and blues singer Bessie Smith. Having considered the mnemonic force of jingles in *S*PeRM**K*T* I also wanted to suggest, with *Muse & Drudge,* that rhyme is too powerful a tool to be abandoned to advertising, greeting cards, or even platinum rap recordings. I hoped to reclaim it. It's interesting that you say *Muse & Drudge* is more accessible. I think that my other books are easier to follow in that they are more coherently organized texts. But the apparently orderly verse form and recurrent tropes of *Muse & Drudge* allow readers to experience it as extended lyric. It has a musical quality that attracted the attention of two composers, T. J. Anderson and Christine Baczewska, who have set parts of *Muse & Drudge* to music.

DK: How important are considerations of race in your writing?

HM: For me, race, class, and gender have been significant issues, but of course they are not the whole of identity, and certainly they are not the sum of my poetry—or of anyone's poetry, for that matter. I can be a black woman while chewing gum and thinking about Disneyland or supermarkets, while reading Stein or Shakespeare, just as I can be a black woman contemplating conventional representations of black women in literature, media, and popular culture. Living in California, where white people are a minority, I'm not so sure that my identity or experience is "marginal." As a woman and as a person of color, I belong to two global majorities, but I'm also aware that throughout most of history, it is not the majority that rules but a privileged minority.

DK: So does identity inform your poetics as much as what might be considered more traditionally formal concerns?

HM: Whatever the content of the poem, identity (not just my own) is as much an aspect of the work as a concern with language, poetics, and form. I think this is evident in all of my work, whether I was consciously constructing a "black voice" or "black literary style" in my first book, *Tree Tall Woman;* writing "the new sentence" in *Trimmings* and *S*PeRM**K*T;* experimenting with "kinky quatrains" in *Muse & Drudge;* or playing Oulipo word games with my *American Heritage* in my latest book, *Sleeping with the Dictionary.* My focus on the clash of feminism with fashion in *Trimmings* and my take on advertising and consumption in *S*PeRM**K*T* were also informed by my perspective as a black woman, and so was my approach to the politics of language and dialect in *Sleeping with the Dictionary.* We often reduce and simplify black expressive traditions, and we must acknowledge the diversity and hybridity of those traditions. I agree with the critic Margo Jefferson when she says, regarding the creation of jazz, "race is not just a series of obstacles, but also a set of possibilities."

DK: Could you discuss your use of word games and Oulipo-inspired procedures in *Sleeping with the Dictionary?* Are these kinds of language games a way of undermining identity and associating oneself with a kind of cosmopolitanism as opposed to a regionalist voice?

HM: Well, I thought I was working "beyond category" (as Ellington said of his compositions that mix jazz and classical influences) in my earlier books. A few of the poems in *Sleeping with the Dictionary* are older than *Muse & Drudge.* As language and identity come together in the work, a concern with collective experience and cultural representation may be more evident in some poems, while wordplay and poetic experiment are more conspicuous in others. I don't know if I'm undermining identity so much as continually rewriting and revising it.

What attracts me to the Oulipo writers, besides their sense of humor, is their systematic effort to demystify the poetic process. In their practice, writing is a pleasurable game that may result in works of "potential literature." Their research reveals that devices we associate with the work of avant-garde or experimental writers are also found in ancient texts, and even in oral forms such as riddles and jokes.

DK: Could you name a couple of these games?

HM: Many quatrains in *Muse & Drudge* began with double entendres, puns, and other polysemic wordplay. Sometimes familiar material is transformed by linguistic scrambling or various kinds of cryptographic writing. In *Sleeping with the Dictionary,* I'm playing with anagrams, palindromes, homophones, and other devices favored by Oulipo. (By the way, I've published critical articles about Sandra Cisneros's cryptographic writing in *Woman Hollering Creek* and the brain-teasing puns in *Oreo,* by Fran Ross.)

DK: When you talk about Oulipo as demystifying the poetic process, I'm interested in your attention to audience, as "demystifying" suggests greater accessibility. Who was your audience in *Muse & Drudge*?

HM: The audience, as always, is any interested reader. But of all my books since *Tree Tall Woman, Muse & Drudge* has the clearest Afrocentric vision. It was in part a response to extreme representations of black women in the media as welfare queens, drug addicts, and skanky prostitutes on the one hand, or as fabulous divas and fashion supermodels on the other. In retrospect, that onslaught of bipolar media images now seems to have been coordinated with the war on drugs, the growth of the prison industrial system, and attacks on affirmative action, welfare, and proposals for universal health care throughout the 1980s and early 1990s. *Trimmings* and *S*PeRM**K*T* are in dialogue with the modernism of Gertrude Stein, whose work influenced Richard Wright and was known to writers of the Harlem Renaissance through their mutual friend Carl Van Vechten.

My sources for *Muse & Drudge* were traditional or familiar materials from African American culture, popular culture, and mass media, but in most cases I sampled and altered the material through some kind of textual device. In composing the quatrains, usually I'd improvise on some fragment of "blacklore":

> tom-tom can't catch a green cabin
> ginger hebben as
> ancestor dances in Ashanti

Sometimes the improvisations are punning riffs on sound, leaning toward a kind of jazzy scat or hip hop style:

> divine sunrises Osiris's irises
> his splendid mistress
> is his sis Isis

In one quatrain, I borrowed Shakespeare's device of writing his name into his sonnets. Some scholars argue that, in addition to punning on "Will" in his poetry, he's subliminally woven his surname into the sonnet that begins "The expense of spirit." There's also a tradition of poets referring to them-

selves in ghazals. I took this idea of a poetic signature when I wrote a quatrain using echoes of my own name, Harryette Romell Mullen:

marry at a hotel, annul 'em
nary hep male rose sullen
let alley roam, yell melon
dull normal fellow hammers omelet

DK: Do you think of *Sleeping with the Dictionary* as a new departure?

HM: As I suppose my title implies, *Sleeping with the Dictionary* explores
my ambivalent relation to language, both standard and vernacular dialects of
American English. The idea is that the dictionary can be not only an authoritative reference, but also a more intimate companion, so to speak. It is literally true that I sometimes fall asleep with books I've taken to bed, including
the big dictionary. It's significant to me that my *American Heritage Dictionary* was compiled with the aid of a usage panel that included African American writers Langston Hughes and Arna Bontemps as well as feminist author
Gloria Steinem. Thanks to my mother, an elementary school teacher, I have
loved encyclopedias and dictionaries since childhood. Along with other volumes, my shelf includes *A Feminist Dictionary,* compiled by Paula Treichier
and Cheris Kramarae, and Clarence Major's *Juba to Jive: A Dictionary of African American Slang,* an important source for the lexicon of *Muse & Drudge.*

DK: I'm fascinated by the fact that you did things that usually are outside
the purview of the author—choosing the cover art of *Muse & Drudge,* for example, or having Henry Louis Gates and Sandra Cisneros "blurb" your book.

HM: The choices I made were part conscious, part intuitive, part seren-
dipitous. A benefit of working with small independent presses is that authors can be more involved in such decisions. In my experience, each cover
has been a collaboration of publisher, author, and artist/designer. Even the
university presses allowed me to choose the cover art, since I was willing to
find the artists and get their permission. All of my publishers have encouraged my active participation, if only because they lack the resources to do
everything themselves. Many poetry books don't get reviewed, so often the
work falls into an abyss of silence. I want to do what I can to help audiences
find my work, including discussing it with readers, critics, teachers, and students as I travel around to various literary events.

DK: You once described to me your idea of an "aesthetic apartheid." Could
you expand on that term, especially as it relates to experimental writing and
social injustice?

HM: As Erica Hunt reminds us in her lucid essay, "Notes for an Oppositional Poetics," aesthetic and political opposition to the status quo do not necessarily go hand in hand, nor are they mutually exclusive. I'm interested in the shared aspirations of social and aesthetic movements that envision a better world. While I celebrate the differences that create distinct aesthetic preferences, I seek to overcome the social segregation that enforces aesthetic apartheid. In Los Angeles, for example, this might require that I drive out of my own familiar neighborhood to see an art exhibit in Little Tokyo or attend a poetry reading at the Institute of Italian Culture—to recall a couple of excursions I've made recently in between taking visitors to the Watts Towers and to the World Stage in Leimert Park.

DK: This sense of political and social engagement is certainly clear in all your books. In *Muse & Drudge* you write, "how a border orders disorder / how the children looked / whose mothers worked / in the maquiladora." Immigration and sweatshop conditions seem to have something to do with the form of that poem. Does thinking about form in some way affect the way you read social and political events?

HM: Human beings create meaning by ascribing significance to difference, however arbitrary. The first line of the stanza makes two observations. The separation of a border defines an order that must be defended, and also presupposes a disorder that continually threatens order. Traditionally it's argued that the container of form creates a boundary or frame that separates order from disorder, art from the mundane. Because our lives encompass a great deal of disorder, we value form and convention. Apparently we need boundaries, even imaginary or arbitrary ones, to define social organization and artistic form. Still, it's impossible to regulate absolutely the movement of people across borders, or even to define with certainty the difference between a work of art and a piece of garbage. It's also true that certain artists are regarded as threats to social or political order.

DK: I suddenly had this vision of your work as proposing a new kind of order. In *Muse & Drudge,* for example, you write, "torn veins stitched / together with pine needles / mended hands fix / the memory of a people."

These lines suggest that one is putting history back together again via the juxtaposition of fragments, which suggest a modernist project in many ways. Do you see your work as blurring the boundaries between the modern and the postmodern?

HM: "Putting history back together again" sounds good, and mending ourselves as well. Of course the fragments, however they are arranged, don't add up to a master narrative. I'm aware that some critics see postmodernism as only a later development of the modernist project. Others would say that modernists mourn a shattered world, while postmodernists revel in its fragmentation and lack of coherence. I suppose my own feeling is somewhere between mourning and reveling. There's no time in the past I'd rather live than now, and I can only hope that we all have room for improvement in the future.

DK: It seems to me that *Sleeping with the Dictionary* might especially appeal to students due to its inclusive use of language games. Might you suggest ways of teaching a specific poem from the book to students?

HM: Pronouns are powerful words. Consider how we use "I" and "you," "we" and "they" to divide or unite ourselves. Sometimes when I'm writing, I'll delete the words "I" or "they" and substitute "we" in a poem. It gives the work a different perspective, makes it more inclusive. One of my students wrote a fine essay on how the use of pronouns includes the reader in the poetry of Adrienne Rich and John Ashbery.

I believe my poetry ideas can be adapted to any educational level, in creative writing as well as in literature classes. I often write poems using the same assignments I give my students. "Dim Lady" and "Variation on a Theme Park" came out of an exercise asking students to write parodies of famous sonnets. With different groups I've used sonnets by Shakespeare or Neruda as models, suggesting that students choose a particular rule for transforming the poem. Instead of having students write a précis or paraphrase in prose, teachers could suggest that students rewrite the poem by plugging other words into the same syntactical and rhetorical structure. Students can use the Oulipo N+7 rule of substituting for each noun in the poem the seventh noun up or down from it in the dictionary. "Variation on a Theme Park" is a "freestyle" version of this Oulipo game. I didn't count up or down, but for each noun and verb in the original text I substituted a different word that begins with the same letter, using free association and the dictionary for inspiration. Students might substitute synonyms or antonyms to alter the diction of a poem, the way I've used synonymous slang words and commercial brand names in "Dim Lady." They could write "inverse translations" of Neruda sonnets, substituting an antonym for each noun and verb in the poem. They could rewrite a familiar poem or story using periphrasis, as I've done in "European Folk Tale Variant." Here my inspiration was Toni Cade Bambara's hilarious black vernacular revision of "Goldilocks and the Three Bears."

The idea of using inversion or antonyms in a poetic way came from Richard Wilbur's delightful collections of poetry for children. I've used *Runaway Opposites,* with collages by Henrik Drescher, in my university classes. Wilbur's humorous couplets highlight his clever use of rhyme and his unconventional sense of opposition:

I wonder if you've ever seen a
willow sheltering a hyena?
Nowhere in nature can be found
an opposition more profound:
A sad tree weeping inconsolably!
A wild beast laughing uncontrollably!

Who else has ever paired as "opposites" a weeping willow and a laughing hyena? One of my poems in *Sleeping with the Dictionary,* "Way Opposite," is an emulation of Wilbur. Another, "Any Lit," uses as its model a fragment of a traditional African American courtship ritual: "You are a huckleberry beyond my persimmon." My poem was created by substitution, playing on the sounds of "you" and "my" in every line.

Many students have tried acrostic poems. Sometimes in my workshops I give everyone a handful of uncooked alphabet noodles to play with. Scrabble tiles are good, too. The students spell out their own names, then use the letters of their names to write anagrams and acrostics. My poem "Ask Aden" is an acrostic I wrote for my nephew Aden when he was about six years old. That's an age when children ask wonderful, often unanswerable, questions, so I decided that each line of the poem would be a question. Originally this was a small handmade book that was inspired by a set of alphabet stamps. On each rubber stamp the letter was a different animal: an aardvark shaped like an A, a dragon for D, and so on. The word *aardvark* sounds like it contains the word *are,* so the first line of the poem was "Are aardvarks anxious?" That became the model for the other lines. From childhood on, I've associated poetry with games and puzzles, with singing and dancing, with codes and ciphers, with riddles and rhymes. I've never lost that sense of play and pleasure in making poetry.

An Interview with Harryette Mullen
by Elizabeth A. Frost

Crossing the lines between often isolated aesthetic camps, Harryette Mullen has pioneered her own form of bluesy, disjunctive lyric poetry, combining a concern for the political issues raised by identity politics with a poststructuralist emphasis on language. Mullen challenges prevailing assumptions about the canons of contemporary poetry and seeks in particular to draw attention to the neglected traditions of African American experimentalism from which her writing emerges. Influences on her work range widely, from Gertrude Stein to the Black Arts Movement, from Sappho to Bessie Smith, from Language poetry to rap. Mullen's allusive, playful texts have gained increasing attention in recent years, perhaps for the very reason that they are often hard to categorize. In her singular approach to poetics, Mullen raises important questions about tradition, innovation, and cultural identity.

Mullen is the author of *Tree Tall Woman* (Energy Earth, 1981), *Trimmings* (Tender Buttons, 1991), *S*PeRM**K*T* (Singing Horse, 1992), *Muse & Drudge* (Singing Horse, 1995), *Sleeping with the Dictionary* (University of California Press, 2002) among other works. Although stylistically varied, these books—most recently written in a fragmented serial form—share a focus on identity and language, race and gender, puns and wordplay. Born in Alabama, raised in Texas, and educated in part in Northern California, Mullen has lived in many regions of the United States and frequently explores the question of borders or margins—geographic, cultural, and linguistic. But her writing consistently avoids direct autobiographical statement. Eliding supposed divisions between "writerly" and "speakerly" texts, and rejecting Romantic "inspiration" and authorial mastery, Mullen often writes by the rules of a game she makes up along the way, as in her often outrageous puns ("deja voodoo queens," "sue for slender," "high on swine," "everlasting arms / too short for boxers," and "forgotten formula cures / endemic mnemonic plague"). The following quatrain from *Muse & Drudge* is an anagram—on "Harryette Mullen": "marry at a hotel, annul 'em / nary hep male rose sullen / let alley roam, yell melon / dull normal fellow hammers omelette" (64). In such passages, rich in sound effects, encoded but ultimately decipherable, Mullen invites readers (as one line from *Muse & Drudge* advises) to "Proceed with abandon."

While Mullen's early work in *Tree Tall Woman* is influenced by the legacy of the Black Arts Movement and focuses on community and family history, *Trimmings* assumes an open-ended, serial form typical of her writing since. In style and subject, *Trimmings* takes Gertrude Stein's *Tender Buttons* (1914) as point of departure, weaving Stein together with the more recent threads of black feminism, Language poetry, and popular culture. Looking at *Tender Buttons* through the "cool dark lasses" of a black feminist perspective, Mullen creates a dialogic text about women's clothing—"girdled loins" wrapped in Steinian "tender girders" (*Trimmings* 26)—complete with everything from dress shields to belts, gowns to "shades." On occasion Mullen literally rewrites passages from *Tender Buttons*, implicitly critiquing Stein's politics even as she pays tribute to her innovations (see Elizabeth Frost "Signifyin(g) on Stein: The Revisionist Poetics of Harryette Mullen and Leslie Scalapino," *Postmodern Culture* 5.3 [1995]). Stein's famous "Petticoat" poem, for example ("A light white, a disgrace, an inkspot, a rosy charm"), is transmogrified:

A light white disgraceful sugar looks pink, wears an air, pale compared to shadow standing by. To plump recliner, naked truth lies. Behind her shadow wears her color, arms full of flowers. A rosy charm is pink. And she is ink. The mistress wears no petticoat or leaves. The other in shadow, a large, pink dress.

In keeping with the sections of *Tender Buttons* ("Objects," "Food," and "Rooms"), Mullen shifts her gaze in *S*PeRM**K*T* from closet to supermarket. Holding a mirror up to consumerism, Mullen progresses through the aisles: "Lines assemble gutter and margin. Outside and in, they straighten a place. Organize a stand. Shelve space. Square footage. Align your list or listlessness." In the poems that follow this first one, Mullen splices together evocations of disparate products with the language of advertising, politics, and the body. In a typical passage, Mullen plays on the "Kills bugs dead" slogan for roach killers, dwelling on its kinship with the language of genocide and wryly observing that "Redundancy is syntactical overkill."

Mullen's *Muse & Drudge* is a long poem in lyric fragments that amalgamate Sappho and the blues, Steinian games with Black Arts radicalism. It is a work I have elsewhere described as exploring hybridity in female identity poetic idiom, and avant-gardism itself ("'Ruses of the Lunatic Muse': Haryette Mullen and Lyric Hybridity." *Women's Studies* 27 [1981]: 465–81). Mullen's diverse sources are spliced together in unpunctuated quatrains, with effects analogous to the rapper's art of sampling. The musical effects range from scat ("mutter patter simper blubber / murmur prattle smatter blather / mumble chatter whisper bubble / mumbo-jumbo palaver gibber blunder" [571] to rhyming toasts ("If you turned down the media / so I could write a book / then you could look me up / in your voluminous recyclopedia" [68]). Inventing a merger of Sappho's lyre and Bessie Smith's blues, the first quatrain of *Muse & Drudge* is dense with references, not all of which, Mullen knows, will be available to a given reader:

Sapphire's lyre styles plucked eyebrows
bow lips and legs
whose lives are lonely too.

Sappho, *Amos 'n' Andy's* Sapphire, Billy Strayhorn ("Lush Life"), Apollo's lyre, Orpheus's bow, lipstick and eyebrow pencil—the list of sources for this passage could go on, epitomizing Mullen's densely layered lines.

Defying categories and camps, Mullen explores the question of inheritance and kinship among a range of writers. As Aldon Nielsen has pointed out, Mullen attempts to draw attention to a tradition of African American experimental writing virtually ignored in constructions of modern and postmodern literature—a tradition that Mullen's work evokes and continues (see *Black Chant: Languages of African-American Postmodernism*). A professor of English at UCLA, Mullen teaches creative writing and African American literature. Mullen has also published the study *Freeing the Soul: Race, Subjectivity, and Difference in Slave Narratives* (Cambridge, 1998).

We met to conduct this interview at the Modern Language Association (MLA) meeting in Toronto in December 1997, where Mullen was giving a poetry reading in conjunction with a panel devoted to her work. We subsequently edited and expanded on that initial conversation.

Q. I'd like to start with the fact that we're meeting for this interview at the MLA convention. You've probably attended this conference dozens of times, but this year you're here not as a scholar but as a poet—to read your work and attend a panel about it. I know that many poets who teach feel a sense of competition between their scholarly work and their poetry. How do you feel about the relationship between the two?

A. This is a good time to celebrate that they definitely have come together in a positive way. When I was a graduate student, there was a weird trepidation about one interfering with the other. There were professors who thought that you couldn't write critically, or write academic prose, and also write poetry. I was at the University of California at Santa Cruz when Norman O. Brown was an emeritus professor. He told me, "Don't ever stop writing poetry. We are still reading poetry that is thousands of years old." That helped get me through some times that were a little bit rough, when it seemed that they couldn't go together.

Q. I guess Nathaniel Mackey was there when you first started.

A. Yes, Nate was there. His signature's on my dissertation.

Q. He must have been a help.

A. Well, the first words he said to me were, "I am on leave." He was supposed to be my adviser, and so I had to get another adviser. And of course when I told him I was going to write my dissertation on slave narratives—I don't know if he'll remember this—he said, "Slave narratives are not literature, and I don't think that they are very interesting texts." But he changed his mind later on. He said when he read my dissertation that he saw what had interested me. Of course, he provided an excellent model of the scholar-poet, and I'm grateful to him for publishing my poetry in *Hambone*.

Q. Did you find as you kept up your research that it made its way into your poetry, conceptually?

A. That research has definitely influenced my thinking about not just poetry but a lot of things. It gave me a deeper sense of where I have come from, individually and collectively. I can remember reading some of the slave narratives and just weeping and thinking that whatever is wrong with my life is nothing compared to theirs. These people went through so much just so that we could exist. It has really become the bedrock for everything else—that grounding in history and collective experience.

Q. I am interested in your articles that deal with the interplay between orality and literacy. That issue makes its way into your poetry too, because there is so much play between the oral and the visual, in almost every line.

A. I am writing for the eye and the ear at once, at that intersection of orality and literacy, wanting to make sure that there is a troubled, disturbing aspect to the work so that it is never just a "speakerly" or a "writerly" text. When we talk about orality, most of the time we are not really talking about orality—we are talking about a mimetic representation. Poetry does come out of song. If it gets very far from song, it is difficult for many people to connect with it. So I am always experimenting with how to be in that space, where it's neither completely spoken nor completely something that exists on the page.

Q. Do you feel that this is also a problem in the way poetry is conceptualized? People are pegged—you are either a speech-based poet or a visual poet, for example.

A. I think so, partly because there are different social scenes that people are participating in. People in one camp don't necessarily even meet people in the other camps. I know that in Los Angeles, for instance, I can go to some poetry readings and see basically the same people, and I can go to other venues and there will be a whole different cast of characters who don't participate in this other literary world. And I like traveling. I enjoy the different perspectives—I have always done that, out of necessity since my childhood. That is actually how I feel most comfortable.

Q. You say out of necessity. How do you mean that?

A. Well, I started in childhood. My family moved around. They were from Pennsylvania. I was born in Alabama, and I grew up in Texas. I lived in New York, now I am living in California, and I lived a little while in New Mexico. My family lived in one neighborhood and went to church in another and we went to school in a third. So I couldn't play with my school friends because none of them lived near me. People in my church didn't live near us. And people in my neighborhood were rapidly moving out because we were black and they were white. You have to find your community wherever you can.

Q. One of the things that I think is particularly important about your poetry is that it crosses camps. In a sense it defies some expectations, raises others, and helps muddy the waters. I wonder if you would talk about what you feel poetically are some of the strands in your work that you are stitching together.

A. Well, you know that I have been influenced by hanging around with the Language crowd. It was their interest in Gertrude Stein that made me want to go back and read Stein again after I was kind of frustrated with her. I think that because I had been listening to a lot of experimental, engaged, innovative poetry, her writing began to make more sense to me and I felt more comfortable reading it. I really was interested in the idea of writing a prose poem. I thought that I would treat the sentence as if it were a line and not worry so much about grammar or punctuation, but just use the grammar and the punctuation in the service of the rhythm of the sentence. That liberated me to try a lot of things I wouldn't have tried otherwise. I was also very much influenced by a certain black tradition, particularly having taken folklore courses with Roger Abrahams at the University of Texas at Austin.

We couldn't take Afro-American literature courses at that time. This was in the 1970s. I took African and Afro-Caribbean literature courses, as well as folklore courses. Now I realize that what was being taught was the folklore of the street culture, and I can remember in some cases feeling really alienated, because the folklore that I knew was the folklore that you know if you go to church, if you are on the school playground, if you are leading a very sheltered, lower middle-class life in a black community. And the folklore that was being taught was collected in prisons, pool halls, or on the street corners. It was the lore of the men on the streets. No wonder I didn't understand it. I didn't know about "Shine and the Titanic." That little piece I published in *Callaloo*, "She Swam on from Sea to Shine," is based partly on a toast which is a folk epic about Shine, a legendary character, who supposedly survived the wreck of the *Titanic*. So that is very much a genre of oral recited poetry that men perform in black communities, and Abrahams actually did collect material in prisons, from poor and working class black men. But I had been working with the idea of folk tradition even before I really knew what it was, because I have a folk tradition—the jump-rope songs and the formulaic greetings that kids have. That was always a part of how I experienced poetry.

I think that I have always felt that what I wrote was somewhere between what I heard and what I read. What I have heard has influenced my sense of rhythm very strongly. Music has always been fundamental to me, as well as folklore and poetry, and the church—*Psalms* and *Proverbs*, the gospels, the spirituals, and all the preaching. My grandfather and my great-grandfather were Baptist preachers; there are two generations of them. So we had a book culture (my maternal grandfather had a shelf of philosophy books and my paternal grandfather was a printer), and my mother and my father's mother were teachers. All my immediate relatives had jobs that required literacy— teaching and preaching, doing office work, or doing social work. There was the street or the playground on one hand and home, school, church, and books on the other. There are always different camps, including the people that don't care about books but want to be able to deal with you face to face. You have to have your wits about you because people are always testing you; if you are walking down the streets in any black community, people just talk to you, in these conventionally formulaic ways, to break the ice. And then you can get into a real conversation, but you have to pass the test. Somebody throws one of these little zingers at you, and you can't just leave. You have to be able to bounce back with something. I was never all that good at it, but I certainly could appreciate what other people were able to do, and I could think of things to say later on, which is why I am a writer.

Q. How old were you when you started to write?

A. At a very young age I was writing the stuff that kids write. I would make cards with lines of verse for everyone's birthdays or holidays, and I made comic books, and I would illustrate and make little stories, invent board games and give them to my friends, with a story that unfolds as you play the game. I created my own alphabet. I was really into the world of symbolism, whether it was a secret code, or coats of arms, or all kinds of riddles or alphabets. We had an encyclopedia that had the history of each alphabet since the beginning of the letter. I wanted to unlock everything that was there, the history. I felt that way about words. Words belong to families, like people.

Q. That sounds like a wonderfully empowered attitude toward language, as opposed to learning in school that a certain way to use language is "correct."

A. Because my mother was a teacher, I knew how to read when I went to school, so I don't even remember learning to read in an institutional setting. When I was in first grade, I didn't know every word—I was increasing my vocabulary. A lot of people have a distinct memory of learning how to read, especially if they had difficulty with it, but I don't have a memory of that experience. I was always checking out books. We went to the library every week and brought home about ten books—that was just normal.

Q. It seems that you got a strong dose on both sides, the sense of a very spoken life and a very written one.

A. I have read drafts of my grandfather's sermons. He wrote them, but he didn't preach them as they were written. We used to say, some preachers just preached the gravy, but he would preach a sermon with both meat and gravy.

Q. That's a good expression.

A. I think about that for myself too. You have the gravy, but you can't just live off the gravy; you need the meat as well.

Q. There is another strand that interests me in your work. You play with theory. But there is never any direct reference. It's as though your work is informed by poststructuralist ideas about language, but those ideas are not directly cited. Somehow the theory is underneath or inside.

A. It probably has to do with how I synthesize information because a lot of times I actually forget where I have read something and who said it. In fact it was devilishly hard when I was writing my dissertation, because I had so many little scraps and notes to myself. Sometimes I didn't even write down the proper citation, and I would have to go back and find it later on. It's unfortunate because my brain doesn't really work in the most efficient way. I am taking in things from all over, and if something fits it goes in.

Q. One can read your work from many different vantage points. One of the things that particularly interests me in *Muse & Drudge* is how allusive it is. For me it gets more and more so every day, as I teach it, because every stanza comes into being as I'm informed about references I might not know. How do you feel about what I might call the politics of allusion?

A. That's a good question. On the one hand, I feel that because *Muse & Drudge* is so fragmentary, wherever parts of the text came from really doesn't matter because it is really not a complete thought about anything. It is very much a book of echoes. Some of the fragments rhyme and some don't, and that is basically the principle of the book—the recycling of fragments of language. I can remember where some things came from. For example, all the Sappho references come from a translation by Diane Rayor. In fact, she and I had a recent conversation—we were at Santa Cruz together when she was beginning her career as a translator of ancient Greek. And she said, you use all those passages with no citation from my book. But what I've used is fragmented, and most of the passages are altered. Her book title, *Sappho's Lyre,* is echoed in the first line of my book. I begin, "Sapphire's lyre styles / plucked eyebrows / bow lips and legs / whose lives are lonely too." That is so very obvious that it didn't need to be attributed in the scholarly way. In fact, in the whole book, there is only one direct quotation, and it was kind of a joke for me to do that because the one thing that was quoted was from a comic book: "fool weed, tumble your / head off." That's from a Krazy Kat comic. There are several things that are taken from Krazy Kat comics, but that one is a complete quotation. Almost nothing else is. Well, "I dream a world" is a complete line and that could have been put in quotation marks.

Q. What is that from?

A. Langston Hughes—and also it's the title of a book of photographs by Brian Lanker of black women, black divas, all looking fabulous and monumental. The title of Lanker's book and photography exhibit is from Hughes's poem. I could put quotation marks around everything, from the folk tradition, or blues songs, or whatever theory I was reading—particular theories of representation. There are also a lot of quotes from my family. But I really like the idea that the only thing that needs quotation is the line from the comic book. George Herriman is also a fascinating figure. He was an African American man from Louisiana whose family had moved to California and passed as white—really, they became white people. Herriman was the creator of Krazy Kat, a comic that I knew about because my mother sometimes called me Ignatz, the name of the mouse that was in love with Krazy Kat. "Hairy man" puns on Herriman's name: "black cat in the family tree / hairy man's Greek to me." Since Herriman rarely spoke of his family or his background, friends and acquaintances speculated on the basis of his appearance that he was Greek, or that he was French because of his Louisiana Creole heritage. Reading the comics one might think he was Jewish since the characters often sprinkle Yiddish words into their speech. Herriman was a melting-pot American. The Hairy Man is an African American folk character similar to the bogeyman in stories told to scare children into correct behavior. The issue of lost kinship, of lineage and the denial of relationship in "passing," is evident in Herriman's story. The quatrain that starts "mutter patter simper blubber" plays on that idea, with homophones of mother, father, sister, and brother. Readers find different meanings in the multivalent references.

Q. It seems that a lot of the language comes out of both shared knowledge and very private knowledge. Where does that put the reader for you?

A. The reader is getting whatever the reader can get. Just as I do when I'm reading. This is about me reading too, getting what I get and passing it on. What I really love, when I read this poem, or when someone else reads it and tells me about their experience, is that different people get different things. If I am in a room with an audience, sometimes the young people are laughing and the old people just stare. And vice versa—the old people will hear things that they know that the young people don't know. Black people get certain things particularly, and Spanish speakers get certain other things. There are people who recognize Sappho lines or Bessie Smith lines.

Q. That's why I have such a great time teaching this book. It makes me think that there is a new kind of reading that you've invented, a sort of collective reading process. I can't think of another type of writing that does this in quite the same way. There is something about the group experience of going through this text that is totally different from reading anything else. It is confusing for some students, because they are used to the idea that there is an authoritative reading. Some of them just run with it, but others are more intimidated. So we brainstorm and come up with all kinds of stuff and that becomes very fun.

A. That's how it should be. I think that there is always a danger of poetry being remote, even painful. I have been in classrooms on both sides when it was painful. People have this fear and anxiety about being wrong, and in this case it is not really about being right or wrong, because the poem allows you to come in and leave at various points. There are times when people will hear something very clearly and know exactly where it came from, and other times sections are obscure. That's okay, because someone else is going to have the same experience, but with different parts being clear or obscure. In fact, some of the things that I wrote, I had just found out myself. I was learning as I wrote *Muse & Drudge*. It came out in 1995, and I probably began at least a little bit of it around the time *S*PeRM**K*T* came out in 1992. So between 1992 and 1995 there was probably one six-month period when most of it was written, and then I did a little bit here and there along the way. When I was busy, I didn't write as much. When I was really going, I was writing every day and everything seemed to rhyme. I would hear something every day, or I would read or remember something that really seemed to fit into the poem. I think that readers should feel free to use whatever competence they have, and I am really delighted when people tell me about their reference points. I may have gotten something from one particular source—for example, the phrase "the other side of far" for me comes from Zora Neale Hurston. For other people it comes from Larry Neal. It's both; Larry Neal may have gotten it from Zora Neale Hurston originally—I don't know. Or a line that I heard in a blues song someone else has heard in a country western song.

Q. When we read the lines "you must don't like my peaches / there's some left on the tree," all my students say, "Oh, Steve Miller Band!" That metaphor comes from Ma Rainey.

A. Most of what I'm using doesn't really belong to any one person or any one group. Some material I think of as African American, and I will go somewhere else and find out it is Irish, or German, or Italian! I think that it's mine. And I realize that I have to share it.

Q. So it's a process of claiming what is yours but simultaneously allowing it to be possessed by others.

A. This whole book is about being possessed by others. It is very much made up of the voices themselves—words of others that I've read, heard, or overheard. I knew this book was not going to be about me; it's about black women primarily, and I am a black woman, so some of those voices could be mine, but I was not writing about myself. If it is me, it's just generic. To a certain extent, a black woman is generic of woman, and woman is generic of humanity. The individual and the collective merge, as in the blues.

Q. Was there some point earlier when you made a deliberate decision that you didn't want to write from the tradition of the first person, lyric "I"?

A. Well, I hadn't done that for the two books before, *Trimmings* and then *S*PeRM**K*T.* It's the culture speaking, definitely.

Q. In some ways I think that those books are less personal than *Muse & Drudge.* There is a very strong sense of subjectivity that runs through *Muse & Drudge,* except that it is plural and keeps changing. In the other books, as you say, it's the culture talking and there is less sense of individual experience.

A. There is the interpretation of the culture. The culture is always babbling at us. And so I was capturing some of the babble and turning it this way and that to see how it could be told.

Q. I also find a lot of sadness in *Muse & Drudge.*

A. People have said various things that sound right to me. Someone said that *Trimmings* was very sad and *Muse & Drudge* was more uplifting, kind of sassy and back talking. Others have said that they see that bluesy sadness in *Muse & Drudge,* and they found more of a liberation in *Trimmings.* So I don't know. For me the tragic and the comic go together. That's true in the blues: you have to make your way out of depression; that is how the blues works as a sort of therapeutic activity. For me the comic is the other side of the coin of tragedy or oppression. They work together. I know people sometimes have a problem when the tone shifts abruptly. Some people find that disturbing, but for me it feels right.

Q. Are there other aspects of the blues that are particularly important that you draw on?

A. Well, there are so many women that have made their mark. Some particular women are the voice of the blues—Bessie Smith is a good example. She is the blues; she lived it and died it. And blues women were very influential and admired as artists before black women were admired on their own— that is important to me. Also, the blues is something that I can identify with even though I didn't grow up with it. We were one of those religious families who thought, "Ooh, this is the devil's music!" I had to really develop my appreciation later in life.

Q. There is so much wonderful scatological material in the lyrics. It wasn't for polite company. But was that true even when you were growing up, through the 1960s and 1970s?

A. My family in that way was very old-fashioned. At home we listened to gospel music, spirituals, classical music. Oddly, we did have a recording of Gershwin's *Porgy and Bess,* so we heard operatically trained black voices. Then we had a whole set of Gilbert and Sullivan operettas, and we listened to the all-American kind of folk songs. We had records of those, because that was something my mom thought children should know. Songs about Casey Jones, or John Henry, "The Erie Canal," "I've been working on the railroad"—that kind of stuff. We were so wholesome. Occasionally, I remember, my mother listened to Sarah Vaughan and Nancy Wilson. I don't think we heard much Dinah Washington. Maybe a little Ella Fitzgerald. And a little Sam Cooke, but he had left the spiritual tradition for the wild life that killed him. I remember the religious people said when he died, "He shouldn't have been into that life!" We heard blues and R&B music when we were getting our hair done, or on the jukeboxes in the soul food restaurants in the black community. (I'm talking about the period before my sister and I developed our own tastes. This was the influence of my family.) I never realized, until much later, that my mother had been in the high school band with Ornette Coleman. It never occurred to her to mention it.

Q. I wanted to ask you who is on the cover of *Muse & Drudge*. To me it looks like a spiritual or gospel performer.

A. Gil Ott, my publisher, had some photographs that a friend of his had taken. She is actually not a performer; she is a woman who attended a public hearing in a big, crowded municipal building—I think it was a hearing about access for people with disabilities—and she is actually in a wheelchair, but you can't see that in the picture. She was participating in a public protest. I liked it because it looks like she could be praying, singing, or clapping. Her eyes are closed, her hands are together. It is an ambiguous image, which I liked. She looked very soulful to me. She definitely looked like a black woman. I put the photo on the Xerox machine and made it bigger, used black marker to crop it, and blacked out everything around her. She kind of shines out of the black background. She seemed just right.

Q. I like that you got the visual pun on blues and sapphire through the background color.

A. I knew that it had to be a black and blue cover.

Q. I am curious what you think about the debate in recent years about the blues as an expression of black culture. The Black Arts Movement rejected the blues because the songs were seen as focused on oppression, and not enough on rage. It is hard for me to believe that you would agree, but it is interesting to see how the blues has been tropes.

A. I think it depends on which kind of blues you listen to, because there are so many different kinds of blues, and many different kinds of people who sang it and continue to sing it. People are revising and editing the blues now. The blues music we are hearing now is probably not the same as when it was sung by people with a living memory of slavery. When you don't feel so oppressed, you sing differently. So the blues has evolved.

It reminds me of Alice Walker's Meridian Hill, a character who stopped going to church as she became politically active. I can remember sitting in the black church singing, "Wash me whiter than snow," with no irony whatsoever. This character in *Meridian* goes back to the black church and says, "The music sounds different. It has changed." That is happening in all forms of black music. Blues was always an improvised music and the lyrics have always been shuffled into different combinations. People felt free to make their own custom version out of the parts of a particular blues song.

Q. It's interesting that you mention the improvisatory quality of blues, because that's apparent in the way the language unfolds in *Muse & Drudge*. But the visual form of the poem is fixed and very symmetrical—those four quatrains per page.

A. It looks more stable than it is.

Q. There are different forces—the connectedness, and the spinning off, the fragmentation. But even in those loose quatrains, there are two forms that I think of: the blues stanza and the Sapphic stanza. Were both of those in your head in some way?

A. Yes, because my whole image was of Sappho as Sapphire singing the blues. It partly had to do with Diane Rayor's translation of Sappho. In American English, Sappho sounds like someone singing the blues. It is that very basic emotion that comes across. So that was the image that informed the book.

Q. Your epigraph to *Muse & Drudge* from Callimachus reads, "Fatten your animal for sacrifice, poet / but keep your muse slender."

A. That comes from another one of Diane's books, *Latin Lyric and Elegiac Poetry*. It is his advice to a poet. It has to do with the economy of poetry. I am very interested in the tropes that people use—here, the idea of sacrifice and fat and slender beauty. When you think about a black woman in this culture, which one is she going to be? She could be either one, the black woman as a beast of burden or as a postmodern diva. There's the black woman who is out of her place, a Josephine Baker, or the supermodels who are admired even as other black women are still being oppressed. That is where the title *Muse & Drudge* comes from. Also, as a woman writing poetry, you are seen as someone else's muse. So there is tension in that as well.

Q. One of the motifs that recur is about the female body, the black female body.

A. And the body as an instrument.

Q. Like the lyre. It seems as though a lot of the images in the beginning, especially Sapphire's lyre, cut both ways. Using the body as an instrument is a kind of feminine strategy—exalted on the one hand, yet undervalued as art. But it is the substitution of that "bodiness" for another kind of self-expression that becomes very tragic.

A. That is how I thought about it, even in terms of the jazz-blues tradition, where the men are playing the instruments and the women are singing. Yet the men are the ones who are usually regarded as great geniuses, because singing is supposed to be less of an art—it's seen as more natural, more intuitive. Although the same thing is also said about instrumental jazz musicians, that they were just born with it, that music just comes out of them.

Q. It interests me that Callimachus is affirming the lyric, the economy of poetry, as you said. At the same time what you have done is write a long poem.

A. I think I realized that somehow I could have both in one—very brief lyrics that I could write in the moment. It's a serial lyric that accumulates the thematic concerns of a long poem.

Q. The page is not necessarily a unit in the book, at least according to my reading. Things stop and start very differently in different sections.

A. There is one whole page about birds; it begins, "sauce squandering sassy cook / took a gander bumped a pinch of goose." And there is one whole page about my mother. There is one whole page of Hollywood's image of black people, and there is a whole section that has to do with a transition in my life. Because it was such a flexible form, I found that I could piece lines, couplets, quatrains together and sometimes have a unit expand into a page, or two pages, or more.

Q. It seems to me that one of the best ways to read this book is not sequentially but almost randomly. Do you like the idea of someone just opening it and starting anywhere?

A. Someone pointed out to me that you could just read the first page and the last page and that would help you to understand the body of the poem.

Q. Especially since Sappho frames it. The final lines, "who you're playing for / what stray companion," echo a Sappho fragment.

A. Yes. I knew the structure, but I did not know which parts would be where. When I wrote the last lines, I probably knew that they were going to be the last lines, and I think that I knew what was going to be on the first page. Everything else just kind of moved around.

Q. Did it feel really different to be working with the quatrain form compared to the prose poem?

A. It felt wonderful because it is such a flexible form. A lot of it is already given—some of the rhymes from the blues songs. It is so ingrained, either quatrains or couplets. A lot of the materials that I am dealing with are already in that form. It allowed me to pluck material from all over the place. I thought when I chose the quatrain that it would help me. As I went through it, I thought, "I could do this forever!" I could find two lines, and then find two more lines. And I could find different ways of writing. Not all of them are *ab*—I could do four *a*'s, or I could do whatever I wanted. I could rhyme *reel* and *leer*, *girl* and *gal*, *radio* and *cielo*, *rubia* and *nubia*. I could rhyme things for some obscure reason known only to myself. There are little motifs that do repeat—birds repeat throughout the whole book, actually. The idea of the bird and the head, all those African masks with the bird com-

ing out of the brow, that fascinates me. And the idea of dreams and imagination, with the bird, the head, the hat, the hair. There is that upward mo-
tion that takes you away from the body. The body has a head, but the head
is dreaming, the head is imagining. The head is flying, like a bird. I began to
discover that motif and I worked those elements into the poem. It is also in
a lot of the material because it is an African motif.

Q. There is also a lot about hairdos.

A. Yes. Well, if two black women are together long enough, they will talk
about hair. I think human beings are obsessed with hair. Hair is so meaningful. We think of it as just this stuff that is on our heads, but we spend a
lot of time working it. It is such a cultural signifier. All the things we do to
our hair, and our feelings about it, are part of who we are.

Q. I was thinking about the relationship between hair and clothes, because
of the two meanings of "ironing" and "pressing." There's the stanza, "my head
ain't fried / just fresh rough dried / ain't got to cook / nor iron it neither."

A. Yes. People say that you get your hair "pressed," and there's the "curl-
ing iron" and "pressing iron," and when we wash our hair and it gets all crin-
kly, it's "rough dried," which is what you say when the laundry comes out,
before it's ironed. Also at the turn of the century a very common occupation
for black women was laundress, and those black laundresses were among
the first workers to organize a strike for higher wages. As much as I hate the
hot comb, look at Madame C. J. Walker, who was a role model for working
black women.

Q. Hair, like nails, is part of the body, but it's not alive, not sentient. And
so it is a kind of object. It has a status similar to clothes.

A. Yes, these are the magical parts of the body. They have a great power,
anthropologically speaking.

Q. There is another motif that is not as pronounced. Some of the stanzas
in *Muse & Drudge* have to do with media events. There is a sequence that I
particularly like: "another video looping / the orange juice execution / her
brains spilled milk / on the killing floor." We get Rodney King, then O.J.,
and a couple of stanzas earlier there's Tawana Brawley: "they say she alone
smeared herself / wrote obscenities on her breast / snatched nappy patches
from her scalp / threw her own self on a heap of refuse." And there is also,
if I am getting it right, Anita Hill: "we believed her / old story she told / the
men nodded at her face / dismissing her case." There is this quick progres-
sion of media constructions of black men and women as projections of some
kind of fear.

A. I actually wrote this before the O.J. trials, but I realized after the O.J.
case that "orange juice execution" was going to be read as having to do with

him. It refers to something that happened in L.A. before the Rodney King riots—when Latasha Harlins was killed for supposedly stealing orange juice from a store; a frightened Korean shop owner killed her. Her death was in the background of the riots. So that is what I was thinking of, but the poem is made so that people can attach to it the things that are already in their minds when they come to read it. Anita Hill and Tawana Brawley came into my mind having to do with what happens when black women speak and create a new version of reality. One of the things people finally began to understand after the O.J. verdict was that black people and white people often don't see things the same way. This was a revelation for a lot of people, but of course this has been going on for a long time. I think the poem partly is about a reality that is sometimes not credible. We are presented with a construction of what reality is, and some constructions can claim more authority than others.

Q. As we were saying, the rhetoric of this book has a more personal feel than *Trimmings*. It addresses a missing female experience, and more particularly a black female experience, that doesn't cross into the public sphere except as performed.

A. I think that's right. Part of what is tricky and difficult is wondering whether we even know what we believe about ourselves. So often we are performing, and we are paid for performing—we are surviving, assimilating, blending in. When are we ourselves? Beyond being either a credit or discredit to our race, who are we?

Q. It raises that difficult problem of authenticity—that there could be something "authentically" black, or authentically anything, and that therefore there is also something inauthentic, which is less often talked about. The search for authenticity seems to me a nostalgic gesture.

A. It is often nostalgic and often points to oppression. That is why I really have trouble with it. I would rather face an uncertain future than go back anywhere in the past. I would rather just make it up as I go and figure that whatever I do is a part of my own black and female experience. There is not a set of black behaviors that I must adhere to in order to be true to who I am.

Q. I had wanted to ask you about the question of audience in your work.

A. *Muse & Drudge* was written to create an audience. It was very deliberate. And when you talk about your class having a collective experience, I think that's great—that is exactly what I was hoping for. The first book that I published, *Tree Tall Woman*, attracted mixed audiences that I would read to, but definitely a good portion were African American women. But with *Trimmings* and *S*PeRM**K*T*, all of a sudden my audience was basically white.

Not that I am against that, but it feels very strange when I walk into a room to read my work, and I am the one person of color in the whole room. That seems odd to me. So I think, for some reason, this work hasn't really spoken to certain audiences. I believe it has something to do with the limited audiences and distribution networks for small-press books, although the Internet is expanding the possibilities. *Muse & Drudge* was written specifically to try to bring different audiences together. I wanted the book to invite more readers. That is one reason why there is a black woman on the cover. Usually the covers of books don't say, Here is a black poet, but I have become very aware of the protocols, the blurbs and what's on the cover. You can tell a black book fifteen feet away, by the cover. The color is usually much brighter than other books, with maybe a kente pattern in the design. Usually there is a black icon or a black person. There are signals that say this is yours or it is not yours.

Muse & Drudge was an attempt to use what Peter Hudson referred to as an "ocean of black signs," and also to go in directions that have to do with poetry generally. What people think of as "black poetry" is set aside from what people think of as "poetry" in terms of tradition and the history of how language is used. People have a very specific notion of what black poetry is. I am finding that more and more as I teach black students who object to or have difficulty with certain poets that I assign. People are so concerned with what is black and what is not black. And to some extent I am concerned with that myself. The question is how blackness is defined and who defines it. There are certain clichés of blackness that I have played with. I thought of this book as a way to use them and free myself from them at the same time.

People are teaching *Muse & Drudge* in American literature courses and in poetry classes, as well as in African American courses. A book that can do that is what I wanted, because I think that the conventional idea of what black people should write is too narrow. The tradition is broader, more eclectic, than people sometimes think, even within the realm of the folk tradition, the oral tradition, going back to African roots. Well, everybody has visited Africa, and people who live in Africa have traveled too. They speak many different languages; there are many different religions, and they incorporate cultural influences from everywhere. And they don't feel that they will be less African if they do that. Here, because we are a minority, and because of our history we fear we are always in danger of losing our identity. When I look in the mirror, I can see who I am. And whatever I do can be connected to that. I remember in the black community some people would say that you couldn't be a professor, because that is a white thing. You can play basketball. But there was a time when we weren't in basketball either. When did basketball become black? When black people were allowed to play basketball.

Q. And now golf, since Tiger Woods.

A. Yes, golf doesn't have to be a white sport. I think we just have to do the things we want to do. And we can do them as black people, and as human beings. There's this idea that a black person and a human being are not the same thing. People say, "This is not a black story, it's a human story"— and what they are really saying is that black is not human, even though that is not what they think they're saying.

Q. That was rehearsed yet again after Ralph Ellison died, and the obituary in the *New York Times* said that *Invisible Man* is not a black story but a universal story as a mark of praise.

A. A human being always comes from a particular time, place, and culture and speaks a particular language. Why is a black person, or an Asian person, seen as anything less than universal? If anything, if we are talking about the earth here, the model should be the Asian woman, because that is who is most numerous.

Q. In *Muse & Drudge* in particular, but also in your other work, there is a balance between two different forces. One is an assertion of identity. The other is what I think of as hybridity—the mixture, the different influences all occurring at once. There is sometimes tension, but there doesn't have to be.

A. If you accept that they go together, the tension evolves into harmony. That is something that we learn from jazz. We learn that from Thelonious Monk when he creates a new sound with discordant notes, allowing us to hear a greater range of possibilities in his music.

Q. Is that something that you can do more easily in your poetry than in your scholarship?

A. I think I do it in my scholarship too. In fact I learned something from my brother-in-law, who is an economist. He has frequently cited *Jet* magazine or *Ebony* when writing academic papers in his field. If it works, it's appropriate. That's another aspect of being confident in who you are—that you know you have a culture. When I was growing up, we were told we didn't have a culture. A lot of my education was my finding out that we do have a legitimate culture. We had the culture that I grew up with, and also the other culture out in the streets that I didn't know about. So that richer version of my culture informed everything else that came to me in my education. We would learn about Europe, and learn about the history of this country, which has always been multiple. It makes this country really interesting. We never quite recognize and appreciate what we have here. Almost unconsciously or accidentally, the elements come together, and you don't really expect it. But that could happen all the time. All this energy could be used productively, but we're too busy fighting each other or being afraid of each other.

Q. Do you have any new poetry projects?

A. I'm writing prose poems again. I think of them as my version of L.A. prose poems.

Q. I've been wondering what L.A. was going to do to your poems.

A. It took a while before I felt settled enough to write. Now I'm writing prose poems, and not in my voice, but as though someone else's words have been overheard, twisted.

Q. Is it a kind of appropriation?

A. Yes, it definitely is appropriation. L.A. is kind of a virtual urban space. Somehow the Internet and L.A. are one proposed combination in my writing of the poem. The language is of this world that I am not a part of, because I've never surfed the Net. There is a whole new vocabulary that intrigues me. There is a geek techie language. Then there is another language that has to do with a representation of spirituality—words like "avatar" and "icon." It is definitely about another way of communicating with people. People want to connect, but they want to do it at a distance. We have been going in that direction for some time now.

Q. And there are the weird possibilities of anonymity or intimacy that doesn't involve a physical presence. Or impersonation.

A. I agree. There are a lot of identity issues, and there is the alienation to overcome *because* of the technology. We can't connect with people in real life. We drive to the Internet café to talk to someone and go back home to bed.

Q. Has living in L.A. been a strange adjustment in other ways?

A. Just the scale of it. Because of the huge number of people all over the place, it can be really crazy at times. I'm enjoying it. I love the diversity. Different parts of L.A. are like different worlds. Downtown is like a third world bazaar. People fear difference, and the city puts out a lot of bad publicity about itself. And difference actually is something to be afraid of, I guess, but you miss a lot if you are just scared all the time.

Q. Since we were talking earlier about music, tell me about the song settings of *Muse & Drudge*.

A. They were composed by T. J. Anderson, who lives in Chapel Hill, North Carolina. He has reorchestrated works by Scott Joplin and written operas and concert music. He's not as well known as I think he ought to be. He was commissioned by a group that was celebrating the centennial of William Grant Still, an early African American composer, and T. J. wanted to use poetry in his piece. He wanted to use Nnenna Freelon, a jazz singer who lives in North Carolina. After two other poets had turned him down, my sister told him that I was a poet, and that he could talk to me directly. I told him, "Whatever you want to do, here is the manuscript." The book was not published yet. He took seven pages and wrote his composition *Seven Cabaret Songs*. He has composed a musical vignette for each one. It was performed in North Carolina in 1995, and I think it was performed at Wright University in Ohio around the same time. Then a group of musicians in San Francisco decided that they wanted to perform it. We had a preconcert talk, before the performance by the San Francisco Contemporary Music Players.

Q. How did it feel to hear your words set to music?

A. I loved it. Nnenna Freelon has a very clear voice. T. J. wrote the piece for her vocal range. There's clarity and warmth in her voice—the clarity of Ella Fitzgerald with the warmth of Sarah Vaughan. Parts of the songs are spoken, and parts of them are improvised—she gets to do some scatting. Parts of it are jazzy, and parts of it are kind of bluesy, but it is definitely a concert piece. It has several different musical influences. The music is very allusive in the way that the poem is also allusive. I think they really understood what the poem meant as well.

Q. I wonder if the experience would have been different if you were writing something that you knew was going to be set to music.

A. I don't know. I like to listen to music when I'm writing, and I felt that this was a poem that had a connection to music. But I didn't think that it was music—it's poetry. But now it's like a great evolution that it's set to music; it's really come full circle.

An Interview with Harryette Mullen by Cynthia Hogue

Cynthia Hogue: I want to start with your origin tale. How did you start writing? Why?

Harryette Mullen: You could say there are several origins. There's the origin of writing, which for me goes far back, since I could hold a pencil. I've been writing to entertain myself and writing rhymes, stories, and cartoons as gifts to other people . . . making booklets for friends, and greeting cards for family members with little rhymed verses in them that I would illustrate. I always had a notebook as a child and I would sketch in it and write in it. This started because my mother was always working. She was the breadwinner. She taught at an elementary school and she would often have to go to meetings and she had other jobs as well. So we always knew we had to be quiet and entertain ourselves. My sister and I read a lot and we both scribbled and drew a little bit. It was a way of keeping us out of trouble.

The first time I had a poem published was in high school and it just happened because the English teacher made everyone write a poem. That was our assignment. She submitted the poems to a local poetry contest and my poem was chosen as the winner. It was published in the local newspaper. So that was my first published poem. As an undergraduate I continued to write for my own amusement and also I went to poetry readings. There were lots of African and African American poets coming to visit the University of Texas and I tried to go to as many readings as possible. Some of my friends were writers too. So I just kept writing. Then one of my friends insisted that I had to do more with my poetry. He was a poet and knew that I was writing, but I wasn't attempting to publish my work, wasn't participating in readings. I was at an open reading one night and he asked me, "Are you going to read your work?" I said, "I didn't bring anything," and he said, "We're going to go home. I'm going to sign you up on the list and by the time you go home and get your stuff it'll be close to your turn." That was the first time I read in public and after that, I really started to think I could face an audience and see myself as a poet; I had been writing forever but not thinking that what I wrote was poetry or that I was a poet, but writing and drawing and reading all went together. They were all part of the same activity.

CH: I want to turn to the evolution of your work. How would you describe that first collection, *Tree Tall Woman*?

HM: The poets I was reading and hearing influenced the book. I was definitely influenced by the Black Arts movement, the idea that there was a black culture and that you could write from the position of being within a black culture. At the time, my idea about black culture was very specific to being Southern, eating certain foods, and having certain religious beliefs. I have a broader sense of what blackness is, what Africanness is, or what a collection of cultures might be, whereas before, I think my idea of blackness was somewhat provincial. Or definitely, it was regional.

CH: "Regional," meaning monologic?

HM: Part of what people were doing with the Black Arts movement was, in a sense, to construct a positive image of black culture, because blackness had signified negation, lack, deprivation, and absence of culture. So people took all of the things that had been pejorative and stigmatized and made them very positive, so that chitterlings, which was the garbage that people threw away from the hog, became the essence of soul food. Words were turned around in their meaning and all the things that were thought of as being pejorative aspects of blackness became the things to be praised. So, that project had created a space for me to write. I didn't have to carry out that project because it had already been done; I didn't have to say "I'm black and black is beautiful." Actually, by the time I was writing, that was getting a little repetitive and almost boring. I wanted to write within the space that had been created without necessarily repeating exactly what those folks had done. At the same time, I now see that I had a kind of restricted idea of what it meant to write within a black culture or with a black voice. The idea of a black voice or black language—black speech—is much more problematic for me today than it was at that time. I felt I knew what it was to write in a black voice and it meant a sort of vernacularized English. I think that it's much more complicated than that. For instance, my family spoke Standard English at home. Educated, middle-class, black speakers are code-switchers, and what we really did was learn to switch from Standard English to a black vernacular in certain situations when that was called for. In our case, my sister and I had people say to us, "You talk funny. You talk proper. Where are you from? You don't sound like you are from here," just because we were speaking Standard English. The idea that there is a black language that is a nonstandard English, that Standard English, therefore, is white, is very problematic. In the work that I am doing now, I'm actually trying to question those kinds of distinctions that are being made between the standard and the non-standard. I wouldn't say that standard American English is in any way a white language. It's a language that is the result of many peoples' contributions. In fact, if you look in the *American Heritage Dictionary*, Langston Hughes and Aran Bontemps are among the people consulted for their usage panel. So people really need to think harder about those distinctions that are being made.

CH: But it was a journey before you began to experiment with the code-switching poetically?

HM: Right. Partly, it had to do with going back to school, going back to graduate school and reading about language. Also, there was, even when I was an undergraduate, a whole movement of sociolinguistics and folklore, partly because there was no African American literature being taught while I was an undergraduate at the University of Texas.

CH: You didn't even read Zora Neale Hurston?

HM: Zora Neale Hurston was not in the canon. She was out of print. Alice Walker was one of the people who helped bring Zora Neale Hurston back into print, and that was happening around the time that I was an undergraduate, but it hadn't yet reached the classroom. I was an English major. I was interested in different kinds of literature. I also took Spanish, so I was reading literature in Spanish. I took courses in classical literature. I didn't know Greek or Latin, but I read the works in English because I wanted to have the background. There was no African American text, even in American Literature classes that I took. We didn't read *Invisible Man*. We didn't read Richard Wright. We didn't read any black women. The places where I was able to read any black writers were in African literature courses because the University of Texas at Austin had a very strong African and Oriental Languages and Literatures Department. They were bringing in African poets like Kofi Awoonor and Dennis Brutus and novelists as well, like Chinua Achebe. There were all these African writers around and sometimes Caribbean writers. So I took a course in Caribbean literature. I took courses in Anglophone African literature, and Afro-American folklore, which was offered through Anthropology. Roger Abrahams, who is known for working on black folklore, was teaching at UT Austin at that time and I took two or three courses with him. My understanding of African American culture really had a lot to do with taking these folklore courses. What's so interesting now, in retrospect, is that I had never heard of most of this Afro-American folklore because a lot of it was based on urban folklore that he had collected from black men on street corners in Philadelphia. He went from there to collecting in prisons because he could get a higher concentration of black men from different parts of the country. He would go to federal prisons and collect twenty different versions of "The Signifying Monkey." His book *Deep Down in the Jungle* is a result of that research. I never would have heard such stuff, because my family's version of black culture consisted of our household, our church, and our school. It wasn't the street corner and it definitely was not the prison.

Here was this white man who was teaching me Afro-American culture, and it was practically all new to me. There were some folktales that I had heard before, but a lot of it—like the toasting tradition—was completely new to me. Now I see, of course, that it is very much a male-centered performance. You don't see a lot of women, especially a lot of middle-class women, going around reciting these toasts. Now I feel that I understand why I kept having this experience of "Why don't I know this? Why is this the black culture and I don't have a real familiarity with it?" This is definitely a black culture that was marked for class and for gender in a way that did not include my own experience, but if you had talked about black people who go to church two or three days a week and who work very hard and are thrifty and try to avoid entanglements with the law, that is the culture that I knew. Partly what was going on was that people were fascinated with those aspects of black culture that were most different from what they saw as white middle-class culture. There was a book that I read at the time actually called *Black and White Styles in Conflict* about people's use of language and their ideas about how they conduct themselves in any kind of discourse. What is described as the "white style" was *my* family's style and we lived totally in the black community. We were segregated in a black community! My parents had gone to a historically black college, Talladega College in Alabama. My mother taught in a segregated black public school in Texas. We lived in a neighborhood that was 99.9 percent black and it was a black world that we lived in, but according to this book, our style was a "white style" and the "black style" was the style of people my mother considered to be not well educated. A certain style was a marker of education and class within the black community, but it was a marker of race within the mainstream. This was what was perceived as black.

It's taken me a while to clarify this distinction in my own mind and to realize it bothers me, because I'm not sure that black children today know that blackness and education are not mutually exclusive. It used to be that we were taught, "Yes, you should be a code-switcher because that way, you could talk to everybody." Now, these kids think, "If I learn Standard English, then I am less black." When they go to get a job, they are less able to qualify for the job if they can't switch to Standard English (if that's the mode of the workplace). Or they have trouble in school, because that is the language of instruction. The idea that Standard English is not just a tool that everyone can use, but is the possession of white people is harmful to black children and anyone else speaking a variant dialect. All of these things bother me now.

CH: You grew up in Fort Worth in the sixties and went to college in the early seventies before the Black Studies movement had reached the University of Texas or widely nationally.

HM: We were marching, protesting for better representation in the student body and the faculty, recruiting more minority faculty. There was an Ethnic Studies course that was required for education majors. We had a black publication that was folded into the school paper. It was the *Daily Texan*, the school paper, and then once a month, we folded in our *Black Print* supplement and I worked on that. I also worked on the *Daily Texan* as an editorial assistant. I wrote editorials for the paper on race subjects usually, and that's what they wanted me to do.

CH: I wonder why?

HM: Yeah, really. I wrote an opinion column and then I worked on the staff for the black publication as well. We had some extremely right-wing regents at that time. It was difficult, and we were forced to develop our political consciousness of who we were and why we were there. Austin was the place of one of the Supreme Court decisions, *Sweatt v. Painter*, and I actually knew the nephew of Heman Sweatt, the man who entered the law school with much resistance to his admission. He was put in this room by himself with law books, and that was their way of complying with the requirement that he be admitted to the law school. He was not allowed to sit in the classroom with the other law students.

CH: And this was what year?

HM: *Sweatt v. Painter* took place in the 1950s, around the time of *Brown v. Board of Education*. Sweatt's nephew was going to University of Texas in Austin when I was there—that was very much living history for us. There were racial incidents happening. The first day that we moved into the dorm, there was a big brouhaha because some white parents didn't want their child in a room with a black roommate. Everyone had gotten a form that said, "Do you mind having a roommate of another race?" and this girl had said she didn't mind, but her parents did mind, so the school moved her out of the room and gave her a white roommate. That set the tone.

CH: Let's talk for a moment about the groups that were bringing in the black artists. There was a group that was publishing the *Black Print* monthly and a Black Arts movement in Austin. Did the University sponsor the readings?

HM: Yes. These were readings on campus that were sponsored by departments. Many of the African writers came because of the strong African Languages Department. Some of them were visiting lecturers and I think that possibly, the English Department sponsored some of the readings even though they weren't necessarily teaching these people's work in the classroom. We also connected, through *Black Print,* with some of the writers. We published, or actually re-printed poems from people like Michael Harper and maybe Nikki Giovanni or Gloria Oden. I remember when Haki Madhubuti came. He was still Don L. Lee at the time. I had come from my English class to the reading with my Shakespeare book. I didn't have any of his books and I couldn't buy any because I was too broke, but I got him to sign my collected works of Shakespeare. He laughed; that is how it was. These writers' work was not in the curriculum but they were there because they were on the circuit and someone had invited them. Feminist poets were coming too. I remember going to see Adrienne Rich read and Audre Lorde. There was also a group in Austin called Women and Their Work, and they did a lot to promote literature and art by women. They were one of the first organizations to sponsor me at a reading. There was also a group called Texas Circuit. I was starting to see that there was a world out there where people were poets and writers and that was their life. I hadn't really thought about that. I just thought, "Okay, I am going to school and I'm going to be a teacher and that will be my life." Then this other possibility opened up. It helped to see African American women who were poets and that was their identity.

CH: You talked yesterday about beginning to hear the Language poets around San Francisco after you started graduate school and how Nathaniel Mackey, himself influenced by Robert Duncan and Amiri Baraka, was an important mentor for you.

HM: He was an important presence.

CR: Presence?

HM: Yes.

CR: And you began to see a different possibility for your poetic voice? Even from your first book, were you already positioning your work, or negotiating your work in dialogue with, rather than in imitation of, what you were hearing?

HM: I think so, because I felt it was possible to enter the space that was created. My identity was part of everything that I wrote, so it gave me a freedom to write a poem about a mother braiding her daughter's hair that was a very black poem, but didn't have to say, "This is a black woman braiding her black child's black hair." There were those poems where blackness had to be asserted and I appreciated what that act of assertion had accomplished. It allowed me to write a simple poem about a mother braiding her child's hair or a poem about a quilt, just the warmth of the quilt. I realized that I was choosing certain subjects that would allow me to explore aspects of black culture and community and family. I think *Tree Tall Woman* is really about relations among black people, whether it's family or intimate relationships or just being in the world as a person who has a particular perspective, but it was not having continually to point out that I was writing from a black perspective. That was just part of the work.

CH: And this is the work that you were writing by the time you were in graduate school?

HM: No, by graduate school I was responding to the idea that identity is much more complex and much more negotiated and constructed. I didn't exactly have an essentialist notion of identity and culture, but I did think that I knew what black culture was, especially since as an undergraduate, I had learned about the other side of black culture that I hadn't really experienced. I felt pretty well-versed. Then, I began to think about the subject as the problem, which was a lot of what graduate school is about, deconstructing the subject. There was resistance on the part of feminists and people of color who were saying, "Just as we are beginning to explore our subjectivity, all of a sudden, we are going to deconstruct the subject and it doesn't matter who is writing?"

CR: Say, "The author is dead."

HM: And it doesn't matter who wrote it; it is language writing itself. There was resistance to that notion. I was really intrigued by it. On the one hand, we used to joke about how there should be a moratorium on certain kinds of writing because we've had enough of that. On the other hand, I thought I should think seriously about how poststructuralism applies to me because I didn't think it applied to me in the same way it would to, say, a white male writer because a white male writer had a tradition to look back upon that I didn't have. I had some tradition as a black writer, but it wasn't regarded in the same way. I had to think about how this discussion of the subject would apply to me. I had to expand my sense of black subjectivity, to see that it is more complicated and dispersed throughout the diaspora. Black people do not necessarily speak the same language or have the same beliefs. There may be some things they have in common, but there is a lot of diversity at the same time. *Muse & Drudge* is the result of that thinking. *Trimmings* and *S*PeRM**K*T* are ways of moving in that direction. Those two books are influenced by Gertrude Stein's *Tender Buttons,* and by my reading as a graduate student, reading the theory, particularly feminist theory, and thinking about language not as transparent but constructed. *Muse & Drudge* in some way allowed me to put together the kind of exploration of black culture that I had been doing in *Tree Tall Woman* and the kind of playing with language and form that I had been doing with *Trimmings* and *S*PeRM**K*T*.

It allowed me to put these things together and also, it helped me to put audiences together because I had lost the audience for *Tree Tall Woman*. I didn't see them when I would read *Trimmings* and *S*PeRM**K*T* because for one thing, I started to get more readings on campuses than in communities. *Tree Tall Woman* attracted audiences in community venues. *Trimmings* and *S*PeRM**K*T* got me a lot of invitations to read at colleges and universities. Part of it might have to do with the fact that I was part of that milieu, as a graduate student and as an assistant professor when I started out at Cornell. I was already known to people. But I would look out at audiences and there would be no people of color. Period. I would be the only person of color in the room—not that there is anything necessarily wrong with that but there is something a little bit odd about it. I would think, "What happened to all the black folks? Why aren't they able to relate to this?" I made sure that my picture was on *Trimmings*—not just to see me, but also to see that a black person wrote this book. It was a shock to go to reading after reading and there would be no people of color in the room. *Muse & Drudge* was written partly to bring the audience back together again.

CH: Did it work?

HM: Yes, it's happening. It's still the case that I am reading a lot on college campuses, but I will see black people, I'll see some Latinos, I'll see some Asian American students there. Part of it has to do with people of color feeling that they can actually deal with literature. People who are bilingual may feel that they have deficiencies in English. Partly it has to do with people being the second and third generation in their family to go to college. When I was a student at UT Austin, most of the people in my cohort were the first in their families to go to college. First generation has to go out and be doctors and lawyers, business people. They have to be able to make back the investment for their families. I think my literary activity is possible because in my family, I was the third generation to attend some type of college. My maternal grandfather was in the seminary. One of my grandmothers went to normal school and was an elementary school teacher. Since I was third generation, that created a certain tolerance in my family for my wanting to be a liberal arts major. Also, the kinds of jobs that people in my family had all had to do with having a respect for literacy. Being a teacher, being a pastor, a printer, and a clerical worker. I never found even one other black student at UT Austin who was majoring in English. I was the only one. In every class that I attended, I was the only black person. And not a single black professor. I took Ethnic Studies to get a black professor. But in the English department, no. We had one person of color, a Japanese American who was teaching Emerson. That's how it was.

CH: No women taught at that time, or very few.

HM: The white women professors I had were definitely inspirational to me. There were certain younger women who were my models and they made me feel that I could do that. They were intellectual and serious. They didn't get tenure. Of the three that I am thinking of, not a one of them got tenure at UT Austin and now one of them is writing Gothic novels. She was a Chaucer scholar.

CH: In *Trimmings* the language becomes more a subject for analysis, rather than a vehicle for expression, or in addition to being a vehicle for expression, and gender becomes a subject that you are really contemplating. Charles Bernstein calls this book "a poetics of cultural modernism." Sandra Cisneros says of your later book *Muse & Drudge* that "language and rhetoric always come up." You are "the queen of hip hyperbole," as she puts it. What interests me is that you kind of burst into this linguistically innovative and thematically feminist verse. You say at the end of *Trimmings* that you wanted to think about language as clothing and clothing as language and that you wondered why women's writing has traditionally been so ephemeral. How did you do that in *Trimmings*?

HM: A lot of it had to do with my engagement with Stein's text, *Tender Buttons*. I remember my earlier attempts to read Stein and thinking, "I can't read this! I can't understand it!" I felt frustrated but it was intriguing. I thought, "She acts like she thinks she knows what she's doing."

CH: Frustrated by the opaqueness?

HM: Right. The language is elusive and there is a secretive quality about Stein's work. She has her own idiosyncratic approach to language, and you get the sense that she definitely knows what she is doing but I felt I just didn't get it. I probably first tried to read Stein as an undergraduate, but I got frustrated and left it. Then when I went back as a graduate student, armed with a lot more theory and a lot more critical attitude about language, all of a sudden, Stein was making sense to me. Also, I really appreciated the elegance of what she was doing, elegance in the way that scientists and mathematicians use it, that you use the fewest elements. An elegant solution is not too complicated. By using words and the syntactical structures over and over again—often there's a series, a list, and the only punctuation is periods and commas—she is boiling down language to the absolute, essential elements.

I began to understand that that was a different way to use language, a way of using language that forces the reader either to throw it down, or else if you stick with it, to enter another subjectivity. The language seems to create an alternate subjectivity. I thought, "This is really powerful, what she is doing with language." I could see how putting items in a series created different ways of reading the sentence. Syntactically, it can be read as items in a series or it can be read as appositives. Are these things contiguous with or equivalent to each other? That is suggested by the way she uses punctuation.

Around that time, I must have read Ron Silliman's *The New Sentence* and I was very interested in the idea of the paratactic sentence and what that sentence is able to do poetically because in a way, the paratactic sentence, because of the compression, is more poetic than a prose sentence. I mean, you could have a prose sentence that uses the paratactic syntax, but there is something about parataxis itself that acts as a sort of poetic compression. I was interested in the technical, syntactical construction and how to use that to allow more ambiguity in the work, to create different levels of meaning using a prose paragraph, a prose poetry paragraph as the unit. Also, I was interested in *Tender Buttons*. The units operate separately and collectively. That really helped me with the form of *Trimmings* because you could read it as separate poems, you could read it as a longer poem that is composed of these units, these paragraphs. In a way, each paragraph is doing the same thing and there is a metonymical construction where the female body is constructed around metonymy.

I was analyzing what Stein was doing to figure out what I could use and I found that on a lot of levels, I could use what she was doing: the structure of the book itself, in terms of using a prose-poetry form, and a paratactic sentence that is compressed, that is not really a grammatical sentence but that makes sense in an agrammatical way, a poetic way. Also, in her use of subject matter, where she is dealing with objects, rooms, and food, the domestic space that is a woman's space and with the ideas of consumption, our investment in objects, our consumer fetishism. At the same time, I read Marx on commodity fetishism. So, all these things came together for *Trimmings*.

S*PeRM**K*T is really the companion of *Trimmings*. On the one hand, it's the woman with the wardrobe and on the other, it's the woman with her shopping list in the supermarket, because women are still constructed through advertising as the consumers who bring these objects into the household. *S*PeRM**K*T* was about my recollections of jingles that have embedded themselves in my brain. We used to have to memorize poetry, the nuns made us do that in Catholic school, and we had to do that also for church programs. It's harder for me to recall some of that poetry than these ads, partly because the ads are just so quick, but twenty-year-old jingles are embedded in my brain and I thought about the power of those jingles, that mnemonic efficiency of poetry, of the quick line that is economical and concise and compressed. Even more than *Trimmings*, *S*PeRM**K*T* is trying to think about the language in which we are immersed, bombarded with language that is commercial, that is a debased language. Those jingles are based in something that is very traditional, which is the proverb, the aphorism. Those are the models, so I try to think back through the commercial and the advertising jingle, through the political slogan, back to the proverb and the aphorism to that little nugget of collected wisdom, and to think about the language that is so commercialized, debased, and I try to recycle it. The idea of recycling is very much a part of *S* PeRM**K*T,* to take this detritus and to turn it into art. I was definitely thinking about visual artists who do that, collage artists and environmental artists, and things like the Heidelberg House in Detroit, where people take actual trash and turn it into a work of art.

CH: The play, or the pun, on "meat market" is most obviously visual but also linguistic. You open signaling the metapoetic moment to the poem: "Lines assemble gutter and margin." Maybe I don't get the poetic lines by that first line, but I certainly do when I get to: "More on line incites the eyes. Bold names label familiar type faces. Her hand scanning, throwaway lines." You read the lines and you read between the lines.

HM: You read as you stand in line.

CH: You read as you stand in line, right—holding your "individually wrapped singles, frozen divorced compartments, six-pack widows." Is it accurate to read this passage as a breakdown of gender relations?

HM: Well, people are hailed, as they say. You are ideologically hailed through your race, your class, your gender. You come to identify the ways that you are hailed and so you are identifying with a particular gender, with a particular race or class, or all at the same time. Or sometimes you are divided up into compartments and sometimes you are hailed for your class, but not your race or your gender. I always wanted to use the pun as a lever to create the possibility of multiple readings. Yes, it's about the lines at the supermarket and about the lines on a page and, well, the supermarket as an environment of language. There is so much writing in a supermarket. There are signs everywhere, labels on products, and I liked the idea of the supermarket as a linguistic realm where there are certain genres of writing. Instructions as a genre of writing. Every trip to the supermarket became research and a possible excursion into language. I wanted to broaden the idea of the supermarket, so that works like clothing in *Trimmings*. The supermarket becomes the reference point, the metonymic reservoir of ways that we see the world and ourselves in it. We are consumers; that's how we are constructed as citizens. People consume more than they vote. It's more important what you buy than what candidates you vote for. That has overtaken our sense of ourselves as citizens in a civic society.

CH: In terms of critically thinking about the discourses that we hear, your work suggests that we consume rather than think through language. At the end of *Trimmings*, you discuss how your identity as a black woman writing about constructions of dominant femininity goes into the book. A word like "Pink," for example, signifies femininity in the dominant culture, but "pink" and "slit" apply equally to a sewing catalog and a girlie magazine. You write that as "a black woman writing in this language, I suppose I already had an ironic relationship to this pink and white femininity. Of course if I regard gender as a set of arbitrary signs, I also think of race—as far as it is difference that is meaningful—as a set of signs. Traces of black dialect and syntax, blues songs and other culturally specific allusions enter the text with linguistic contributions of Afro-Americans to the English language." So you were already thinking about how to infuse traditionally poetic language, and we might even say, the tradition of poetic innovation—if we look at Gertrude Stein's *Melanctha* with traces of black dialect and syntax.

HM: This is another frustrating Gertrude Stein experience! Is she racist or is she just playing with the idea of race?

CH: I taught that novella in New Orleans to a fairly diverse class and I had to stop teaching it. We couldn't get past its representations of race.

HM: Too much contention?

CH: Well it wasn't the contention; it was pain. It was an undergraduate class. Black students were very used to the thoughtless expression of racism in New Orleans, but they hadn't experienced it at that level of conscious expression. It was too painful for them to discuss. I ended up just stopping the attempt to discuss and analyze.

HM: Wow. I know that Richard Wright championed this work and actually, if you think about it, there are some similarities between it and *Native Son*, even though they had very different agendas. The naturalistic mode in which he was working also put blackness into a kind of stark relief in a way that happens in *Melanctha* as well, although she does it in a seemingly more playful manner. He seems very deadly serious. They both seem to be interested in the cultural significance of blackness and whiteness and the whole set of signifiers that are called into play when you question the whole idea of difference.

CH: Before we get into *Muse & Drudge*, how did that come into play in *Trimmings* and *S*PeRM**K*T*?

HM: In *Trimmings,* I actually found myself at a certain point becoming alarmed, because I wanted the book to be about feminist ideas, a feminist exploration of how femininity is constructed using clothing, how the clothing itself speaks to, or is emblematic of, certain kinds of constraints on women's bodies. That is one of the issues I wanted to deal with: the overlap at that time of pornography and fashion, the kind of photography that was very trendy in fashion magazines. There was a lot of S&M imagery in the eighties. We read *The Story of O* in a graduate seminar at Santa Cruz. I was horrified and fascinated because all of a sudden, the discourse of pornography and sadomasochism was taking over the feminist conversation in the same way that pornography seemed to be taking over fashion. So I was really wondering, "What does this mean?" The other thing had to do with the critique by black women and other women of color of the very way that feminism was constructed around the needs of white women without always considering the sometimes very different needs of women of color who were not middle class, or working-class white women who also had problems with academic feminism. I think a lot of us were puzzled by why we were reading *The Story of 0* in a women's studies class. Does this really make sense? I actually found that book hard to read, it was painful to read. Partly my book was really setting out to be an explication of white feminism, but then I felt kind of uneasy doing that. I was thinking about the dominant color code for femininity. It is pink and white. English literature is full of the "blush." I felt that I had to include images of black women. *Trimmings* grew from my response to Stein. One of my poems even cannibalizes Gertrude Stein's "Petticoat" poem. My reading of Stein's "Petticoat" poem also brings Manet's "Olympia" into the picture. I had an insight that she might have also been thinking about that painting, with her "Petticoat" poem.

CH: Would you read that passage from your poem?

HM:

A light white disgraceful sugar looks pink, wears an air, pale compared to shadows standing by. To plump recliner, naked truth lies. Behind her shadow wears her color arms full of flowers. A rosy charm is pink. And she is ink. The mistress wears no petticoat or leaves. The other in shadow, a large, pink dress.

I'm using the language of Stein. She has a "light white," "an inkspot," "a rosy charm." So I put those words into my poem. Then I expanded to give the reader an image of Manet's painting of the white nude with the black woman in the shadows who's obviously a servant. Manet contrasts the white woman's body and the black woman's body with the white woman's body constructed as beautiful, feminine, seductive, and also a little outrageous. The black woman is basically just a part of the decor but her presence seems to enhance the qualities that are attributed to the white nude. In a way, the whole book is really built around this: both my active and my somewhat critical engagement with Stein, my problematic relation to the Western icon of beauty and the black woman's relationship to that, and my interest in representation itself; whether it is a visual representation or a representation in language. I didn't think it was enough just to have that, so I put some other things in here that were definitely meant to investigate alternative female images. I put in the Josephine Baker poem and the "bandanna" poem because it was unsettling to me just to investigate this white femininity without some kind of black experience being represented as well. There are also "cool dark lasses" wearing their shades, maybe jazz divas, someone like a Billie Holiday. I have "the veiled woman" at the end. I remember at this time in graduate school, I read a book, *Veiled Sentiments,* by Lila Abu-Lughod, about the Arabic traditions of veiling women, so that was in my mind as well. It's a way of taking a woman's body out of circulation but she's still being controlled in the culture.

CH: But not being specularized?

HM: Right. She is outside of the gaze or she is protected from the gaze. Some of the radical Islamic fundamentalists think that they are actually liberated by wearing the veil. I was using this work to explore such questions and problems. This book is connected to *Muse & Drudge* because *Muse & Drudge* is a book about the image and representation of black women, and *Trimmings* has more to do with the representation in the dominant culture of white women, although there are black women here and there. *Muse & Drudge* is intended to think about folk representations, popular culture representations, self-representations of black women, and to think about how to take what is given. There is a whole set of codes, a whole set of images that we really don't control as individuals. They are collective and they are cultural. The problem as a writer is: How do you write yourself out of the box that you are in? *Muse & Drudge* is an attempt to take those representations and fracture them, as I try to do with breaking up the lines and collaging the quatrains together, sometimes from four different sources. It was an attempt to use this language as representation, to use it in a self-conscious way as code, as opposed to taking the code as something that is real. The body exists but there is a way that your body is interpreted based on a historical and social context. I take that and use it as material, as opposed to saying well, that defines you; that's what makes you who you are. I have a certain faith as a writer that we can use language in a liberatory way to try to free ourselves. But at a certain point, I was concerned that I was continuing to be trapped, in the prison house, right? A lot of the strategies had to do with my breaking out. I had to take things and riff on them, as a musician improvises on a melody and really creates a new song. It's based on the same old traditional standard but sounds new when it is performed in this way.

CR: Aldon Nielsen, in his recent book *Black Chant,* and Elizabeth Frost, in a recent essay in *Women's Studies,* have both discussed your work as fundamentally reconfiguring our understanding of black cultural productions. Frost characterizes *Muse & Drudge* as a hybrid serial-poem, a "heteroglossic series," structured by the blues quatrain but working with Bahktinian heteroglossia, with a lot of languages, various cultural registers. I will confess to you that when I read *Trimmings,* I missed many of the references to black identity until I had read some of your criticism, even though I was really thinking about it. For example, in the section that you just read, I noted "shadow" when I first read the passage, but it didn't signify anything more than the literal meaning. After reading your criticism, the light lit. It's not possible for a white reader to miss the signifying in *Muse & Drudge.* You talked the other day about the practice of code-switching, and I wanted you to talk a bit more about how you are working with that in *Muse & Drudge,* the significance of including black dialect with the simultaneous invocation of Sappho as the poem opens up.

HM: With "Sappho and Sapphire"? Because Sapphire has been a pejorative figure for black women ever since the old Amos & Andy television comedy, and before that, a radio program with white men doing their version of black dialect. So it was actually an extension of the minstrel tradition where "black face" was done linguistically instead of in a visual way. Later black actors performed these stereotypes in the television comedy. So the black woman, Sapphire, was a loudmouth, aggressive, the image of the supposedly emasculating black woman with the husband who is henpecked. She was a shrill harpy and she always dressed in grotesque outfits as well, with hideous hats. So in the sixties, when people were reversing the signification of these pejorative terms, black women reclaimed Sapphire as an assertive, vocal black woman who stands up for her own opinions. You know, just take that negative stereotype and make it positive. Sapphire is actually an entry in the *Feminist Dictionary* with a discussion of this process of inversion. Of course, there is an African American writer who has taken this as her pseudonym as a poet and a novelist also. I definitely wanted to think about Sapphire singing the blues and Sapphire as Sappho, singing the blues. One of the people, my cohort at UC Santa Cruz, Diane Rayor, translates ancient Greek and has published a book called *Sappho's Lyre*. I transformed her title in my first line, "Sapphire's lyre," to think about a crossroads of ancient lyric poetic tradition. If we think of ancient lyric poetry, we have to think of Sappho. This is a place where a woman is actually one of the forerunners and foremost practitioners of the art. We don't have too many areas where that is the case, so I'm honoring this woman and I'm also thinking about the blues tradition and Diane Rayor's translations, really, because she is trying to bring Sappho into a very contemporary American language. It seemed to me that Sappho is singing the blues. Sappho's like a blues singer, to me, in translation. So, that was the conceit that allowed me to go on with this poem and to investigate my own connections with this tradition, which was actually called into question by people like the Language poets who feel that the lyric poem is too much entangled with a subject they want to deconstruct. I have a certain attachment to the lyric subject, but the lyric subject in this poem is multiple, not singular. It is many voices and contradictory voices. It is a heteroglossia or maybe a cacophony of voices.

CR: And it's very playful. You have lines like, "Up from slobbery," which are very funny and playful, yet at the same time, very critical of a particular voice.

HM: Yes. *In Up from Slavery,* Booker T. Washington talks about learning "the gospel of the toothbrush" and part of what those educators thought they were doing was teaching people how to be decent and clean. In order to qualify for the rights of American citizens, you have to be decent and clean. That's assuming that blacks weren't already, but had to be taught how to do this!

CH: And also placed. It allowed them to be placed in a perennially subservient position.

HM: Yeah, his entrance exam was, in a sense, to sweep the floor. He talks about how he was assigned to sweep a floor when he came to apply for admission to Hampton, implicitly an admission requirement. So even to gain admission at this school, he had to be willing to sweep the floor, which is very appropriate considering what they trained people to do. Each one of those lines is a kind of tag for a whole possible conversation that the poem doesn't stop to engage in. It just gives the tag and keeps moving.

CH: Why?

HM: Partly because I wanted the poem to have that quality of quick movement from one thing to another, from one subject or thought to another, from one mood or emotion to another. Partly because I wanted things to be in flux, a state of flux, a state of change. If you stand still too long, they will put chains on you, so you want to keep moving. This is one of the things that is most fascinating to me about the slave narratives I was studying while I was writing my dissertation. The true freedom in the slave narrative is at the point of deciding to escape and the journey north. Once they get to the North, they are, again, part of a hierarchy and they are still at the bottom of that hierarchy. If everyone is free in the North and you are still working as a servant and living in someone else's house and having to obey the master of the house, you are earning wages, but you are still at the bottom of the hierarchy. The freedom that people experience is actually when they are on the road, in flight. I associate that with writing, for myself. The time that I am free is when I am writing. The poem is running; the poem is flying. There is an expression that is part of African American folklore—when people are telling tall tales they say, "If I'm flyin', I'm flyin'" because they are pushing the limits of language.

CH: We theorize identity as being fluid and that seems very pertinent to your work, through the punning and the word play. A word is never fixed; it's always bleeding into a new identity by the process of association but in practice, once we fix that theory of identity as fluid, then it solidifies into something more inflexible.

HM: Right, it's a paradox.

CR: I'm also fascinated by what seems a new spiritual register in the collection. Maybe I'm missing it in the earlier collections.

HM: I think it is more deliberately in use in *Muse & Drudge* than it had been.

CH: I recognized some of the references to Yoruba and Achebe's "ancestor dances," references to Orishas and the "deja voodoo queens"—that kind of wonderful word play that you are always engaging in! I wondered how that functioned in the poem as a whole. Would you talk about that a bit?

HM: Partly those things are allusions. They work in the poem as allusions to the African diaspora, cultures, and spiritual traditions. They expand the idea of blackness. They suggest both continuity and discontinuity. That is knowledge that I have acquired through reading, through study. It is not knowledge that I have directly through experience or practice. My family is Baptist. That is the religious or spiritual base that I come from regardless of whether I currently go to church or not.

CH: Your grandfather was a Baptist minister?

HM: My grandfather and one of my great-grandfathers also. My grandmother was the daughter of a Baptist minister and she married a Baptist minister. My family is very, very deeply religious. I think that I am spiritual; I am not religious in the same way that they are and I am not tied to the church in the same way that they are. I am interested in these African spiritual traditions partly because I think that in some ways, there are continuities for people who call themselves Christians. In my family, there was this other side of spirituality that I now understand to be retentions of African spiritual systems. In my family, because we were always so much involved with the church, there was the sense that those things were dangerous and that we don't really want to deal with them, but we also don't dismiss them.

CH: These things?

HM: Voodoo. Christians didn't believe this stuff and just dismissed it and also educated people didn't believe this stuff. My ideas about it have changed, partly because of what I see in my own family. They used to say to us that we should not eat food in other people's houses because you don't know who in the community might have a grudge against you or someone in your family. If we were with our family and invited to have dinner with some friends, that was one thing, but as children just wandering around at that time, people would invite you in. You could be playing with some kids and they would have you over to eat or old ladies might invite you in for teacakes. My mother would warn us not to do that. She said they could harm you that way, through your food. At the time we thought, "Well, what are they going to do, poison us? Or does she think their kitchen isn't clean enough?" This is what we would think, but now I realize that my mother meant they could harm you through the food. There was also an experience I had with a Nigerian when I was an undergraduate. He was a graduate student in computer engineering. He was completely technologically adept, a totally modern contemporary person who also believed in all sorts of ghosts and spirits and magical practices at the same time. It was perfectly compatible. These are some of the things that made me think in more complicated ways about black identity or just human capacity for holding contradictory thoughts. I began to think about the meaning of the whole world of spirits. What do they actually do for people?

As an artist, it's a whole set of metaphors. It's a system of metaphors that allows people to think in certain ways. The fact is that people can think in these metaphoric ways and then they can shift into completely scientific ways of thinking. To me, that is fascinating, and it's one of the things that black people and people of color have to offer, that tolerance of the dichotomy between the material and the spiritual or scientific ways of thinking versus ways of thinking that are thought to be superstitious or primitive. Some of the excesses of the twentieth century have to do with devotion to the scientific or mechanical and actually, in a way, worshipping *that*. Actually, we are closing off a part of ourselves, the metaphoric, the intuitive, the poetic aspects of our thinking process in order to enhance the other part. For instance, there is a great book by the anthropologist Karen McCarthy Brown. She studied women who practice Haitian voodoo. They have emigrated from Haiti to New York City; they live in Brooklyn and they are keeping their community together through these practices. One of the things that is interesting is that they have many Loa or spirits. Everyone can pick the Loa with which they are most compatible, and there are certain qualities that respond to human attributes that people want to feed or enhance and when you are feeding the Loa, you are feeding these qualities in yourself. By bringing these offerings, you are giving yourself permission to express these qualities, these human qualities that are part of yourself. One of the things that she suggested as a feminist scholar is that there are as many female deities as there are male. This gives many opportunities for expression of female being in the world because there are so many goddesses that you can worship. If you are a woman who is very feminine and coquettish, and very much involved with enhancing your erotic powers, there is a deity for that. If you are really into being a mother, there is a deity for that. If you are out there being a career woman, there is a deity that will support that aspect of your being. That's one way I understand certain spiritual practices. It was kind of mystifying, to have the sense that it really has to do with your life, here and now, on earth and that these are modes of expression of human aspiration, and that these gods are so humanlike. They have favorite foods, favorite liquor that they prefer. Some of them like beer and some like rum and some like whiskey. Some like cigars and some like a certain brand of perfume and they are very specific in their likes and dislikes and I am fascinated by the idea of indulging the preferences of these spirits. The people probably also feel that it reinforces their sense of themselves as being very particular and having very specific likes and dislikes and that you indulge yourself the way you indulge the Loa.

CH: You had mentioned that in your study *Gender, Subjectivity, and Slave Narratives,* gender and the subjugated body have influenced your poetry. Can you discuss at a bit more length some of the ways that the two languages were mutually influential, perhaps, or have you found that your critical, theoretical work influenced your poetry?

HM: When you go into graduate school and you learn how to do critical writing, in a sense, what you are learning is an alternative aesthetic for writing. I remember when I first thought that a lot of critical writing is awkward and ugly. It is densely compacted. The kind of critical writing that I aspired to seemed to cram a lot of information into a sentence. There were incredibly complicated sentences, and you had to really keep your wits about you, especially when writing on a computer screen. I'd think, "Could I diagram this sentence?" In a way it's kind of the opposite of the paratactic sentence, the hypotactic sentence. It has many connectors, many clauses, subordinate and coordinate clauses and you have to know where you are in the sentence to keep it all together. Then you have to have many of these sentences adding up and accumulating. The academic training altered my sense of what in writing is pleasurable. The pleasure that I got from writing before I went to graduate school had a lot to do with rhythm, musicality, the usual poetic qualities that we think of when we think of literature. It was an aesthetics of beauty. Critical writing gave me an aesthetics of intellectual engagement, of complexity of thought and a corresponding complexity of syntax and structure, the complexity of argument as opposed to metaphor. Metaphor is complex in its own way; argument has another way of creating complexity. It was significant that I learned to enjoy and to love this writing that at first struck me as so ugly, so lacking in rhythm, so lacking in beauty and harmony, and also, so demanding. You don't sit down and read critical theory for escape or for the kind of pleasure that people get when they read Wordsworth. You are in a different zone. I think that my poetry after graduate school is drawing on this different connection to writing, this critical connection to writing. In these more recent books, the writing engages both with what I think of as the pleasure centers—those things that really have to do with the heartbeat and with the singing quality of language, the voice, song, the rhythmic speech—and something that is happening from your eye to your brain, where your voice is not even necessarily involved. I try to combine those two qualities together in the poetry. I think it was very important; I could not write the poetry I am writing now, without having gone through that academic experience.

But in some ways I think I'm ruined, because the kind of poetry I was writing before has much more mass appeal. Recently, I was reading in the L.A. Book Festival and because I realized there would be very few people there, since I was reading at nine in the morning, I chose to read from *Tree Tall Woman*. I talked with one man there who complained, "Poetry is so hard to understand. I feel like they are really trying to trick me and I don't know what they are talking about." But he loved those poems and I thought, "Boy, if I had read other stuff, he wouldn't have felt this way." My mother used to say, "You can sling that lingo but can you write it so that anybody's grandma can understand?" To her way of thinking, that was the great writer. The great writer is the person who can write in a language that is accessible to anyone who is literate. So I'm always feeling a certain tension because poetry "should" be accessible, simple in certain ways. Plain speech. An American style really is a plain speech style. That is what we think of as American as opposed to European.

CH: As Marianne Moore said, "A language dogs and cats can read."

HM: Yes, but on the other hand, there is the dazzle of the intellect and there is the complexity of the thought or the kinds of connections that can be made when you are working on different levels of signification or different rhetorical levels. I hope that this is a productive tension or conflict. I think that I don't lose sight of the fact that everyone didn't go to graduate school and some people just want to read something and feel a very direct and uncomplicated pleasure. I want some aspect of that kind of pleasure in my work and when I am revising my work, I am thinking about the people I am leaving out and am thinking about how I can bring them back in. I want the work I do to be intellectually complex, but at some level, the form is open to allow people to enter wherever they are. Especially with *Muse & Drudge,* I thought a lot about what is going to exclude readers and what is going to include readers. At various times, people will feel very strongly their exclusion and that will trouble them and be uncomfortable. There are other aspects of the book that will allow them to stick with it, to persist through the rough passages. There will be moments of insight and moments of familiarity and connection with the text as opposed to those moments of alienation, estrangement, and feeling left out. I wanted there to be enough of those moments of inclusion for everyone so that they can tolerate the moments of feeling their exclusion. In some ways, the experience of the reader parallels my experience in the world and perhaps everyone's experience in the world. In some conversations, I feel right at home. In other conversations I know I'd better sit quiet and listen for awhile because they are talking about things I really know little of and maybe at some point later, I can speak in this conversation, but at the moment, I'm better off just listening and understanding where they begin. I think more and more, as the world becomes a global village, it doesn't mean that we have the simplicity of the village. It means that we are interacting with a lot of people we really don't understand.

CH: We may even think we understand and discover later that we missed some key codes.

HM: It happens more and more often, but I've noticed as black codes are entering the mainstream, they are altered once they get there. The process of entering the mainstream alters them and that is partly what I am thinking about with *Muse & Drudge.* What happens when you take these codes and use them in a context, in a way that they are actually fractured and collaged with other materials so that they don't mean what they would mean in a coherent system because they are now in an incoherent system? This book is really about what creates coherence and what is felt as incoherent. The quatrains and the use of rhyme are things that help people, things that make a poem look orderly, make the poem seem familiar, that give it elements of convention that people can deal with while they are reeling from the unfamiliar and incoherent.

CH: Who have been your major influences?

HM: Definitely Stein is an influence on *Trimmings* and *S*PeRM**K*T.* Gwendolyn Brooks is such a deep influence on me that sometimes I don't even know that it's there, but it's there and it has been pointed out by a couple of people, like Stacey Hubbard in her review of *Trimmings*. I think Langston Hughes as well, for what he was trying to do—you know, the things that we now take for granted about using a culturally marked, black language and bringing this colloquial speech and blues and jazz elements into poetry, and also for being political, trying not just to entertain people with poetry, but also to get them to think. People like Bob Kaufman and Amiri Baraka have been very useful to me. I would say Lucille Clifton. She was at Santa Cruz when I was there. Nate Mackey, Lucille Clifton, and Al Young were all teaching there, at least part of the time that I was there. I think that all three of them were in different ways very important to me. They did different things but in different ways. They all suggested to me that there is a subtlety in the African American contribution to poetry. I came kind of late to reading Melvin Tolson's work, but Melvin Tolson was a revelation. And Jean Toomer.

There is a canon that is constructed now and there are certain people who are marginal to the canon or who get left out of the canon or else they are not taught as often as other writers. There are certain works that are at the center and other works that are more at the periphery and so one of the things I really started to do as a graduate student was to recover this tradition of innovation within African American poetry. The poetic practice that Jean Toomer was doing was very experimental work. I knew of *Cane*. I had found *Cane* in a used bookstore when I was an undergraduate. I used to scour the used bookstores looking for those black books that I was otherwise not going to read in the classroom and I had my own library. I was on a mission to find this literature. I can't understand when my students say, "I'm trying to get into your class. I haven't been able to take your class yet so I can read this book that you are teaching." If I waited until a class was offered, there would be a whole bunch of books I never would have gotten around to reading. I was free to form my own opinion about a lot of these works because there was nothing in the classroom about them. Then, as a graduate student, it was a question of recovering those things that were really at the margin of what was considered black literature, so I became interested in people like Bob Kaufman. I just taught a course that included Stephen Jonas. I haven't seen a single black critic discussing his work at all. Bob Kaufman tends to get marginalized. Melvin Tolson tends to get marginalized. There are different stages of the recovery project. We all try to connect to something but because this information is missing, people don't know that there is a tradition, so each time someone is doing work that is considered innovative, it seems to come out of nowhere or as if all of the interesting innovation comes from the white people that the black writers were hanging around with. Innovative black poets don't seem to have any black antecedents. I'm constructing retrospectively a tradition that I can say is a black tradition. On the other hand, as Nate Mackey points out, there are actually connections that are made through these boundaries of race. A lot of the poets who really did influence my thinking about my work in a different way were white poets, the Language poets. For example, people would say to me, "Oh, do you know Erica [Hunt]? Have you met Erica? You must know Erica." Erica Hunt had been in California, but she had moved to New York by the time I got to California. So, no, I didn't know Erica. I later met her, but people assumed that she and I must know each other but we didn't. We had white friends in common.

Eventually we read together in Detroit and I got to know her and I'm writing about her book, *Arcade,* and about Will Alexander for the first European MELUS conference in Germany. Will is here in Los Angeles and Will and I have a connection because of Nate Mackey and *Hambone.* It's as if now there is beginning to be a quorum. Cecil Giscombe, who edited the special issue of *American Book Review* on so-called black postmodernists, was poetry editor for *Epoch* magazine at Cornell when I was there. I taught his book in my course this year. It was he and Nate and Erica and Will, plus Bob Kaufman, Stephen Jonas, Ed Roberson, Amiri Baraka, and Ntozake Shange, along with Marlene Philip and Kamau Brathwaite. We also have had to ask, *What are the qualities that are considered to be "black" in literature*? If Erica Hunt is writing in Standard English, about an urban experience and a female experience with very few markers of blackness in the work, then is this not to be read as a black text? Will Alexander is writing in the tradition of surrealism. There is Jayne Cortez, who also has connections to surrealism, but is seen as being really engaged with a black political consciousness in a way that moves her work in another direction. Those are some issues that we have had to think about now that we have an established canon with the *Norton Anthology of African-American Literature.* Nate Mackey is in it. Baraka is in it, but some other poets I taught just recently at UCLA in my graduate seminar are not in it.

CH: In your opinion does that narrow the voices of black writers?

HM: The *Norton Anthology* does not include people who are atypical, although it's a fairly exhaustive anthology. It's not just a poetry anthology; it's got all the genres in it. It is trying very hard to include a lot of things, but the nature of anthologies is that they can't include everything; they are supposed to be selective and there are particular criteria. Henry Louis Gates, the chief editor of this anthology, has a particular theory that privileges orality in the text, what I call mimesis of orality in the text. So what if a work does not do that and does not allude to African American culture or diaspora culture? Or does it in ways that seem strange, unfamiliar, or difficult? There are certain things you have to do in order to be visible as a black writer. That necessity does eventually become constraining. I don't think we have completely run out of things we can do within those constraints but we will find them eventually more constraining and I think that, for the future, I'd want to encourage as wide and as inclusive as possible a view of what black poetry, black literature, black language can be. When I am writing I'm sometimes thinking about that.

CH: You mentioned earlier that language and poetry can be liberatory. I wondered how you position your work in terms of a politics of poetics or a poetics of politics. It's so clear with a poet like June Jordan or Adrienne Rich, for that matter, and it's that subject-driven element, if you will, that has become very controversial with the poets who are writing with a transformative politics in mind, a very impassioned and committed poetry that engages in formal experiment. How do you position your work? What are you trying to do?

HM: These are questions that I think about a lot both as a writer and as a teacher and as a reader also. I think that political discourse and the rhetoric that accompanies it really can be in a productive tension with the aesthetic qualities of poetry and literature. I think that there are different intentions that are political that have to do with political discourse and rhetoric that assume that the audience is in your own time and space, that you are addressing living human beings who are capable of performing a particular action that will change political reality. I think that that is a good thing to do and a necessary thing to do and something that we really are compelled to do about our political circumstance. To my way of thinking, literature can do those things but literature also has other things that it wants to do that go beyond the address to the people who are my contemporaries. Partly I am writing for unborn readers in my most optimistic view that the world will still exist, that we will still have literature, that people will be literate, that people will want to read, and that my work will last beyond my lifetime. These are all very optimistic assumptions but if all of that should come to pass, then I am not just addressing the situation that exists in my lifetime. I'm addressing human beings who don't exist yet and so, to me, that means that literature has a larger horizon than political discourse. Political discourse is very important, very necessary, and can be compatible with some but not all of the intentions of literature. When I'm writing, I am usually thinking more about the unborn than those people who are my contemporaries, and my approach to writing really is influenced by this belief, this hope, this optimistic aspiration on my part that my work will continue. In a way, for me, that is a spiritual belief and to the extent that literature has a spiritual intention, then the language operates differently. Language is not so instrumental. Language is not so intently focused on reality. Language is not so much a tool of persuasion to move people to think, act, or behave in a particular way or to focus their energy on a problem that exists now.

Because I live now and I don't live in the future, my framework is my own political reality, my social reality, my cultural reality, so that aspect is there already as far as I am concerned. Literature, art, is ideological even when it has no political agenda. There is a certain implicit politics that is inherent in any work that engages with reality in any sense. Who I am is a political question, but who I can be is a question that literature can help me to answer. I think that art involves a struggle between all of the things that engage us now and all of the things that we can't even imagine because they don't exist yet. For me, for literature to be powerful beyond its present moment, the conditions of its making, there has to be some space or acknowledgment of the possibility of this future, which politics cannot really encompass. Maybe that is the naive position of someone who is an artist, who would like to believe that literature has this power beyond politics, although a visionary politics can be part of literature just because how we live is determined to some extent by these circumstances that both confine us and allow us expression at the same time.

23

"I Dream a World"

A Conversation with Harryette Mullen
by Nibir K. Ghosh

Q. How does it feel to be black and female in the most powerful democracy in the world?

I belong to a race that has been enslaved, segregated, and deprived of rights in a nation calling itself "the land of the free." Yet I am aware of my privileged status as a writer, my comfortable life as an educated, middle-class American in the twenty-first century. My writing addresses the paradox that your question implies. In recent poems, I avoid overtly confessional or didactic writing, but I often focus on identity in a critical way to highlight the contradictions of my existence in this time and place.

Q. Do you feel the contemporary African American writer still needs to confront the idea of Du Bois's "double consciousness"?

When Du Bois wrote *The Souls of Black Folk,* black people were barely acknowledged citizens of the United States. Few Americans understood how profoundly Africans have influenced Western and "mainstream" American culture. My black ancestors could have been among the Africans who arrived in colonial Virginia as indentured workers as early as 1619. We have been in America longer than other immigrant groups, including most Europeans. Researching my family's history, I've found an African American ancestor, a former slave, who was a Union soldier in the Civil War. Another black relative, also a former slave, was elected to the Texas legislature during Reconstruction. Du Bois knew that the problem isn't that we are black. The problem is that the dominant culture often finds it expedient to exploit and exclude a visible minority.

Q. In your own career as a writer and academic have you ever faced the challenges that stem from prejudice on color lines?

Until sixth grade, I attended schools in Texas that were racially segregated by law. My identity as an African American was formed in part through that experience. The difficulty with prejudice is that, particularly in a "post–Civil Rights" context, it isn't always easy to detect. Often it operates silently, through unspoken assumptions. As a writer and teacher affiliated with UCLA, I rarely encounter direct racism aimed at me personally, but institutional racism is a more subtle and pervasive force. California has a very diverse population; but black students and faculty are still underrepresented in the University of California system. Race and culture, class and economics all play a part in determining who is most likely to be accepted into the university.

Q. Four decades after the Civil Rights Act of 1964, how far do you think is the African American community from the dream that Martin Luther King Jr. envisaged in his famous speech?

Langston Hughes wrote, "I dream a world," even before King said, "I have a dream." At the time of his death, King was shifting from a protest movement for black equality to a broader human rights struggle. Although legal discrimination has been struck down, other barriers remain, especially for undereducated, poor, and minority communities.

Q. Within the African American community there has always been a strong undercurrent of conflict along gender lines. How do you respond to such conflicts?

Conflict between men and women is a reality, regardless of race or nationality. I'm not sure there is more conflict in black relationships, although it's possible that we are more outspoken in voicing our disagreements. Certainly our internal disagreements can be aggravated by social factors that undermine the health and stability of our families and communities. It helps to listen with compassion as well as to speak with clarity about our differences and our shared concerns.

Q. What events or factors motivated your choice of the poet's vocation? Who among poets or writers would you like to name as your literary ancestors?

It all began with my family. My parents and grandparents were very caring and articulate adults who read to me when I was a child and imprinted me with a love for language. They gave me books, records, music lessons, and art supplies. They encouraged me to read, write, draw, and paint. They told me that I was intelligent, artistic, creative, and imaginative. I had the idea that I would do something creative, and writing seemed to be my talent. I abandoned the clarinet and the piano. I loved drawing and painting, but I didn't think I was good enough for art school. My writing always got a good response from family, teachers, and friends. It was something I had always done, even before I ever thought of writing as an art form. Because of that early encouragement, I was very open to the influence of the poets who visited my university campus, especially the black, Latino, and feminist poets. I attended as many readings as I could, and then I began to find the local poets in that university town. I joined a community of poets and artists mainly because I enjoyed their company. Two influential living poets who have connected me to whole worlds of literature, music, and culture are Lorenzo Thomas from my Texas days and Nathaniel Mackey from my time in Santa Cruz, California, where I was a graduate student. I'd call them mentors rather than ancestors. As black poets with a global vision, they have been exemplary influences. (Lorenzo Thomas died in 2005.)

Q. Who are your favorite writers?

There are so many writers whose work I love and so many writers I love as friends, it's really hard to mention just a few. I read all sorts of things and I'm always delighted to find new favorites. So maybe I'll just respond by recommending a handful of black writers whose work I've enjoyed for many years: Kamau Brathwaite for poetry, Toni Cade Bambara for short stories, August Wilson and Adrienne Kennedy for drama, Chester Himes for pulp fiction, Toni Morrison for novels. I also love Ishmael Reed's *Mumbo Jumbo*.

Q. What do you recall as your singular contribution as a member of the Texas Commission on the Arts and Artists in the Schools program?

The Artists in Schools program helped me to earn a living while establishing a statewide reputation as a poet. Along with other artists, I led workshops with students and teachers in the public schools. I visited different Texas cities during my years as an emerging poet, so I became acquainted with writers and artists in communities across the state. I was never a member of the Texas Commission on the Arts. I served for one or two years on a literature peer-review panel, which I also chaired. Although panelists were selected for our supposed expertise, our votes were not binding. The state arts commission could and sometimes did ignore our recommendations for funding community arts organizations. I can't point to any singular accomplishment. Perhaps it is enough to say that I continue to write and teach, and I am still on good terms with the multiethnic community of writers that befriended me in Texas.

Q. As a child of the civil rights era, how did you react to works like Richard Wright's *Native Son*, Ralph Ellison's *Invisible Man*, and James Baldwin's *Fire Next Time*?

I have always preferred Baldwin and Ellison to Wright, and I prefer Wright's autobiographical writing in *Black Boy* and *American Hunger* to his novel *Native Son*. It is amazing to me that I found and read these books on my own, although I majored in English and I have a doctorate in literature. They were not taught in any of my undergraduate literature courses. Even as a graduate student, I found few courses that included African American authors, although there were a couple of nineteenth-century American literature courses that looked at the slavery issue from black and white perspectives. It's different now for my students. The curriculum is much more inclusive.

Q. At the turn of the century, what would you identify as dominant trends in contemporary African American writings?

We are grasping our freedom to explore the world, to experiment with style, form, and subject matter, to express ourselves in a variety of ways. With the worldwide recognition of Toni Morrison, Derek Walcott, Wole Soyinka, and other writers of African descent, we have less need to write prescriptively, didactically, or defensively.

Q. Which writers would you like to single out as dominant trendsetters?

I don't know about dominant trendsetters, but I could mention some adventurous editors who have published interesting work in their journals: Nathaniel Mackey in *Hambone,* Giovanni Singleton in *Nocturnes,* Renee Gladman in *Leroy,* Juliana Spahr and Jena Osman in *Chain,* Mark Nowak in *Cross-Cultural Poetics,* Summi Kaipa in *Interlope,* Jordan Davis and Chris Edgar in *The Hat,* Brian Kim Stephans in *Arras,* Michael Magee in *Combo,* Kreg Hasegawa and Daniel Comiskey in *Monkey Puzzle.*

Q. If one were to go by current statistics the African American family seems to be in a real state of crisis. What, according to you, are the causes and remedies for such a malady?

California, where I live, is a "state of crisis." African Americans, individually and collectively, may be in crisis. The family as an institution may be in crisis. Currently the United States is experiencing something called a "jobless economic recovery." There's a saying among black Americans, "When America sneezes, we catch pneumonia." That's partly because, ever since slavery was abolished, we have been America's surplus labor, "the last hired and first fired." I'm not sure that the answer is a return to some ideal "traditional family" that possibly never existed. I think it's more important to respond, individually and collectively, to such basic needs as food, clothing, housing, education, employment, health care, and other human rights.

Q. Your *Muse & Drudge* has for an epigraph Callimachus's statement: "fatten your animal for sacrifice, poet, but keep your muse slender." How exactly would you interpret "slender"?

As I recall, Callimachus was comparing lyric poetry favorably to the weightier epic. In his time the latter was the dominant poetic mode. In our time the reverse is true, as novels, film, and video have taken over narrative. *Muse & Drudge,* a book-length poem of lyric fragments, is an attempt to synthesize the personal and individual voice we associate with lyric and the collective identities we associate with epic. African American blues and spirituals work in a similar way to merge individual and collective expression. Taken out of its original context of classical Latin poetry and placed in relation to this work about people of color, specifically African American women, the quote can be read as a comment on contemporary discussions of physical beauty, body image, health, obesity, dieting, and eating disorders. The epigraph also highlights the oppositional images of earthy versus ethereal women to which my title refers.

Q. In the "afterword" to *Trimmings,* you refer to an ironic relationship with "pink" and "white" femininity. Could you please elaborate?

In part, I was speaking of my relationship to a traditional literary canon. With the notable exception of Shakespeare's sonnets to a mysterious "dark lady," much of European poetry is devoted to pale ladies and blushing maidens. Even when he writes against it, Shakespeare knows the ideological force of aesthetics as a system that shapes our perception of physical and lyrical beauty. What I enjoy about those sonnets is Shakespeare's dissection of conventions that determine what is worthy of praise. Shakespeare shows how we resist convention in order to gratify our desire and how we modify desire to conform to convention. Gertrude Stein in *Tender Buttons* examined another set of conventions regarding women's identification with objects in domestic space. Stein expresses "unspeakable" desire through women's identification, metaphorically and metonymically, with common household objects. Following Stein's attention to objects, I focused on women's clothing and accessories. In my book *Trimmings,* I tried to take apart and examine certain ideas about femininity and masculinity that determine the representation of women in art, literature, media, and popular culture.

Q. Where does your primary interest lie: in the lyric mode of expression or in using words as "weapons"?

For me there is no need to oppose these two possible interests, although I'm more likely to think of writing as a tool or instrument rather than a weapon. I'm always interested in what Roman Jakobson called the "poeticity" of poetry. Poeticity is not exactly the same thing as "lyric mode of expression," which is only one of several different modes of poetry. Although Jakobson gives a redundant definition—poeticity is whatever it is that makes poetry poetic—as a linguist he offers useful ideas about the structure and function of poetic language. I am interested in the variety of poetic language expressing the diversity of human experience. I prefer to explore diversity and variety rather than universality or consistency.

Q. Affirmative Action and other similar legislations have successfully created an elite group of writers and intellectuals who seem to be in a class of their own. Ironically, this elite group seems to keep itself at a safe distance from being involved in the general predicament of the African American community. Do you find this attitude analogous to the "tendency of the literate to view the illiterate and the oppressed as 'voiceless'"?

Are writers, artists, and cultural critics to be classed as elites because some (not all) of our labor is creative and/or intellectual? Yes, we are fortunate to have work that we enjoy. We also, compared to other professionals, receive less income and less respect for what we do. Many of the writers, artists, and intellectuals I know are workers, teachers, mentors, advocates, and activists in communities, schools, arts institutions, prisons, public interest organizations, and social agencies. In addition to the normal workload at our regular jobs, many of us frequently offer our services for low fees or no fees to support the arts and to help struggling organizations in our communities. Affirmative Action is widely misunderstood. This country's elite consists of a class of people (still predominantly white and male) who were educated with the expectation that they would run the world. Affirmative Action is intended to provide greater opportunity for others who are underrepresented in higher education. The chief beneficiaries of Affirmative Action have been white women. It's true that Affirmative Action doesn't go far enough. Can we imagine a world that isn't dominated by a few wealthy families and multinational corporations, and then can we create institutions to empower the rest of us as we remake the world?

Q. How would you describe your process of creativity? Do you proceed from an idea and give it a concrete shape or does a poem emerge as a spontaneous overflow of powerful feelings?

In poetry I hope to merge the pleasures of reading and writing through an interactive critical and creative process. I often use association, improvisation, and disjunctive syntax in word collages composed of original and recycled scraps of language. Some poems I construct around a single idea or literary device. I work with an expansive notion of rhyme that allows a variety of rhetorical tropes and compositional moves. We're accustomed to think only of rhyming similar sounds, but I've begun to think of rhyme in the larger sense of any trope that implicitly or explicitly compares, contrasts, juxtaposes, or opposes sounds, words, ideas, images, memories, and experiences.

Q. In a land where the Statue of Liberty proclaims to the world the avowed principles of life, liberty, and the pursuit of happiness, how do you explain an African American poet losing his poet laureateship on account of his poetic utterances?

Anyone familiar with the life and work of Amiri Baraka would not be surprised to read "Somebody Blew Up America," his response to the terrorist attack of September 11, 2001. I can only guess that the politicians who insisted on his dismissal had never read Baraka's work before his appointment as New Jersey's poet laureate. Composed almost entirely of rhetorical questions rather than declarative statements, his text clearly intends to prompt critical thinking. Beginning with the words "They say," the poem opposes official and unofficial versions of current events, showing how rumors and conspiracy theories circulate in the absence of truth and information:

"They say (who say? Who do the saying)." It seems that many of our politicians are as unaccustomed to reading poetry as they are uninterested in protecting our Bill of Rights. We could call Baraka's provocative poem a test that the politicians failed.

Q. While composing a poem do you have a particular audience in mind? Your poems often seem to adopt the postmodernist stance of obscurity. In writing for the community, don't you think obscurity of poetic expression could be a luxury?

I don't believe that obscurity is a luxury or that simplicity is a necessity. I write for anyone who cares to read or listen to my work. I hope that present and future readers will share my delight in what happens to language when it becomes poetry. I've written poems that are immediately accessible, as well as others that require more attention. Although some readers may find it puzzling, I honestly don't think that my work is difficult. I certainly don't intend to be difficult or obscure. At the same time, I am aware that many readers do not share the assumptions, experiences, or values that influence how I think and write. Poetry invites readers and writers to consider unconventional uses of language. We comprehend poetry in ways we can't always articulate. For whatever reason, some find it difficult to trust this other way of reading and understanding.

Q. Your story "She Swam on from Sea to Shine" ends with the statement: "Revolution is a cycle that never ends . . . Plato opens utopia to poets on opiates." Is your attitude in fiction writing akin to that of a romantic idealist in contrast with your approach to poetry?

"She Swam On . . ." is one of the longer prose works in *Sleeping with the Dictionary*. It was first published in *Callaloo* when the journal editor, Charles Rowell, requested an autobiographical essay. I think of this piece, which summarizes my life in language, as a hybrid genre: a mixture of prose poetry, autobiography, folklore, and fiction. A few of my more conventional short stories have been published in anthologies of Texan, southwestern, or western writers.

Q. How would you chart your poetic voyage from *Tree Tall Woman* through *Trimmings* and *S*PeRM**K*T* to *Muse & Drudge* and *Sleeping with the Dictionary*? Is there an essential transformative pattern?

My writing has changed over the years as I respond to the influence of different people, places, events, and interests. I've become more interested in reading and writing across differences that normally create barriers to understanding. Instead of being daunted by diversity, I try to incorporate it into my own process of critical reading and writing.

Q. Rap music is too often associated with sex and violence. Artists like Tupac Shakur were an integral part of the world of crime. "Gangsta rap" has become quite popular in contemporary America. What are your views on these attributes of rap music that tend to undermine its artistic merit?

Rap music is an expression of contemporary African American youth culture. In addition to music and spoken word, this creative articulation of black experience—known as hip hop—includes dance, fashion and beauty culture, slang, and graffiti art. In its original expression, hip-hop represents the experience and values of black youth in America's desolate inner cities. Growing up without arts instruction in neglected communities, hip-hoppers created alternative art forms that violate conventions of self-expression in urban public space. While gang culture influences rap music, many hip-hop artists are strong opponents of gangs, drugs, and violence. Hip-hop is critical of mainstream hypocrisy. Its attitudes are rooted in this population's disillusionment with America's broken promises. Yet some of the most popular performers embrace prevailing American values of "getting paid" and "living large." They celebrate conspicuous consumption "by any means necessary," with this dictum of Malcolm X now stripped of revolutionary intent. It is intriguing to consider that hip-hop has become the popular expression of youth culture all over the world. However, as hip-hop is packaged for a global mass market, black performers are rewarded for providing images of ghetto life that ultimately affirm the complacency of the middle-class consumer. The worst of it mirrors the mainstream culture's obsession with celebrity, materialism, voyeuristic sex, and formulaic violence.

Q. Do you think there is a need for serious rap artists to combat increasing commercialization to save this popular form from aesthetic decay?

We need to be more selective about our choices. If there were no audience for "gangsta" rap music, those artists and producers would create a different product. Artists can resist the mass-market mentality by creating alternative venues and networks for producing, performing, and distributing their work. Audiences can choose to support creative artists who don't sell a million copies.

Q. How will the new information technology and things such as cyberspace shape and affect black poetry of the future?

Computers, videos, and compact discs are already displacing books and magazines as dominant media, creating mass markets for spoken word and performance poets. Many younger black poets are making compact discs and releasing videos rather than books. Their work may be easier to find on the internet than in printed books or literary journals. My nephew, a student at University of North Carolina, just produced a rap CD with some friends. They call their group Language Arts. My younger nephew, a high school student, has a guitar solo in the mix. Cave Canem, an organization founded by poets Toi Derricotte and Cornelius Eady, has tried to unite black poets of "page and stage" through readings, workshops, panels, and a poetry book publishing prize.

Q. Do you find any essential difference between African American writing and other black writing around the world?

Perhaps we are the most obsessed with the contradictions between freedom and oppression.

Q. What has been your most significant contribution as a professor in the creative writing program? Do you think creative writing can really be taught?

In a writing workshop, students can practice writing, expand their knowledge of poetry, and learn how to give and receive constructive criticism.

Q. Does teaching creative writing affect your own mode of writing?

My reading and writing habits influence the way I teach creative writing, especially because I never attended a poetry-writing workshop as a student. I learned how to write poetry by reading poems, listening to poets, and scribbling continually in my notebooks. I recommend these habits to my students. I have a somewhat analytical approach to writing because of my training as a student of literature, but I've never lost the sense of joyful spontaneity and play that I felt as a child who read and wrote poetry for pleasure.

Q. What is your advice to younger upcoming African American poets?

Get the best education you can. Read literature from all times, all places, all races. Go to readings. Talk to poets. If you feel you must write, then write.

Bibliography

Adele, Lynne. *Black History/Black Vision: The Visionary Image in Texas.* Austin: U of Texas P, 1989.

"The African-American Experience in Ohio, 1850–1920." The Ohio Historical Society. Accessed 02 Jan. 2012. <http://memory.loc.gov/ammem/award97/ohshtml/aaeohome.html>

Alexander, Eleanor. *Lyrics of Sunshine and Shadow: The Tragic Courtship and Marriage of Paul Laurence Dunbar and Alice Ruth Moore.* New York: New York UP, 2001.

Alexander, Elizabeth. *Body of Life.* Chicago: Tia Chuca, 1996.

———. *The Venus Hottentot.* Charlottesville: UP of Virginia, 1990.

Alexander, Will. *Above the Human Nerve Domain.* Scotia, N.Y.: Pavement Saw, 1999.

———. "Alchemy as Poetic Kindling." In *A Poetics of Criticism.* Ed. Juliana Spahr et al. Buffalo: Leave Books, 1994. 173–177.

———. *Arcane Lavender Morals.* Buffalo: Leave Books, 1994.

———. *Asia & Haiti.* Los Angeles: Sun & Moon, 1995.

———. "Poetry: Alchemical Anguish and Fire." In *Writing from the New Coast.* Ed. Peter Gizzi and Juliana Spahr. *Oblek* (Spring/Fall 1993): 15–16.

———. *The Stratospheric Canticles.* Berkeley: Pantograph, 1995.

———. *Towards the Primeval Lightning Field.* Oakland: O Books, 1998.

———. *Vertical Rainbow Climber.* Santa Cruz: Jazz, 1987.

Allen, Paula Gunn. *The Sacred Hoop: Recovering the Feminine in American Indian Traditions.* Boston: Beacon, 1986.

Andrews, William L. *Sisters of the Spirit: Three Black Women's Autobiographies of the Nineteenth Century.* Bloomington: Indiana UP, 1986.

Aptheker, Herbert. *American Negro Slave Revolts.* 1943. New York: International Publishers, 1983.

Baraka, Amiri (LeRoi Jones). "Expressive Language." In *Home.* New York: Morrow, 1966.

Barrigan, Barbara. "'Hewing the Void': Linguistic Rebellion in Will Alexander's *Asia & Haiti.*" *Hambone* 14 (Fall 1998): 201–6.

Bass, Ruth. "Mojo" and "The Little Man." In *Motherwit from the Laughing Barrel.* Ed. Alan Dundes. New York: Prentice Hall, 1973.

Bastide, Roger. *The African Religions of Brazil.* Trans. Helen Sebba. Baltimore: Johns Hopkins UP, 1978.

Bernstein, Charles. *Content's Dream: Essays, 1974–1984.* Los Angeles: Sun and Moon, 1986.

———. *A Poetics.* Cambridge: Harvard UP, 1992.

The Big Chill. Dir. Lawrence Kasdan. Columbia, 1983. Film.

Blackmer, Corinne. "African Masks and the Arts of Passing in Gertrude Stein's 'Melanctha' and Nella Larsen's *Passing.*" *Journal of the History of Sexuality* 4, 2 (1993): 230–236.

Bloom, Harold. *The Anxiety of Influence: A Theory of Poetry.* New York: Oxford, 1973.

———. *A Map of Misreading.* New York: Oxford, 1975.

Bontemps, Arna. *Black Thunder.* 1936. Boston: Beacon, 1968.

———. "The Relevance of Paul Laurence Dunbar." In *Singer in the Dawn: Reinterpretations of Paul Laurence Dunbar.* Ed. Jay Martin. New York: Dodd, Mead, 1975. 45–53.

Brawley, Benjamin. *Paul Laurence Dunbar: Poet of His People.* Chapel Hill: U of North Carolina P, 1936.

Braxton, Joanne M., ed. *The Collected Poetry of Paul Laurence Dunbar.* Charlottesville: UP of Virginia, 1993.

"The Browning of America." *Time* special issue (Fall 1993): 3–12+.

Brown, Karen McCarthy. *Mama Lola: A Vodou Priestess in Brooklyn.* Berkeley: U of California P, 1991.

Brown, Sterling. *The Collected Poems.* Ed. Michael Harper. New York: Harper and Row, 1980.

———. *The Negro in American Fiction.* 1937. Port Washington, N.Y.: Kennikat, 1968.

Caples, Garrett. "Is the Analysis Impure?" *Lingo* 7 (1997): 74–76.

Carby, Hazel. *Reconstructing Womanhood: The Emergence of the Afro-American Woman.* New York: Oxford, 1987.

Chase, Truddi. *When Rabbit Howls.* New York: E. P. Dutton, 1987.

Chesnutt, Charles. *The House Behind the Cedars.* Ridgwood, N.J.: Gregg, 1968.

Chopin, Kate. "Desiree's Baby." In *The Complete Works of Kate Chopin.* Vol. 1. Ed. and introduction by Per Seyersted. Baton Rouge: Louisiana State UP, 1969. 240–45.

Cohen, Milton. "Black Brutes and Mulatto Saints: The Racial Hierarchy of Stein's 'Melanctha.'" *Black American Literature Forum,* vol. 18, no. 3 (1984): 119–121.

Cole, Norma. Backcover. *Above the Human Nerve Domain.* By Will Alexander. Scotia, OH: Pavement Saw, 1999.

Cortez, Jayne. *Somewhere in Advance of Nowhere.* New York: High Risk Books, 1996. 92–93.

Costanzo, Angelo. *Surprizing Narrative: Olaudah Equiano and the Beginnings of Black Autobiography*. New York: Greenwood, 1987.

Cunningham, Virginia. *Paul Laurence Dunbar and His Song*. New York: Dodd, Mead, 1947.

Davis, Charles T., and Henry L. Gates Jr. *The Slaves' Narrative*. New York: Oxford UP, 1985.

Davis, Leslie. "Interview with Will Alexander." *Cups: A Café Journal* (April 1994): 8–10.

DeJongh, James. *Vicious Modernism: Black Harlem and the Literary Imagination*. New York: Cambridge, 1990.

Douglas, Ann. *Terrible Honesty: Mongrel Manhattan in the 1920s*. New York: Farrar, Straus, and Giroux, 1995.

Douglass, Frederick. *Narrative. The Classic Slave Narratives*. Ed. Henry Louis Gates Jr. New York: New American Library, 1987.

Dupriez, Bernard. *A Dictionary of Literary Devices*. Toronto: U of Toronto P, 1991.

Durand, Marcella. Review of *Asia & Haiti*. *The Poetry Project Newsletter* 1996. N. p.

Ellison, Ralph. *Invisible Man*. New York: Modern Library, 1992.

Equiano, Olaudah. *Travels. The Classic Slave Narratives*. Ed. Henry Louis Gates Jr. New York: New American Library, 1987.

Fabre, Michel. "Ted Joans: 'The Surrealist Griot.'" In *From Harlem to Paris: Black American Writers in France, 1840–1980*. Urbana: U of Illinois P, 1992. 308–23.

Flashdance. Dir. Adrian Lyne. Paramount, 1983. Film.

Freire, Paulo, and Donalda Macedo. *Literacy: Reading the Word and the World*. South Hadley, MA: Bergin and Garvey, 1987.

Frost, Elisabeth. *The Feminist Avant-Garde in American Poetry*. Iowa City: U of Iowa P, 2003.

Fry, Gladys-Marie. *Stitched from the Soul: Slave Quilts from the Antebellum South*. New York: Dutton Studio Books/Museum of American Folk Art, 1990.

Gates, Henry Louis, Jr. *Figures in Black: Words, Signs, and the "Racial" Self*. New York: Oxford UP, 1987.

———. *The Signifying Monkey*. New York: Oxford UP, 1988.

Greimas, Algirdas-Julien. *Structural Semantics: An Attempt at a Method*. Trans. R. Schleifer and A. Velie. Lincoln: U of Nebraska P, 1983.

Hammad, Suheir. *Born Palestinian, Born Black*. New York: Harlem River P, 1996.

Head, Bessie. *A Question of Power*. London: Heinemann, 1974.

Howells, William Dean. "Life and Letters." *Harper's Weekly* 40, no. 2062 (27 June 1896): 630–31.

Hughes, Langston. "Passing." In *The Ways of White Folks*. New York: Knopf, 1979. 49–53.

Hunt, Erica. *Arcade*. Berkeley: Kelsey Street, 1996.

———. *Local History*. New York: Roof Books, 1993.

———. "Notes for an Oppositional Poetics." In *The Politics of Poetic Form*. Ed. Charles Bernstein. New York: Roof Books, 1990.

Jackson, Rebecca Cox. *Gifts of Power: The Writings of Rebecca Jackson, Black Visionary, Shaker Eldress*. Ed. Jean McMahon Humez. Amherst: U of Massachusetts P, 1981.

Jacobs, Harriet. *Incidents in the Life of a Slave Girl*. In *Classic Slave Narratives*. Ed. and introduction Henry Louis Gates Jr. New York: New American Library, 1987.

Jarrett, Gene. "'Entirely *Black* Verse from Him Would Succeed': Minstrel Realism and William Dean Howells." *Nineteenth-Century Literature* 59.4 (2005): 494–525.

Joans, Ted. *Black Pow-Wow*. New York: Hill and Wang, 1969.

Joans, Ted, and Joyce Mansour. *Flying Piranha*. New York: Bola, 1978.

Johnson, James Weldon. *The Autobiography of an Ex-Colored Man*. In *Three Negro Classics*. New York: Avon, 1969.

Joron, Andrew. "On Alexandrian Philosophy." Introduction to *Towards the Primeval Lightning Field*, by Will Alexander. Oakland: O Books, 1998. 7–15.

Kellner, Bruce. *Carl Van Vechten and the Irreverent Decades*. Norman: U of Oklahoma P, 1968.

Kemble, Frances Anne. *Journal of a Residence on a Georgian Plantation in 1838–1839*. Ed. and introduction by John A. Scott. New York: Knopf, 1961.

Larsen, Nella. *Passing*. New York: Negro UP, 1969.

Lazer, Hank. *Opposing Poetries* Vol. One *Issues and Institutions*. Evanston: Northwestern UP, 1996.

Lindberg, Kathryne. "Bob Kaufman, Sir Real, and His Rather Surreal Self-Presentation." *Talisman: A Journal of Contemporary Poetry and Poetics* 11 (1993): 167–82.

Lippard, Lucy R. *Mixed Blessings: New Art in a Multicultural America*. New York: Pantheon Books, 1990.

Lowe, Donald. *History of Bourgeois Perception*. Chicago: U of Chicago P, 1982.

Mackey, Nathaniel. *Bedouin Hornbook*. Lexington: U of Kentucky P, 1986.

———. *Discrepant Engagement: Dissonance, Cross-Culturality and Experimental Writing*. Cambridge: Cambridge UP, 1993.

Major, Clarence. "Three Lives and Gertrude Stein." *Par Rapport* 2 (1979): 53–66.

Martin, Jay, Ed. *A Singer in the Dawn: Reinterpretations of Paul Laurence Dunbar*. New York: Dodd, Mead, 1975.

Martin, Jay, and Gossie H. Hudson, eds. *The Paul Laurence Dunbar Reader*. New York: Dodd, Mead, 1975.

Melhem, D. H. "A Melus Profile and Interview: Jayne Cortez." *MELUS Journal* 21, 1 (Spring 1996): 71–79.

"Misplaced Zeal." *Dayton Tattler* 1, no. 2 (20 Dec. 1890): 3.

Mullen, Harryette. "'A Collective Force of Burning Ink': Will Alexander's *Asia & Haiti*." *Callaloo* 22, 2 (Spring 1999): 417–426

———. "Hauling Up Gold from the Abyss: An Interview with Will Alexander." *Callaloo* 22, 2 (Spring 1999): 391–408.

———. "Optic White: Blackness and the Construction of Whiteness." *Diacritics* 25, 2–3 (Summer/Fall 1994): 71–89.

———. *Recyclopedia: Trimmings, S*PeRM**K*T and Muse & Drudge*. St. Paul, Minn.: Graywolf, 2006.

———. Review of *Arcade* by Erica Hunt. *Antioch Review* 56, 2 (1998).

Mullen, Kirsten. "The Persistence of Vision." In *Rambling on My Mind: Black Folk Art in the Southwest*. Dallas: Museum of African-American Life and Culture, 1987.

Mullin, Michael, ed. *American Negro Slavery*. New York: Harper and Row, 1976.

Nasisse, Andy. "Aspects of Visionary Art." In *Baking in the Sun: Visionary Images from the South*. University Art Museum. Lafayette: U of Southwestern Louisiana, 1987.

Nat Turner. Ed. Eric Foner. Englewood Cliffs, N.J.: Prentice-Hall, 1971.

New York Review of Books' Reader's Catalog. Review of Will Alexander's works. Accessed 02 Jan. 2012. <http://www.readerscatalog.com/>.

Nielsen, Aldon. *Black Chant: The Languages of African-American Postmodernism*. Cambridge/New York: Cambridge UP, 1997.

———. *Reading Race: White American Poets and Racial Discourse in the Twentieth Century*. Athens: U of Georgia P, 1990.

Nordloh, David J., ed. *Paul Lawrence Dunbar*. Boston: G. K. Hall, 1979.

North, Michael. *The Dialect of Modernism: Race, Language, and Twentieth Century Literature*. New York: Oxford, 1994.

Oliver, Akilah. *The She Said Dialogues: Flesh Memory*. Boulder: Smokeproof Press/ Erudite Fangs Edition, 1999.

Osofsky, Gilbert. *Puttin' on Ole Massa: The Slave Narratives of Henry Bibb, William Wells Brown, and Solomon Northup*. New York: Harper and Row, 1969.

Patterson, G. E. *Tug*. Saint Paul, Minn.: Graywolf, 1999.

Perelman, Bob. *The Marginalization of Poetry: Language Writing and Literary History*. Princeton: Princeton UP, 1996.

Peterson, Carla. "The Re-making of Americans: Gertrude Stein's 'Melanctha' and African-American Musical Traditions." In *Criticism and the Color Line: Desegregating American Literary Studies*. Ed. Henry Wonham. New Brunswick, N.J.: Rutgers, 1996. 140–157.

Pines, Jim. *Blacks in Films: A Survey of Racial Themes and Images in the American Film*. London: Studio Vista, 1975.

Piper, Adrian. "The Triple Negation of Colored Women Artists." In *New Generation: Southern Black Aesthetic*. New York: Southeastern Center for Contemporary Art, 1990.

Reed, Ishmael. *Catechism of D Neo-American Hoodoo Church*. London: P. Breman, 1970.

———. *The Last Days of Louisiana Red*. Garden City: Doubleday, 1974.

———. *Mumbo Jumbo*. New York: Random House, 1972.

Riffaterre, Michael. *Semiotics of Poetry*. Bloomington: Indiana UP, 1984.

Saldivar-Hull, Sonia. "Wrestling Your Ally: Stein, Racism, and Feminist Cultural Practice." In *Women's Writing in Exile*. Ed. Mary Lynn Broe and Angela Ingram. Chapel Hill: U of North Carolina P, 1989. 181–198.

Schuyler, George. *Black No More*. New York: Collier, 1971.

Scroggins, Mark. "Logolatry." Review of *Asia & Haiti*. *American Book Review* 17, 3 (Feb.–Mar. 1996): 7.

Shange, Ntozake. *Nappy Edges*. New York: St. Martin's, 1978.

———. *Sassafrass, Cypress & Indigo*. New York: St. Martin's, 1982.

———. *Three Pieces*. New York: St. Martin's, 1981.

Silliman, Ron. *The New Sentence*. New York: Roof Books, 1987.

Silverman, Debra. "Nella Larsen's *Quicksand*: Untangling the Webs of Exoticism." *African-American Review* 24 (1993): 599–614.

Simone, Timothy Maliqalim. *About Face: Race in Postmodern America*. Brooklyn: Autonomedia, 1989.

Smedman, Lorna J. "'Cousin to Cooning': Relation, Difference, and Racialized Language in Stein's Nonrepresentational Texts." *Modern Fiction Studies* 42, 3 (1996): 569–588.

Spahr, Juliana. *Everybody's Autonomy: Connective Reading and Collective Identity*. Tuscaloosa: U of Alabama P, 2001.

Stein, Gertude. *Selected Works of Gertrude Stein*. Ed. Carl Van Vechten. 1962. New York: Vintage Books, 1980.

———. *Tender Buttons*. 1914. Los Angeles: Sun and Moon, 1997.

Stepto, Robert B. *From Behind the Veil: A Study of Afro-American Narrative*. Urbana: U of Illinois P, 1979.

Stowe, Harriet Beecher. *Uncle Tom's Cabin*. New York: Viking, 1982.

Stuckey, Sterling. *Slave Culture: Nationalist Theory and the Foundations of Black America*. New York: Oxford UP, 1987.

Szymborska, Wislawa. *View with a Grain of Sand: Selected Poems*. Trans. Stanislaw Baranczak and Clare Cavanagh. New York: Harcourt Brace, 1995.

Taussig, Michael. *The Nervous System*. London: Routledge, 1992.

Thompson, Robert Farris. *Flash of the Spirit*. New York: Vintage Books/Random House, 1983.

———. "The Song that Named the Land: The Visionary Presence in African-American Art." *Black Art: Ancestral Legacy*. Dallas Museum of Art. New York: Harry N. Abrams, Inc., 1989. 97–141.

Toish, Luisah. *Jambalaya*. San Francisco: Harper and Row, 1985.

Tuma, Keith. "Noticings." Review of *The Stratospheric Canticles*. *Sulfur* 39 (Fall 1996): 171–173.

Turner, Darwin T. "The Poet and the Myths." In *Singer in the Dawn: Reinterpretations of Paul Laurence Dunbar*. Ed. Jay Martin. New York: Dodd, Mead, 1975. 59–74.

Wagner-Martin, Linda. *Sylvia Plath: A Biography*. New York: Simon and Schuster, 1987.

Wahlman, Maude Southwell. "Africanisms in Afro-American Visionary Arts." In

Baking in the Sun. Ed. Herman Mhire. Lafayette: University Art Museum, U of Southwestern Louisiana, 1987.

Walker, Alice. *In Love and Trouble.* San Diego: Harvest/Harcourt, Brace, Jovanovich, 1973.

Wardlaw, Alvia, ed. *Black Art / Ancestral Legacy.* New York: Harry N. Abrams, 1989.

Weinberger, Eliot. "Will Alexander." In *Written Reaction: Poetics, Politics, Polemics.* New York: Marsilio, 1996. 182–183.

Wilde, Oscar. "The Critic as Artist, Part II." In *Intentions.* New York: Boni and Liveright, 1891.

Wilson, Harriet. *Our Nig.* New York: Random House, 1983.

Wright, Richard. *Black Boy.* New York: Perennial/Harper and Row, 1966.

Young, Al. "Chicken Hawk's Dream." In *New Black Voices.* Ed. Abraham Chapman. New York: New American Library, 1972.

Young, Kevin, ed. *Giant Steps: The New Generation of African American Writers.* New York: Perennial, 2000.